TAKEN HOSTAGE
STORIES AND STRATEGIES

TAKEN HOSTAGE
STORIES AND STRATEGIES

*What Families, Employers,
and Governments Should Do*

LARRY BUSCH

Library of Congress Control Number: 2016906997
ISBN: Hardcover   978-1-5144-8938-3
               Softcover   978-1-5144-8937-6
               eBook   978-1-5144-8936-9

Illustrations by Alexandra Lowe

Print information available on the last page.

Rev. date: 05/26/2016

To order additional copies of this book, contact:
Xlibris
1-888-795-4274
www.Xlibris.com
Orders@Xlibris.com
731515

This book is dedicated to the many hostages who graciously consented to speak with me and were willing to relive their captivity and their horrors. Their bravery and their honesty are very much appreciated, and as promised, their identities and their secrets will be kept. It is dedicated to those hostages who fought, suffered, survived, and returned home. It is also dedicated to those who did not return, for they too fought and suffered. And it is dedicated to the many hostages still out there.

CONTENTS

A WORD FROM THE AUTHOR

I'm not sure when it happened—when I had to find out why people do really bad things to other people. Maybe it came naturally, living in a dysfunctional family where my parents' fights were legendary in the neighborhood. Maybe it came after joining the Royal Canadian Mounted Police (RCMP) and responding to domestic complaints in other kids' homes—wrestling drunken mothers and fathers, sometimes both at the same time, out of the house, into the police car and then wrestling them into separate cells. Maybe it was listening to them the next morning as they held hands through the bars, cried, and professed their love for one another. Was it at a traffic accident and hearing the screams of people writhing in pain, with family lying dead next to them as the drunken driver of the other vehicle sat in the back of the police car and asked for a cigarette?

After investigating suicides, assaults, stabbings, and murders, there were always the rapes and sexual assaults. My interest in the psychological whys of these behaviors was matched only by my interest in the hows. I was often the go-to autopsy guy in the office because I wanted the physiological answers to what causes a person to die. When the lead investigator didn't want to attend the autopsy, I would. There are a lot of very good police investigators out there, but some can't attend an autopsy for ten seconds after the first cut.

I began with part-time university courses and then summer courses and correspondence courses. Eventually, the RCMP sent me to university full-time to help me finish my bachelor of science degree in psychology. During those years, I was selected for the National Negotiation Team. I attended numerous domestic and international negotiation courses and received critical incident training as well as tactical debriefings and many aircraft-hijacking training scenarios. I spent days with the Canadian Hostage Rescue Team (HRT) Joint Task Force 2 (JTF2) and watched as they fast-roped from helicopters, intercepted moving vehicles, and performed explosive entries. It was instructive being a scenario hostage in a full-size airliner and looking out the window to see if I could detect the HRT that I knew was coming. Or was it more interesting being on the outside of the aircraft the next

LARRY BUSCH

time as I watched the HRT do its sneak-up and entry? I have stood in closed battle quarters (CBQs) in the pitch black during live-fire hostage rescues. I spent weeks with SWAT teams responding to all manner of gun calls, barricaded persons, and suicide attempts. I also attended the RCMP's air marshal course, arguing that if I were a negotiator on the outside of a hijacked aircraft, I needed to know what the air marshals on the inside were trained to do. I studied deviant criminal behavior, terrorism, cults, and the psychology of suicide bombers.

I do know when I became interested in posttraumatic stress disorder (PTSD) and torture. One day in 2001, while on a United Nations (UN) peacekeeping mission in East Timor, I was walking down the road and saw an elderly woman walking, head down toward me, carrying a bag of food. As we approached, I said good morning. In an instant, her deadpan face immediately lit up; she smiled and said good morning, and just as quickly, her face returned to its expressionless mask as she walked away. It was instant, dramatic, and remarkable. I knew then and there that she had learned to survive among her captors. To her, I was just another uniform, just another occupier. That was my epiphany. From then on, I saw the mission in a completely different light. From that moment on, I needed to learn everything I could about PTSD, and you can't fully understand PTSD without a solid understanding of the physiological and psychological aspects of torture.

A few months later, while deployed at the UN headquarters in New York City, I began research at the UN library regarding previous UN missions where there was evidence of civilian torture. I researched the UN Lessons Learned Unit and then scoured the Manhattan bookstores.

When I returned home from the year-long mission, I requested RCMP headquarters to permit me to interview any released Canadian hostages in an effort to better understand what physical and psychological treatment they'd been subjected to so that as a negotiator, I would be better able to do my job. There are many more people taken hostage than the general public sees on the television news or reads about in the newspapers.

xvi

This book is the culmination of my thirty-five years of service with the RCMP, personal negotiation experiences, three UN peacekeeping missions, interviews with released hostages and their families, plus the published works of released hostages, all made sharper through the focus of academics.

PROLOGUE

The very idea of being a hostage is so extremely remote that people prefer to watch these dramatic situations unfold on the evening news or at the movies. In the mid-1990s, civilians taken hostage were likely to be airline passengers flying to some remote country or aid workers in some third-world country. More recently, with the advent of global terrorism, hostages may very well be taken on a domestic airliner or cruise ship or in a school, coffee shop, or movie theater in their hometown. Worldwide, people are traveling more frequently and farther than ever before. This is true for vacationers, businesspeople, and unfortunately, for terrorists as well. Hostage taking and terrorism used to happen on the other side of the world; now they walk among us.

This book is for travelers who are more concerned than ever about their security and survival; it is for those who seek the answers behind today's events and tomorrow's headlines, and it is for those with loved ones in harm's way. This book was written generally with the civilian in mind but not specifically so. With some modification, they are just as relevant and applicable to the soldier on a mission as they are to nongovernmental organizations (NGOs) providing services around the globe. These survival strategies are designed to respond to mid-term and long-term hostage situations predominately in the Middle East; North, East, and West Africa; and to a lesser extent, Central and South America. Mid-term and long-term hostage situations can last for periods of a few weeks to many years. However, these same hostage survival strategies are applicable to situations where young girls and boys are abducted off the street in their own hometowns and held as companions to replace a lost child or an absent spouse. In short, the strategies are universally applicable to anyone taken against his or her will, regardless of age or circumstances.

The survival strategies in this book offer no guarantees; however, they are based upon science. These stories of survival come only from those who lived. But why did they live and others die?

These strategies are the product of reports from tortured political prisoners, tortured hostages, and prisoners of war. They are based upon the debriefings, testimonies, and stories of released hostages and escaped hostages. Many survived by using these strategies, some survived only by luck, and some survived until rescued. What made the difference? Was it because of what some did and others did not? Of course, history tells us that for many, it was, in fact, just by chance—one prisoner was sent one way and another prisoner was sent another way; one died and one lived.

The first few chapters of this book instruct business travelers on the essential predeployment training and planning they should undertake prior to their departure and security practices to follow while traveling. For hundreds of released hostages, it is not enough just to survive the months or years of confinement while enduring physical and psychological abuse. After their release, they must then face possibly an even greater challenge—reintegration; returning home as a changed person to a changed family.

The final chapters of this book are dedicated to this psychological aftermath. Some hostage survival strategies are specific to being abducted and confined, and others are specific to returning to a normal life. It is an emotional tragedy and puzzling to us all why, when a repatriated hostage or a combat soldier returns home, that person must still find the will to live. These chapters provide both categories of survivors—the repatriated hostage and the waiting families—with guidelines on how to approach one another, mentally decompress, manage the press, and support one another.

The strategies in this book come from those who survived, seemingly against the odds, when others did not. Was it a physical difference or a mental difference? Was the only difference that one had the will to live and the other did not? And how does one get this will to live? Are some born with it and some not? This book will answer these questions.

INTRODUCTION
HOSTAGE SURVIVAL STRATEGIES

The strategies in this book are presented as an option; hostages have used them and survived. Admittedly, their stories of survival—and the strategies derived from those stories—are biased. They are the recounting of events recalled from fallible human memories formed under circumstances of extreme anxiety. That said, the stories recount the hours and days of excruciating pain caused by barbaric physical torture and sexual abuse suffered at the hands of one human being against another, which makes one wonder how they could be forgotten. We are left with the stories only of survivors, be they true, exact, embellished, or fictitious. And what of the stories of those who did not survive? What strategies failed? Did they do everything, or did they do nothing? Sadly, we are left only to imagine, to wonder, and to make assumptions.

When a medical vaccination exposes your body's immune system to a harmful virus, it provides your immune system with the opportunity to physically experience and chemically examine the virus—your immune system responds and builds the appropriate physiological resistance. A psychological inoculation, for the purposes of this book, exposes the reader to real-life stories of hostage takings that include the mental and physical abuses many hostages suffered at the hands of their captors. I will identify and examine a variety of strategies used by these and other hostages to survive what, at times, seemed unsurvivable. I will explain in detail how to apply these strategies and survive a broad range of physical and mental traumas. This book will offer explanations as to why hostages are taken in the first place and provide an understanding of the many stages of capture and confinement a hostage is likely to encounter.

Emergency and first-responder professionals such as police, firefighters, hospital trauma teams, military personnel, and airline pilots train extensively in scenarios that closely resemble real-life situations so that when they come face to face with similar circumstances in the future, they can quickly apply their skills in a calm, professional manner to resolve the situation—and save lives. Psychological inoculation serves hostages by affording them the ability to recognize the situation and adapt more quickly. By using predictability as a buffer against being overwhelmed, the victim can make sense of the situation and improve their psychological ability to cope. A better understanding of what lies ahead decreases the likelihood of panic, thereby reducing the possibility of physical harm and increasing the chances of survival.

The strategies in this book will provide options for how to act during every stage of the hostage taking. In regard to their day-to-day physical treatment, hostages will be able to play a more active and positive role. They will be better able to maintain positive mental health. This mental state will have a positive impact on their ability to endure the days and months of excruciating boredom and the stress of prolonged family separation, physical abuse, and the mental anguish of an uncertain future and the always-present fear of death.

Psychology is the science of the mind and the applied science of individual behavior. It uses proven scientific study techniques to understand and predict, with some degree of certainty, how a person will act given a particular set of circumstances. Psychology takes that knowledge and extends it to predicting how individuals are likely to act toward other individuals and groups. Sociology is the science of social behavior and social interactions. It is the science of understanding how and why people act together in a group, how they form relationships with one another, and how they relate with a larger group and institutions. The reader will recognize how both psychological and sociological principles are directly related to each of the survival strategies I describe. The reader will understand and identify how some strategies pertain to only the individual hostage and others pertain to the hostage's interactions with a guard or a group of guards. Later in the book, I will present ways in which these same strategies can be adapted when there is more than one hostage held under the same circumstances.

A number of government publications, as well as many private security companies, identify four stages of a hostage taking, with a two- or three-line narrative of what a hostage should or should not do at each stage. I describe five stages in this book because I include the planning stage. I do so as a means to educate travelers in what preparations and activities the kidnappers must go through as they select a target, a time, and a place; work to gather intelligence; choose kidnap personnel; and acquire the necessary equipment. I believe that if travelers can recognize and identify these activities for the threat they are, they can adapt their behavior immediately and accordingly—forewarned is forearmed. I describe each of the five stages in detail, providing several survival strategies for each, supported by examples and quotes from hostage interviews, scientific studies, and hostage publications.

Police and intelligence surveillance teams routinely detect surveillance teams from other police and intelligence services actively working their own targets. People who are trained and experienced in carrying out surveillance operations are the best ones to pick out other persons' conducting surveillance. That is my training philosophy here—if you know how the other guy does his work, you can more easily pick him out when he's doing his work. As any good sports buff will attest, if you know your opponent's offensive strategies, you can apply the appropriate defensive strategy.

The strategies presented in this book will provide the reader with scientifically proven approaches that have been used successfully by hostages in a variety of hostage situations. Some strategies are particular to hostages' physical needs and others to their mental needs; the behavioral strategies are directed toward their day-to-day demeanor and frame of mind. The psychological makeup, the experience, education, and intentions of the captor group as well as the hostages' reasons for travel and their own psychological frame of mind will determine which strategies are best suited to assist the hostage in surviving their ordeal.

The scenarios I refer to in this book are presented only as instructional examples focused principally around the many situations forced upon a single civilian kidnapped in a Middle Eastern or African country by religious fanatics or criminal gangs. Religious fanatics come in all shapes and sizes. They are not exclusively Muslim jihadists. As we have seen throughout history, religious fanatics act upon particular passages, teachings, or doctrines of a selected religion and apply an interpretation that best suits their political, religious, or social beliefs. These fanatics will justify and defend any and all of their actions as righteous, as actions mandated by their religion or their politics. They may belong to, or be affiliated with, ISIS (Islamic State/Daesh), al-Qa'ida, the Taliban, or Al-Shabaab or whatever terrorist group jumps onto the world stage tomorrow. Whether these are the actions of true religious believers or the excuses of criminal actors looking to justify their activities and absolve themselves of any criminal, religious, or social wrongdoing is for the reader to decide. These jihadists—persons in armed opposition to occupation or acting under religious orders—reject authority in all fashions but their religion. They use unconventional warfare tactics—hostage taking is but one.

The size and affiliations of these groups will also differ. The groups might be composed of only two or three persons following a specific doctrine or a few hundred persons following a much broader principle. These groups might act alone in a loosely knit structure of two or three, be in an organized cell of six or seven, or follow a charismatic leader in a well-structured organization made up of hundreds or even thousands.

Criminal groups in these regions will often justify their actions on financial or political grounds. As an example, Al-Shabaab is a religious extremist group in Somalia that takes hostages for both ransom and political leverage; Somali pirates, who live in the same area, take hostages strictly for ransom. Both groups are Muslim, but they are enemies.

There are a variety of reasons certain people are kidnapped. Civilians are kidnapped for one of three main reasons: political leverage, ransom, or human shields. Politicians are usually kidnapped for two reasons: political leverage and ransom. Soldiers are kidnapped or captured for one reason—they are soldiers—and they are held for all three reasons: political leverage, ransom (trade), and human shields. Because of these variances, it is impossible to predict exactly how each hostage will be treated, how long each will be held, and what it will take to regain their freedom.

Understanding the hostage survival strategies outlined in this book will serve the reader as a form of psychological inoculation. They are intended to provide the reader with an understanding of what is likely to happen at each stage of a hostage taking, to assist hostages in recognizing what is happening at each stage, and to prepare them for what may happen next. Such understanding and preparation is essential to reducing the confusion and the numbing fear and panic that hostages always experience.

Hostages cannot rely solely on the benevolence, humanity, or sympathies of the hostage takers for their release. That is just unrealistic. At the same time, hostages cannot afford to sit back and dispassionately spectate at an event that involves their very lives. They cannot afford to leave their lives in the hands of their company's senior executives, their own government, or even their families and friends. These efforts must be complemented by their own efforts on the inside. Their thoughts must always be of survival—to live and return home safely. They must establish a plan of behaviors and strategies that will influence their captors to improve their treatment and increase the likelihood of their early release. Just as everyone back home plans their day of business filled with meetings and phone calls or their day at home planning family meals, kid's pickups, and drop-offs, so must hostages plan their day in captivity. *They must take an active role in their own survival; to do otherwise may mean giving up.*

This book does not speak directly to the very different circumstances of military personnel being taken hostage or captured. Military personnel have a different purpose for being where they are, and they have specific training for what they are doing. Military personnel from around the world undergo a type of Survival, Evasion, Resistance, and Escape (SERE) or Conduct After Capture (CAC) training. Both of these are general predeployment programs with added outdoor survival, first-aid training, and interrogation preparation; the training is mission-specific. Obviously, different countries train their military personnel differently, but the basics are pretty much the same. There is also a very different set of abductors who capture and hold military personnel, and they interrogate them for very different reasons; how they are treated is another situation altogether. That said, many, if not all, of the survival strategies in this book are still very relevant to military personnel, with the necessary modifications. Hostage survival training may soon become mandatory for frontline military personnel.

It is up to you as the reader to recognize how each strategy may or may not apply to your particular circumstances. As a hostage, you have more information than anyone else, your situation is unique, and you are the best one to decide what you should do. I present only history, information, and options.

CHAPTER 1
WHY ARE HOSTAGES TAKEN?

The act of taking people hostage has been around for hundreds of years, although initially they were not referred to as *hostages* per se; they were just called prisoners. In Roman times, captured enemy soldiers were taken prisoner and sold as slaves; civilians captured when cities and countries were conquered were kept as slaves or concubines or trained as gladiators for entertainment. Captured soldiers were crucified or impaled on poles

and displayed along roadsides as a warning to other armies who might dare contemplate an invasion. This practice was common throughout history—the empires of Western Europe would routinely imprison soldiers of attacking armies for years in cramped dungeons and ransom those of the most senior ranks. Especially valuable were members of royalty such as dukes and earls or even knights. Soldiers of low rank and, therefore, little value were sold as slaves or simply put to death.

Medieval Europe also invented most of the infamous machines of torture that would literally burn, beat, hack, or squeeze a confession from any person. Torture became an art. During these earlier wars, and later, during the First and Second World Wars, the Korean War, and the Vietnam War, prisoners were subjected to years of confinement and all manner of physical and psychological torture.

Hostage takings from the 1960s through to 2010 were likely to be of civilian airline passengers on board hijacked airliners in the Middle East (see Table 1).

Table 1
Airline Hijackings Worldwide by Decade

Years	Number of hijackings	Number of fatalities
1950–1960	26	23
1960–1970	146	15
1970–1980	347	344
1980–1990	244	220
1990–2000	196	237
2000–2010	76	275
2010–2014	10	0

Source: Adapted from Aviation Safety Network (2015). A service of Flight Safety Foundation, aviation-safety.net/statistics/period.

These hijackings were almost always political in nature. The airliner was taken over by armed men and flown to a sympathetic or neutral country, where the terrorists could negotiate in relative safety for the release of political prisoners. The term *political prisoner* is still used today, as it most often refers to captured fighters. The physical constraints of an aircraft and the logistics involved in the care and feeding of a hundred or two hundred passengers plus the captors forced these hostage takings to be relatively short—two to maybe five days.

There were a number of notable politically motivated hostage events during this time, such as the September 1970 coordinated hijacking of four US-bound airliners by the Popular Front for the Liberation of Palestine (PFLP). But it was the hostage taking and killing of eleven Israeli athletes at the 1972 Summer Olympics in Munich, West Germany, that was watched by a television audience estimated at more than nine hundred million, from over one hundred countries, that really brought terrorism and the media together. The media and terrorism have been wedded, for better or for worse, ever since. Following these events, there was the hostage taking of foreign oil ministers at the 1975 OPEC (Organization of the Petroleum Exporting Countries) conference in Vienna, Austria, where sixty hostages were taken and three were killed.

The aircraft hijackings in the United States during those same years were often for the purpose of obtaining a flight to Cuba. The hijackers didn't necessarily want hostages; they just wanted the aircraft as a conveyance. Still, the hostages served as protection—they were human shields. The same can be said for the 9/11 hijackers. They didn't want the passengers as hostages per se; they were more interested in the aircraft—as weapons.

After 9/11, the Shoe Bomber in December 2001, and the Underwear Bomber in December 2009, airline security was increased, including secure cockpit doors plus the other numerous changes to airline procedures, including the use of air marshals. These measures have led to a dramatic decrease in aircraft hijackings. Hostages must now be found elsewhere.

Table 2
Incidents of Terrorism, Worldwide

Type of attack	2007	2008	2009	2010	2011
Attacks worldwide	14,415	11,663	10,968	11,641	10,283
Attacks resulting in at least 1 death, injury, or kidnapping[1]	11,085	8,361	7,874	8,259	7,453
Attacks resulting in the death of at least 10 individuals	353	234	236	193	193
Attacks resulting in the death of at least 1 individual	7,229	5,040	4,761	4,704	4,502
Attacks resulting in the death of only 1 individual	3,982	2,870	2,695	2,691	2,550
Attacks resulting in the death of 0 individuals	7,186	6,623	6,207	6,937	5,781
Attacks resulting in the injury of at least 1 individual	6,231	4,831	4,530	4,724	4,333

Attacks resulting in the kidnapping of at least 1 individual	1,156	948	882	1,118	795
People killed, injured, or kidnapped as a result of terrorism, worldwide	71,803	54,290	58,720	49,928	43,990
People killed as a result of terrorism, worldwide	22,720	15,709	15,311	13,193	12,533
People injured as a result of terrorism, worldwide	44,103	33,901	32,660	30,684	25,903
People kidnapped as a result of terrorism, worldwide	4,980	4,680	10,749	6,051	5,554

Note: Adapted from United States Department of State, National Counterterrorism Center: Annex of Statistical Information, office of the coordinator for counterterrorism. *Country Reports on Terrorism 2011*, report, July 31, 2012.

On June 19, 2015, the US Department of State released *Country Reports on Terrorism 2014*. Statistics in the report showed extremist violence in the Middle East, Africa, and Asia had increased by 35 percent since 2013.

In the past year, nearly 33,000 people were killed in almost 13,500 terrorist acts around the world, up from just over 18,000 deaths in nearly 10,000 attacks in 2013. Twenty-four Americans were killed by extremists in 2014, and abductions soared to 9,428 in the calendar year from 3,137 in 2013 (Lee and Klapper 2015).

Over the past decade, Afghanistan has proved the world's deadliest country for aid workers. Between 2004 and 2014, 430 attacks targeted aid workers in Afghanistan, with 57 losing their lives last year alone. Altogether in 2014, 190 attacks occurred across 27 countries, killing 120 aid workers. A further 88 were wounded while 121 were kidnapped (Niall McCarthy 2015).

Table 3

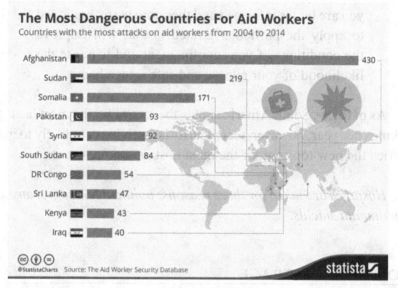

The Most Dangerous Countries For Aid Workers
Countries with the most attacks on aid workers from 2004 to 2014

Afghanistan — 430
Sudan — 219
Somalia — 171
Pakistan — 93
Syria — 92
South Sudan — 84
DR Congo — 54
Sri Lanka — 47
Kenya — 43
Iraq — 40

@StatistaCharts   Source: The Aid Worker Security Database

statista

This chart shows the countries with the most attacks on aid workers from 2004 to 2014.

On the criminal side of hostage taking, often, hostages were taken as a result of botched criminal acts, such as a bank robbery. Of course the crooks only wanted the bank's money, but when something went wrong with the heist, taking hostages was the best option available. As many police officers will attest, there is more planning dedicated to carrying out the robbery than to the getaway. In the late 1970s to the mid '80s, as police response times to bank alarms in the United States became faster and faster, hostage taking during bank robberies became more frequent. Therefore, in the United States, police standard operating procedure in response to these alarms was changed so they would not arrive too early, thereby trapping the robbers inside, essentially compelling them to take hostages. Arriving later gave the robbers time to escape the bank premises.

(As an aside, the police didn't just wait for the robbers to step outside and into a gunfight; new technologies such as video surveillance, exploding dye packs, and electronic tracking equipment were used to track and identify the bank robbers.)

Understanding why you've been taken hostage is vital to your survival. When you understand why, you are better informed and therefore better equipped to apply the particular strategies that will improve the conditions of your confinement and increase the likelihood of your release and safe return home.

As of today, South America holds the record for the most hostage takings per year; however, recent terrorist activities are likely to gain Africa the new top spot for the most hostage-taking events.

Hostages are taken for three reasons: political leverage, ransom, and human shields.

POLITICAL LEVERAGE

Political leverage allows the hostage takers to get something in return, to force political or social change that is otherwise unlikely to happen or not happen soon enough without that leverage.

Political leverage is gained through local and international embarrassment of a country or ruling government so as to affect trade deals or focus attention on human rights abuses. Hostages are taken to bargain for the release of political prisoners or enemies of the state; to force political change; or to give back entitled lands or for the recognition of state, culture, language, or religion. In the case of rising environmental terrorism, this political leverage is often justified simply as social activism and purely ideological. Well, so is wanting to overthrow a government.

You only have to watch the news for an ongoing list of political issues that spark heated debate, confrontation, anger, or protest. Depending upon the country and whether it is a democracy, theocracy, or monarchy, socialist or communist, public or political opposition may not be permitted.

Terrorists often shift the blame for their actions to other countries, other governments, big businesses, or other religions as justification for their actions. The abduction of Western hostages serves the terrorist group's propaganda strategy, as news of their capture and the propaganda value of parading them as trophies almost guarantees international media coverage.

Propaganda is political leverage; propaganda does not have to be true to be believed or to be effective.

RANSOM

Ransom is most often cash money—a straight financial gain. Ransom provides the huge amounts of money necessary to finance today's terrorist organizations or organized crime activities. In many countries, ransom pays police and government officials for their influence, favors, or complacency.

Ransom is often distributed among the local inhabitants and neighbors and to the poor or less fortunate in an attempt to buy their favor and cooperation. For kidnappers holding a hostage, it is a significant benefit to have their neighbors looking out for their privacy by informing them of any military or security forces in the area or strangers asking questions. Many hostages have escaped their immediate captors, only to be turned in by sympathetic neighbors or villagers.

Terrorism is expensive. Often the terrorists or freedom fighters, revolutionaries, or activists—whatever name they might go by—have little or no income and must seek the support of sympathizers through donations or logistical support or acquire monies through the kidnapping and ransom of hostages.

In many South American and African countries, taking hostages for ransom has evolved into the much safer crime of extortion. Nowadays, the criminals simply demand annual payments from large corporations as protection for *not* taking their employees hostage. Considering the risks criminal groups take to kidnap, confine, guard, and negotiate for the lives of foreign workers, this modern organized-crime approach makes perfect sense.

Organized crime, terrorists—or warlords, as they are referred to in some countries—force farmers to grow illegal crops, which, when cultivated, generate substantial profits for both the criminals and the farmers. Organized crime groups and terrorists often raid international aid convoys of food and medical supplies and either give them or sell them to the civilian population to gain their support. Sometimes they hold the convoy drivers as hostages; sometimes they do not.

It is important to understand that not all terrorist organizations kidnap, hold, and ransom their own hostages. In many countries where hostage taking is more prevalent, such as Mexico and South American countries where it is estimated there are almost one hundred kidnappings per day, terrorist groups often hire criminal organizations to kidnap selected targets and hold them while they assume responsibility for ransom negotiations. In today's business vernacular, hostage taking is being outsourced. This is because not all terrorist groups have the experience, the skills, or the facilities for short-term or long-term hostage maintenance. This is strictly a business agreement between the terrorist group and the criminal organization. That said, this arrangement complicates hostages' personal efforts to seek their own release through humanizing and social bonding strategies, cultivating religious or political sympathies, or building human compassion or logic. This is a straight business deal, where over 70 percent of hostages are released upon payment of the ransom. These strategies will be discussed in later chapters.

In all kidnap situations, hostages must recognize that they are strictly a commodity, but one that needs to be fed, watered, and even protected. Even in this respect, there are strategies that can improve hostages' treatment and even save their lives. As a commodity, hostages might be sold between criminal or terrorist groups. Selling occurs when hostage maintenance costs become a burden, the group loses faith in negotiations, or the group senses the risks are becoming too great. There is also the risk that another more powerful terrorist or criminal group will demand that a high-value hostage be turned over to them. This starts the hostage transport and confinement cycle all over again—new captors, new rules.

Often, hostage takers justify ransom monies as fair and just compensation for political, social, or religious injustices; lost income; or a negative impact on living conditions. They often cite government intervention, inaction, or corruption when permission is given to international logging or mining corporations. Or they might view the ransom as compensation for financial or environmental losses suffered through reduced fishing yields, the loss of farmlands or lost income from historical hunting grounds, hunting techniques, or threatened cultural activities. Sometimes, ransom just serves as a penalty for interference.

Ransom monies can also be acquired through theft or seizure of raw materials or manufactured products. Somali pirates are one of the most recent examples of the significant financial gains to be made through ransoming humans, multimillion-dollar ocean vessels, and millions of barrels of oil. However, if they were to hold these captured ships without human crew as hostages, negotiations would drag on for many years while the ships rusted where they lay. Likely the insurance companies would just write them off and buy another ship. It's the human hostages that make the difference.

One Somali pirate leader admitted that the reason he asked for US$50 million ransom for a ship and its crew was because he wanted to buy a new house and a Hummer. Ransom requests are not always reasonable, and hostage takers are not always rational.

One side of the Somali pirate argument accuses the local government of unregulated and unenforced international fishing off the coast of Somalia, which results in significantly reduced fish catches, thereby plunging the local fishermen into near starvation. The fishermen's only recourse is to seize the cargo and crew of international ships in their local waters and seek ransom payment as compensation. The other side of this argument is that it's a good way to make lots of fast cash in a country with a weak government and an ineffective legal system.

Pirate hostage takers defend these large ransoms as the cost of doing business, because they rationalize that large international corporations and insurance companies have vast financial resources and can easily afford the huge ransom demands.

Jessica Buchanan (*Impossible Odds* 2014, 80)[1] sums up the choices faced by many Somali men.

---

[1] On October 25, 2011, thirty-two-year-old humanitarian aid worker Jessica

You can become a kidnapper and play the long odds,
or you can bend over and take it from the whole world.
Three choices greet you: Scrape out a life in the legal
way, chew *khat* [a flowering shrub native to northeast
Africa whose effects are euphoria, increased alertness
and excitement] and wait for the deliverance of death,
or take a desperate gamble.

The definition of *ransom* is also subjective; many Somali pirates prefer to use the term *tax.* They rationalize this by arguing that all companies pay taxes; therefore, they are just collecting taxes on shipping through their waters. Collecting taxes is not a crime, not a sin.

Possibly the most world-famous kidnapping for ransom was the 1932 kidnapping of Charles Augustus Lindbergh Jr., the twenty-month-old son of the famous American aviator Charles Lindbergh. Ransom demands increased from the initial $50,000 to $70,000 and then $100,000, a significant sum indeed during that time. The child's disappearance and the eventual arrest, conviction, and execution of his murderer induced the American Congress to pass the Federal Kidnapping Act, better known as the Lindbergh Law, making kidnapping a federal crime. There is a strong suggestion that the term *kidnapping* was first coined with respect to this case (Federal Bureau of Investigation 1932).

Some terrorist organizations deliberately seek to capture more hostages prior to peace talks or cease fire negotiations so that they can offer the release of hostages as a show of good faith.

Buchanan was kidnapped at gunpoint and held for ransom by a band of Somali pirates. For the next three months, Jessica was terrorized by gangsters, held in filthy conditions, and starved while her health steadily deteriorated. After ninety-three days of fruitless negotiations and with Jessica's medical state becoming a life-or-death issue, President Barack Obama ordered Navy SEAL Team Six to attempt a rescue operation.

Human Shields

Hostages provide hostage takers with a level of physical security and protection. Hostages are kept in close proximity to the "fighters" to prevent their enemies, governments, and militaries from using long-range or more sophisticated and powerful weapons against them. Having human shields eliminates the high-tech weapons advantage of militaries, thereby leveling the playing field. Terrorists target citizens of the specific nations fighting against them, as these citizens afford a higher value and, therefore, serve as better human shields than hostages from uninvolved nations. As hostages die while serving as human shields or by some other means, more are abducted to take their place.

Hostages taken by South American fighters are often held for years and forced to march with them through miles of dense jungle. This practice prevents government military forces from using airborne strafing or carpet bombing against suspected militant hideouts. As such, the military are forced to enter the jungle on foot and fight a conventional ground war in unfamiliar surroundings.

In February 2002, Franco-Colombian presidential candidate Ingrid Betancourt was taken hostage by the Revolutionary Armed Forces of Colombia (FARC). She was rescued six and a half years later, in 2008, along with three American military contractors and ten others. In April 2012, FARC released ten soldiers and police personnel, all of whom had been held in the jungle for at least twelve years.

With the use of human shields, hostage takers are better able to control the where and how of an enemy attack or rescue attempt. Regardless of the reason a particular person was selected and eventually taken as a hostage, for either political leverage or for ransom, all hostages serve as human shields to some degree. It is how they are treated and where they are housed that influences a clearer distinction of purpose.

In Mexico and South American countries, organized crime commits the majority of kidnappings and, regrettably, often with the assistance of the police. These countries suffer from widespread police and political corruption, low wages, high unemployment, and extreme poverty. Mexico and Central America have some of the highest rates of "express kidnappings" and "lightning kidnappings"; these also occur worldwide, just not as frequently as in Mexico and Central America. Express kidnappings are often carried out by taxi, where the occupant is driven to a bank machine (ATM) and threatened into withdrawing as much cash as the person's credit and debit cards will allow. Then the individual is released—quick, easy money. They can also happen when the kidnapper sticks a gun in someone's back and walks the person to a nearby ATM. Years ago, ATM robberies were very common in the United States, especially in California. The advent of ATM cameras has all but eliminated such crimes, but variations still exist.

Lightning kidnappings involve grabbing a hostage off the street and driving around for a few hours until the ransom is paid. These kidnappings last only a few hours because the ransom demanded is only a few hundred dollars—again, quick and easy money with few complications.

A variation on express and lightning kidnappings is taking a bank manager's family hostage and thereby forcing the manager to rob his own bank.

In Mexico, there are hundreds of kidnappings each week. Kidnapping has become so widespread that it is now seen almost as a "reputable" business, at least among the criminal element. Kidnapping brings in much-needed cash without offending the existing drug cartels and the ensuing turf wars and murders associated with them. It is important to note, however, that kidnapping for ransom continues to be successful because the hostages are often freed alive. The criminal groups that commit these kidnappings are successful because they have a reputation for bargaining in good faith. That is, they have built credibility; if the ransom is paid, the hostage is released. This is important for anyone taken hostage by these groups to know. Again, knowing who your kidnappers are and why they have taken you is invaluable to you as a hostage because this knowledge will affect the decisions you make, which will directly affect your chances of survival.

Many of the terrorist groups in South America and Africa are fighting against foreign oil companies and foreign mining companies that are being given huge tracts of land for exploration and exploitation. The activities of these companies pose a significant immediate and long-term threat to the people's livelihood and to the environment. Some of these groups fight against resource exploitation and in defense of the environment; other criminal groups just take the opportunity to steal from the oil companies and benefit from their own country's rich oil revenues. In West Africa, terrorism is against oil exploration; in East and Central Africa, Boko Haram is kidnapping schoolgirls in retaliation against Western education. In North Africa, terrorism is related to political and religious instability and the want of statehood; in East Africa, it is Somali pirates and religious fanatics such as Al-Shabaab. In Central Africa, Al-Shabaab is kidnapping children as child soldiers in South Sudan. In the Middle East, the Palestinians want statehood and lands returned; in many Eastern European and Mediterranean areas, there are grievances that go back hundreds of years. There are many countries, such as France, Turkey, and Cyprus, that have ongoing disputes about territory, language, political separation, and statehood. India and Pakistan have decades-old disputes regarding Bangladesh. There are Pakistan, India, and Kashmir; there are China and Tibet, Russia and the Baltic States, Georgia and Crimea . . . and that's just a partial list of ongoing situations in the region.

More recently, Islamic extremists, also referred to as militants or jihadists, have been at the forefront of terrorist activities. Although there were jihadist rumblings for many years in a number of the Middle Eastern and North African countries, these terrorists exploded onto the world stage, committing their attack against the United States on September 11, 2001, now referred to worldwide as 9/11. Since then, the whole world has heard of al-Qaeda and Osama bin Laden. Most every fledgling Islamic terrorist group since 9/11 says it is affiliated with al-Qaeda in some fashion. This claim of affiliation is often an effort to enhance the group's reputation among other terrorist groups, improve recruitment, and develop its credibility as a force to be reckoned with. These al-Qaeda–inspired terrorist groups have taken hostages in various countries and held them for varying lengths of time for a variety of demands.

Since 9/11, there has been a relatively slower growth of new terrorist organizations. This was until the June 2014 self-declaration of ISIS (Islamic State of Iraq and al-Sham), often referred to as ISIS or ISIL (Islamic State of Iraq and the Levant) or simply the Islamic State. Their numbers swelled from only few hundred members operating in isolated areas to today's many thousands due to the scores of migrating fighters from the many regional conflicts. ISIS is a sadistically brutal terrorist organization that is on a ruthless path to building a caliphate across the Middle East, beginning with Iraq, Syria, and Libya. Its sheer brutality against Western hostages, nonaligned religious sects, military prisoners, local citizens, Christians, and tribespeople is alarming and terrifying indeed.

Daesh is the name commonly used by many enemies of IS/ISIS. Accordingly, it has become the standard descriptor used by many Middle Eastern countries. The French government has officially encouraged its use, although the French media has not warmed to the change. *Daesh* is a loosely translated Arabic acronym for Islamic State of Iraq and the Levant (al-**D**awla **a**l-**I**slamiya al-**I**raq al-**Sh**am). It was first used in April 2013 by Arabic and Iranian media hostile to the jihadist movement. A principal reason for using the acronym was to remove the words *Islamic* and *State* in reference to the group in a bid to stop Muslims in war-torn Syria and beyond flocking to its ranks. Worldwide, *ISIS* is still the most recognized label for this terrorist group; therefore, this book will use this term.

ISIS's use of hostages thus far has been mostly for spectacle—beheadings, immolations, and crucifixions. These atrocities are both a testament of their commitment to the world and a warning that no one dare stand in the way of their forming a religious statehood. Although it is forbidden in the Koran (religious text of Islam) for a Muslim to kill another Muslim, ISIS is killing Muslims by the hundreds, video-recording it, and proudly presenting it to the world. Such was the case with the video-recorded murder—immolation—of the Jordanian pilot Lieutenant Muath al-Kasaesbeh, the execution of Iraqi soldiers, and the beheading of twenty-one Egyptian Christians in Libya in February 2015. They defend what is prohibited in one part of the Koran by the words in another part of the Koran, which state that any blood, even Muslim blood, can be spilled if they stand in the way of a caliphate. This practice is referred to as deterrence. "We made it a law . . . that the killing of a person for reasons other than legal retaliation or for stopping corruption . . . is a great sin . . ." (Koran 5:32).

Extremists in these regions do not always select their hostages based upon their political affiliation, religion, or relevance to their cause. White-skinned foreigners are sought out for their propaganda and ransom value. Recently, hostages have been humanitarian workers taken solely because they were easy to capture and they were North Americans, Europeans, or Asians. As such, terrorists gain sought-after international exposure by using North Americans and Westerners as propaganda. Hostages do not always have to represent a terrorist group's national or international enemies. The UN reports that in 2014, ISIS made over US$50 million from hostage ransom alone. Its 2015 and 2016 ransom incomes are probably double that amount.

Hostage taking—at least civilian hostage taking—is internationally recognized as a war crime. The International Convention against the Taking of Hostages defines hostages and hostage taking as follows:

ARTICLE 1

1. Any person who seizes or detains and threatens to kill, to injure or to continue to detain another person (hereinafter referred to as the "hostage") in order to compel a third party, namely, a State, an international intergovernmental organization, a natural or juridical person, or a group of persons, to do or abstain from doing any act as an explicit or implicit condition for the release of the hostage commits the offence of taking of hostages ("hostage-taking") within the meaning of this Convention.
2. Any person who:
    a. attempts to commit an act of hostage-taking, or
    b. participates as an accomplice of anyone who commits or attempts to commit an act of

hostage-taking likewise commits an offence for
the purposes of this Convention.
(United Nations General Assembly Official Records 1979)

Also, Articles 34 and 147 of the Fourth Geneva Convention,
August 12, 1949, state that taking civilians hostage is a grave breach
and will be considered as a war crime.

Hostage negotiators term the motives for taking hostages as either
instrumental or *expressive*. Instrumental hostage takings are when the
kidnappers expect to receive something in return for the safe return
of the hostage. That something might be the straight financial gain of
ransom, the release of a prisoner, or media coverage for some social
or political cause. Expressive hostage takings can be just venting
or expressing anger against a person, company, or government for
perceived injustices. Barricaded persons taking hostages are also
categorized in the same manner. However, people who are mentally
ill and take hostages often act out in response to their particular
disorder, sometimes following instructions and voices in their heads.
The strategies outlined in this book do not speak directly to hostage
takers who are barricaded or suffering mental illness.

Hostage negotiation is a complicated synthesis of sciences that
requires years of dedication and practice by those with a particular
skill set. As such, it is beyond the purpose of this book to go further
than the occasional mention. However, hostages must remember
that as they apply their survival strategies on the inside, hostage
negotiators are applying their strategies on the outside. This fact is
frequently made known to hostages, as a frustrated captor will often
confront the hostage and complain that negotiations are not going
well or have broken down. Hostages should take this as good news
because it means everyone back home knows you are still alive, and
it makes you aware that negotiations are ongoing. Any news from the
outside world regarding your situation is a bonus—it provides hope.

As part of your predeployment training and awareness, it is
incumbent upon you to familiarize yourself with the history of
terrorist and organized crime factions in the area you are planning
to visit. Knowing the organization and its purpose for the kidnapping,

the history of ransom demands, the length of confinement, and negotiation processes previously employed will better prepare you and your employer, should you become a victim of a hostage taking.

> Kidnappings and hostage events involving U.S. citizens have become increasingly prevalent as ISIL, al Qa'ida and its affiliates have increased attempts to finance their operations through kidnapping for ransom operations. ISIL, al-Qa'ida in the Arabian Peninsula (AQAP) and al-Qa'ida in the Islamic Maghreb (AQIM) are particularly effective with kidnapping for ransom and are using ransom money to fund the range of their activities. Kidnapping targets are usually Western citizens from governments or third parties that have established a pattern of paying ransoms for the release of individuals in custody. (United States Department of State 2015)

From 2011 to 2014, the incidence of kidnapping Chinese nationals has more than doubled worldwide, with the majority happening in the Philippines and Nigeria. Chinese companies have a more adventurous business attitude and are more likely to push into regions where other companies are reluctant to travel. Chinese companies and families have a history of paying ransoms relatively quickly with little negotiation, which is partially responsible for this significant increase. Also, quick ransom payments have caused kidnappers to renege on their release promises and demand a second ransom payment.

WHO IS LIKELY TO BE TAKEN HOSTAGE

First, a hostage must represent some value to the hostage takers. The hostage may be a citizen of a country whose government is somehow aligned with the hostage taker's own government and, therefore, directly related to the grievance. The hostage may be an employee of the international company at the center of the disputed mining action or a company that best represents that grievance. Often, the higher the hostage's ranking within a particular government or corporation, the higher the value of that hostage.

The hostage may be an enemy soldier who serves as the hostage taker's propaganda. This demonstrates the terrorist organization's superior fighting skills and results in improved status among other terrorist groups, increased recruitment, and increased financial donations. An enemy soldier provides excellent value as a human shield, as his fellow soldiers and his home government are far less likely to attack a terrorist hideout if there is a risk of killing one of their own military personnel. A Western, NATO, or Alliance soldier provides significant trading power.

The hostage's value is assessed against these three factors: political leverage, potential ransom value, and the level of protection the hostage may provide as a human shield. Each traveler must assess his own hostage value with due regard to the region, the types of activity he will be engaged in, and the length of his stay, offset by the level of security planning and preparations undertaken.

Figure 1 shows a quick summary of target selection and planning vis-à-vis the target's security practices.

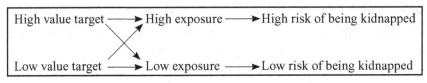

Figure 1. Risk potential for being taken hostage.

If the hostage is considered a high-value target for political leverage, ransom, or as a human shield and does not take the appropriate security precautions and/or remains in the theater of risk for an extended period of time, he is highly exposed and therefore at a high risk of being kidnapped. However, if a high-value target takes the necessary security precautions and does not remain in the theater of risk for extend periods of time, he is at a lower risk of being kidnapped.

If the hostage is a low-value target, takes appropriate security precautions, and does not remain in the theater of risk for extended periods, he is at a low risk of being kidnapped. However, a low-risk target who does not take security precautions and remains in the theater of risk for an extended time is highly exposed and, therefore, at a high risk of being kidnapped.

> Terrible forces were in play, as dangerous and random in their violence as lightning strikes. For anyone in range of this storm, victimhood was a matter of timing and location. (Jessica Buchanan, 81)

> What we had failed to recognize in taking this trip was the simple but vital fact that although our organization had been providing for these communities for years, not only had that not been sufficient to prevent this; it had attracted it to us. (Jessica Buchanan, 89)

CHAPTER 2
WHAT IS A "TERRORIST" GROUP?

This book uses the word *terrorist* often and broadly when speaking about groups who take hostages, whatever their purpose. Taking foreign citizens hostage is often political and, therefore, falls under the definition of terrorism. Even if the kidnapping is solely for ransom, taking a citizen of a foreign country hostage always involves that hostage's home government and the government of the country in which the kidnapping occurred. (To learn more about the responsibilities of the country in which the hostage taking occurred, see appendix 5, Author's Note 3.)

The survival strategies outlined in this book focus on situations faced by hostages that have been held for many months—or even years— by religious fundamentalist groups, for mainly political or financial purposes. That said, the strategies are also applicable to criminal organizations that abduct persons to be kept as hostages for financial or political gain. Hostage takers may modify their ransom demands from political to financial or a mix of both, depending on the identity of the hostage and the fluctuating social or political issues of the day.

This book uses the terms *kidnapping* and *abducted* to mean "taken against one's will." Also, following the current convention in legal writing, this book uses male pronouns to refer to either sex.

DEFINITIONS

There are numerous definitions of *terrorism*; Canada has its own, as do the United States, Great Britain, the European Union, and so on. However, it is significant and instructive to recognize that the UN has no internationally agreed-upon definition of *terrorism*.

In Canada, Section 83.01 of the Criminal Code defines *terrorism* as an act committed "in whole or in part for a political, religious or ideological purpose, objective or cause" with the intention of intimidating the public "with regard to its security, including its economic security, or compelling a person, a government or a domestic or an international organization to do or to refrain from doing any act" (Criminal Code 1985). Activities recognized as criminal within this context include death and bodily harm with the use of violence; endangering a person's life; risks posed to the health and safety of the public; significant property damage; and interference or disruption of essential services, facilities, or systems.

In the United States, *terrorism* is defined as consisting of activities that "involve acts dangerous to human life that are a violation of the criminal laws of the United States or of any State . . . intended to intimidate or coerce a civilian population; influence the policy of a government by intimidation; or . . . affect the conduct of a government by mass destruction, assassination, or kidnapping" (*Country Reports on Terrorism 2014*).

The Department of Homeland Security (Homeland Security Act 2002) (DHS) publishes its own definitions of *terrorists*, *extremists*, and *facilitators* as well as what it defines as *homegrown violent extremists*, *lone offender*, and *radicalization*. Accordingly, DHS has recently reclassified the shooting at Fort Hood and against the military recruiting station in Arkansas as terrorist acts.

Title 22, Section 2656f of the United States Code (USC) also requires the Department of State to include in its annual report "to the extent practicable, complete statistical information on the number of individuals, including United States citizens and dual nationals, killed, injured, or kidnapped by each terrorist group during the preceding calendar year." In compiling the figures of terrorist incidents that are included in the *Country Reports on Terrorism* (CRT), the National Counterterrorism Center (NCTC) uses the definition of *terrorism* found in Title 22, which states that terrorism is "premeditated, politically motivated violence perpetrated against non-combatant targets by subnational groups or clandestine agents" (*Country Reports on Terrorism 2014*). Interestingly enough, the

DHS states, "There is no one definition of *terrorism* accepted by the federal government." (See related information at https://info.publicintelligence.net/DHS-Extremist Lexicon.)

The legal definition of *terrorism* in the European Union can be found in the EU Framework Decision on Combating Terrorism (The Council of the European Union 2002), which identifies *terrorism* as activities with the aim of "seriously intimidating a population, or unduly compelling a government or international organization to perform or abstain from performing any act, or seriously destabilizing or destroying the fundamental political, constitutional, economic or social structures of a country or an international organisation." Activities that may be deemed terrorist under this framework include attacks on people resulting in death, kidnapping, or hostage taking and extensive destruction to a government or public facility.

> The United Nations has not been able to come to a consensus on a definition of terrorism.

> The definitional impasse has prevented the adoption of a Comprehensive Convention on International Terrorism. Even in the immediate aftermath of 9/11 the UN failed to adopt the Convention, and the deadlock continues to this day.

> The prime reason is the standoff with the Organization of the Islamic Conference (OIC). The Arab Terrorism Convention and the Terrorism Convention of the Organization of the Islamic Conference (OIC) define terrorism to exclude armed struggle for liberation and self-determination. This claim purports to exclude blowing up certain civilians from the reach of international law and organizations . . .

> On November 7, 2014 the Chairman of the General Assembly Working Group—that was established to finalize a draft convention on international

terrorism—circulated an oral report in which he named the outstanding issues. He highlighted the OIC demand "to distinguish between acts of terrorism and the legitimate struggle of peoples under foreign occupation and colonial or alien domination in the exercise of their right to self-determination." (*Human Rights Voices*, n.d.)

I believe it is unlikely the UN will agree on a definition for some time, especially when some Middle East states wish to "exclude blowing up certain civilians" as an act out of reach of international law.

The UN often faces this conundrum. If it moves too quickly, it is accused of meddling in a nation's affairs; if it moves too slowly, it has let innocent people die.

Speaking on behalf of the OIC on October 7, 2014, the Egyptian delegation was again explicit about the standoff:

The group reiterates once again the need to make a distinction between terrorism and the exercise of the legitimate right of peoples to resist foreign occupation. (United Nations, General Assembly Working Group 2014)

Likewise, Iran, speaking on behalf of the nonaligned movement, said,

Terrorism should not be equated with the legitimate struggle of peoples under colonial or alien domination and foreign occupation, for self-determination and national liberation. (United Nations, General Assembly Working Group 2014)

This pretty much leaves the door wide open for any and all militant actions against any government in power through any process, legitimate or otherwise—democracy, theocracy, or monarchy, civilian or military.

The common theme in the Canadian, American, and United Kingdom definitions is the unlawful use of force or violence against persons or property to intimidate or coerce a legitimate government, the civilian population, or any segment thereof in furtherance of political or social objectives.

Most definitions of terrorist groups state that their violent acts require an element of terror. The group must commit an act so terrible that it provokes a sense of terror among the local citizens or the government in order for them to be labeled as terrorists. It has become widely understood that *terror* means the significant loss of life, often directed at the general civilian population. Often, a rising terrorist group feels it needs to enter the world stage by coming up with more and more gruesome acts of violence that strike more and more terror into the general population. This is why we continue to see bombs going off in marketplaces, in train stations, on public transport, and at schools.

Recall the Fatah terrorist who, when asked about the violence, explained, "I regarded armed actions to be essential, it is the very basis of my organization . . . The aim was to cause as much carnage as possible. The main thing was the amount of blood. An armed action proclaims that I am here, I exist, I am strong, I am in control, I am in the field, I am on the map" (Post 2007, 61).

It is important at this juncture to identify relevant terms or definitions that are frequently used when discussing terrorist events. When civilians are killed, as they were in the American attacks of 9/11 or London's 7/7, on Madrid's railway, in a Moscow theater, or in a Paris restaurant, music concert, or the Brussels airport, they are referred to by politicians and the media as "innocent civilians." To the terrorist, however, there are no innocent people; the country is treated as whole. *Innocent* is a term the affected country uses to vilify the act and the cowardly perpetrators who kill unarmed civilians who are not direct actors against a terrorist group such as military or police personnel. Terrorists believe, again this is purely as justification for their actions, that civilians voted for the government that now attacks their country; the citizens' taxes pay for the soldiers that kill their friends and family; the citizens' taxes buy the planes and the bombs that blow up their homes. Therefore, civilians are legitimate targets.

It is imperative, when hostages find themselves face to face with their kidnappers, they are aware that their very survival may depend upon terminology. Terms such as *terrorism, war, occupation, soldier, evil, fault, religion*, and *innocence* change with perspective. One slip of the tongue can set religious fundamentalists off on a verbal tirade or evoke an immediate physical retribution. In all dealings with your captors, remember—*perspective.*

Government leaders are quick to label attacks against any of their political representatives, political personnel, senior government officials, government sites, or military personnel as *terrorist.* This is often a rallying cry for political support, a legal authority to act plus increased security spending.

Events like the 2014 attack in Canada at the National War Memorial and the Parliament Building plus the 2013 attack in Britain against uniformed soldiers do not always have the same impact on public opinion as attacks on numbers of innocent civilians, but they unite citizens in support for those who serve. In 2009, the United States saw attacks at military recruiting offices in Little Rock, Arkansas, and Port Hood, Texas, and in 2015, a similar attack in Tennessee. Soldiers should not be considered to be in harm's way when at home. However, when at home, they are less vigilant and, as such, can be considered as a soft target.

While passing the 2015 National Defense Authorization Act at the end of 2014, lawmakers changed the definition of an *attack* to include attacks "inspired or motivated by foreign terrorist organizations." Hence, in December 2015, FBI Director James Comey announced that the Navy Recruiting Station attacks in Chattanooga, Tennessee, in July 2015 have been reclassified from homegrown violent extremism to a foreign terrorism event. It had initially described Abdulaziz as a homegrown violent extremist.

Political parties have difficulty agreeing on terrorism as defined by the act alone. It would be much easier to identify and define an act as terrorism if the violence was carried out in conjunction with an expression of fundamentalist membership or ideology, but such is not always the case. Often the ensuing investigation uncovers an interest in a political or religious ideology, and sometimes it just uncovers a history of mental illness. No clear answers.

HOMEGROWN TERRORISM

Around the world, an accusing finger is pointed at the Internet as one of the pipelines of homegrown terrorism because it makes terrorist propaganda available from any number of online sources. Where there used to be imaginary friends and imaginary playmates for troubled teens and adults, the Internet is now a 24-7 community where everyone who feels disenchanted or disenfranchised can find a home, a friend, acceptance . . . and a message.

A recent theory of homegrown terrorism suggests that parents that emigrated from war-torn Middle Eastern countries may hold dual citizenship, but they remain fully aware of the horrors of the civil wars, oppressive regimes, and the sectarian violence they left behind. Although their dual citizenship connects them to their old country, they have no intentions of going back. Their children, however, being born in their new country, hold only single citizenship. This effectively severs them politically from their old country. They may begin to feel like a foreigner, alienated from their cultural lineage, their roots. This situation often results in a natural curiosity about the political and social goings-on in the old country, and the resulting conflicted emotions make them more susceptible to influence. This influence may cultivate feelings of guilt, foster an identity crisis, and create a moral obligation to return, to be a somebody and fight—to fight *for* something or fight *against* something.

This situation may be exacerbated by the children living in an ethnocentric community within their new country which may inhibit building a "new" sense of identity and allegiance to the new country—in effect, counterassimilation.

For years, Western countries had a certain protection from terrorist acts on home soil because of what is called *covenant security*, i.e., not committing terrorist acts in the country in which you live. However, it may not be long until "homegrown" terrorism in North America and the EU involves hostages abducted and held on home soil. Canada remembers the Front de Libération du Québec (FLQ) October Crisis in Quebec in 1970, when Pierre Laporte, the deputy premier and minister of labor for Quebec, was kidnapped and killed; British diplomat James Cross was also kidnapped but was later released. The United States remembers the 1974 abduction of Patty Hearst by a previously unknown terrorist group that called itself the Symbionese Liberation Army. After the Army members were arrested for bank robbery, Patty Hearst was also charged because the bank video showed she was present at the bank, holding an automatic rifle. Although she did nothing else but stand with the rifle, her trial defense team argued that brainwashing and Stockholm syndrome had won her over. Her controversial conviction sent her to jail, although she later received a presidential pardon.

The use of terror is not only intended to affect the opinions and actions of a government but also to instill fear and terror into the general population so they, in turn, will exert pressure on the government. After the attacks of 9/11, people around the world are more afraid of flying than ever before, and everyone understands why. This fear will remain for generations to come. Airport security measures around the world are a daily reminder of these events. Subway riders in Spain and public transportation users in London will be nervous for years to come.

Populations worldwide are continually reminded of these terrorist attacks as the media recounts, over and over, the death and destruction during the anniversaries of every major terrorist event. These media replays help the terrorists celebrate their victories over and over again and provide valuable propaganda for their cause. The citizens of Paris were anxious to put the events of November 13, 2015, behind them—not to forget but to reclaim their city and their way of life. The media wouldn't let them. There were media reports from the scene every hour on the hour for days, interviews with witnesses, updates and one-day anniversaries, two-day anniversaries . . . and one-week anniversaries. Each replay increases the media's ratings, each replay increases the terrorist's ratings, and each replay reaffirms the public's fear.

The term *international terrorism* used in this book means terrorism involving citizens or the territory of more than one country; the term *terrorist group* means any single group that may have significant subgroups that practice international terrorism.

For the legal and theoretical purposes of this book, the basic definition of *terrorism* will suffice. That said, it is vitally important for hostages to remember a common phrase: *"One man's terrorist is another man's freedom fighter."* Therefore, for the practical purposes of this book, hostages must recognize that the definition of *terrorism* is subjective and never static.

The meanings of *terrorist* and *terrorism* continue to be debated at various committees and organizations within the United Nations and are often referred to differently within the context of each dispute. With respect to the Koran's justification for armed resistance, "Permission to take up arms is hereby granted to those who are attacked; they have suffered injustice. God has all the power to give victory" (Koran 22:39).

If a bomb is dropped from an airplane, it is called war; if a bomb is hidden under your clothes, it is called terrorism. If you kill an enemy soldier within the "recognized" geographical boundaries—the theater of the war—it is called war; if you kill an enemy soldier outside those boundaries, it is called terrorism. All this pretty much means that the definition of *terrorism* is very subjective and effectively in the eye of the beholder. Each act may have to be decided on its own merits and by the International Criminal Court.

I also use the generic terms *Westerners* and *the West* when referring to many of the people taken as hostages. This term includes Europeans, citizens of most countries surrounding the Mediterranean, Russians, North Americans, Australians, and New Zealanders. There are fewer Asians taken as hostages in the Middle East than Westerners, but they are included as well. For the purposes of this book, hostages are, for the most part, foreigners.

While we're talking about definitions, even the meaning of *hostage* is not always accurate when discussing many terrorist attacks. Traditionally, *hostage* was meant to describe a person held captive until an agreement to exchange them for money or some other concession can be agreed upon. During the terrorist attacks against internationals at the hotels in Mumbai (2013), in Mali (2015), in Burkina Faso (2016); the music concert in Paris (2015); and the shopping mall attack in Nairobi (2013), it was never the intention of the terrorists to abduct or exchange any persons for any political or monetary concessions. They captured people solely for the killing, a spectacle intended to add an exclamation point to their conviction and determination.

Police forces around the world have changed their operational approach when engaging terrorists who have captured civilians. Traditionally, the police standard operating procedure (SOP) was to surround the building, make contact with the captors, and begin negotiations while collecting information and intelligence in hopes of a peaceful resolution. The events of the Columbine High School shooting in the United States and other similar events around the world involving students or disgruntled employees shooting students or fellow employees in their own office building have highlighted the problems of police responding quickly to the site but then waiting outside until there were sufficient officers and equipment to safely enter and confront the offenders. This practice, however, allowed the perpetrators inside to continue killing people relatively unimpeded. Now, SOPs require the police to take immediate action in order to reduce the number of civilian causalities. These situations are defined as active-shooter events, and many police forces around the world now train extensively in active-shooter scenarios.

These active-shooter events have put police forces in a catch-22 situation. Historically, police hostage negotiation principles in the West didn't really come of age until the mid to late '70s and early 1980s in the New York Police Department, pioneered by psychologist Harvey Schlossberg and Captain Frank Bolz. Prior to then, police SWAT teams would storm the building, the bank, or the store and shoot the perpetrators, often with death and injury to civilians. Public pressure and professional ethos forced the police to change these tactics. The new SOP directed the police to take up a holding position outside and begin negotiations toward a safe resolution. The new hostage philosophy around the world became "contain and negotiate." Hence, many hostage situations went on for days and even weeks, but many lives were saved.

Nowadays, terrorist attacks around the world take prisoners solely for slaughter. The police must now quickly decide if this is a criminal event with hostages or a terrorist event with prisoners.

Police first responders are now under immense pressure to enter the building, not knowing how many shooters there are or where they might be. They are likely outgunned and relatively unprotected with only a hand gun and a patrol-level vest. They must put themselves at extreme personal risk. These active-shooter events necessitate that law enforcement respond with greater tactical capacity; critics, however, accuse the police of militarizing. When the smoke clears, the police must justify their actions as being neither too soon or too late and with a minimum of collateral damage. Negotiate or assault? No easy decision.

It seems the earlier 1970s and '80s terrorist tactic of hijacking an airplane or occupying an embassy and negotiating released hostages for political concessions has evolved. Today's major terrorist groups don't want a few political concessions . . . they want the whole country.

SELF-IDENTIFICATION OF HOSTAGE TAKERS TO THE HOSTAGE

"Terrorism is sustained by three elements: (1) grievances, (2) a conspiratorial interpretation of the grievances, and (3) a license to act, which may be given by religious authority" (Marvasti 2008, ix).

I am not aware of any hostage takers who identified themselves up front to their hostages as terrorists. Rather, they always told the hostage they were fighters for some legitimate social, political, or religious cause. Given the UN's difficulty in providing a definition of *terrorism* that is acceptable to all 188 member states, in the face of the argument to exclude armed struggle for liberation and self-determination, it is little wonder that politically motivated groups who take hostages can justly argue they are fighting for a worthy and just social, political, or religious cause. This lack of clarity also provides the terrorists with an argument against accusations of war crimes or crimes against humanity, as they see themselves in a "legitimate struggle of peoples under colonial or alien domination and foreign occupation, for self-determination and national liberation" (United Nations, General Assembly Working Group 2014).

> Cast perpetually on the defensive and forced to take up arms to protect themselves and their real or imagined constituents only, terrorists perceive themselves as reluctant warriors, driven by desperation—and lacking any viable alternative—to violence against a repressive state, a predatory rival ethnic or nationalist group, or an unresponsive international order. (Hoffman 2006)

Case study interviews, research, and my experience all confirm that a hostage does not have to wait long before being informed about the group's identity and purpose. Hostage takers have a compulsion to justify their actions to the hostage and—coincidently, it seems—to reaffirm that purpose to themselves. The hostage takers will also take this opportunity to dictate the rules of the hostage's confinement, which usually contain the threat of death should the hostage attempt to escape.

The leader of the group, or whoever is giving this introductory speech to the hostage, may also take this opportunity to insult and berate the hostage, accuse the person of being a spy, and possibly beat the hostage. This is as much a demonstration of his power over the hostage as it is venting his frustration for all the planning, time, and expense it has taken to abduct the hostage.

> "We know that you are a Mossad spy." As I started to protest, he interrupted me: "Don't waste your breath. You have twenty-four hours to decide whether to tell the truth and die with a clear conscience . . . or go to your death as a liar. That is your choice. Think it over." (Taylor, Scott, *Unembedded* 2009, 314)[2]

> Through a Translator, Judith Tebbutt is informed "They are Somali pirates." He seemed to study my face for a reaction. "You are very lucky. Somali pirates, they don't kill people, don't torture people. They just want money. That's why they took you. When they get money you will go home." (Tebbutt, Judith, *A Long Walk Home* 2013, 85)[3]

---

[2] In September 2004, Canadian journalist Scott Taylor was seized by Iraqi mujahedeen and sentenced to death. Chained to a bed frame, awaiting execution, the one-time art student reflected on the events that had culminated in his imprisonment in Iraq.

[3] In September 11, 2001, Judith Tebbutt and her husband, David, were kidnapped while vacationing on a beach resort forty kilometers south of Somalia. Judith was torn away from David by a band of armed pirates, dragged over sea and

What motivates an individual engaging in terrorist activity is the quest for significance. The hunger to feel recognized or significant is not exclusive to terrorists however, Kruglanski's assertion puts into perspective why terrorism doesn't need to be associated with a specific kind of ideology. The ideology can be religious, ethno-nationalistic or political in nature, because the ideology merely provides the means to justify the quest for significance. The ideologies used to justify terrorist activity largely have three common aspects; a grievance (a wrongdoing towards a certain group or community), an enemy (someone who is responsible for the grievance) and a method (the belief that terrorism is the most effective way to attain significance). (Kruglanski et al. 2013)

(Professor Kruglanski, from the University of Maryland, is a recognized expert on the mind of a terrorist.)

On a psychological level, this self-identification serves hostage takers' need to absolve themselves of their illegal or unethical actions, which are often in direct conflict with their espoused religious beliefs. The group will go to considerable lengths to justify its actions to the hostage, often providing numerous examples of why their cause is righteous and just. In the case of many Islamist fundamentalists, they will quote religious scriptures as proof of their righteousness. Believing Iran's and Egypt's earlier UN position that "the activities of the parties during an armed conflict, including in situations of foreign occupation" and the "legitimate struggle of peoples under colonial or alien domination" (United Nations, General Assembly Working Group 2014), do not constitute terrorism gives the hostage takers plenty of room for espousing political as well as religious

---

land to a village in the arid heart of lawless Somalia, and there held hostage in a squalid room, a ransom on her head. But though she was isolated, intimidated, and near-starved, Judith resolved to survive, walking endless circuits of her nine-foot prison, trying to make her captors see her as a human being, keeping her faith at all times in Ollie, her son.

righteousness. They inform the hostage how their captivity is related to their cause and then go on to explain the terms and conditions of the hostage's release. Again, this is just as much a justification to the hostage as it is a reaffirmation to their fellow terrorists in attendance.

Your prime interrogator will absolve himself and his fellow kidnappers of any fault. It was the actions of your country, your government, or your company that forced them to kidnap you. If anything happens to you, it is not their fault; there is no blood on their hands. How many psychopaths and sociopaths explain away their actions by blaming their victims? How many sexual deviants and rapists absolve themselves by blaming their victims? These kidnappers, these religious fanatics, these criminals are no different. The psychological term for this internal struggle is *cognitive dissonance*. This is a state of psychological conflict or anxiety resulting from a contradiction between a person's simultaneously held beliefs or attitudes—an illogical conflict, as it were. "I'm a good person, but I'm doing bad things." In order to resolve this internal conflict between what they have done and what they know is right, they must find an answer—but an answer that absolves them of any blame. So they come to the conclusion that the fault must be an outside person or force. Their perspective changes from "Why have I done these things?" to "Who is responsible and forcing me to do this?" Once they have come to this decision, this reconciliation, they can proceed without any concern for their actions, their conscience, or their feelings of guilt. Dissonance is a strong theory in criminology, as many individuals or criminal groups absolve themselves of any wrongdoing because they have come to blame everyone but themselves for their situation.

This compulsion by the hostage takers to identify themselves and justify their actions benefits hostages by helping them understand the "who" and "why" of their kidnapping. This knowledge provides a very important first step in hostage survival, as they can now begin to select and apply the appropriate strategies for their treatment and release. That said, it is widely known that some hostages are taken in an act of mistaken identity or opportunity, just by being in the wrong place at the wrong time. Regardless of whether their selection was planned or opportunistic, they will still be informed as to the hostage takers' identity and purpose.

⌒✯⌒

In some Middle Eastern countries, terrorist groups and organized crime groups may be referred to as "warlords." Their followers are often composed of family members or formed along ethnic or tribal lines. They flourish in countries where the government is unstable, weak, or indecisive; where there is political and police corruption or complicity; where the military may not have the willpower or political support to act; where there is an ineffective judicial system, a poor economy, plus helplessness and hopelessness among the population. Their reasons for taking hostages are most always financial.

Terrorism and hostage taking can be seen as a source of easy money, adventure, or the only means of fighting back against political or religious oppression. Terrorists and organized crime groups often blame the poor economy on existing or foreign government activities. Terrorists will continue to justify their actions by blaming big businesses or other religious or ethnic groups as justification for their actions. Uniting citizens against a common enemy is always a good recruitment philosophy for terrorist groups and for rogue governments, as it diverts attention and blame.

SOCIO-ECONOMIC FACTORS

From an economic standpoint, the years of war, civil unrest, and terrorism have had a significant negative impact on the economy of the entire Middle East region and neighboring states. Unemployment is very high and unlikely to improve in the foreseeable future. The prevailing social custom in these areas is that the eldest son must quickly establish himself financially and, soon thereafter, find a wife and start a family. For the eldest son as well as his younger siblings, this course has essentially become unattainable. This situation affects not only the men of the household but also the girls, who have little chance of being courted by a man of prospect. Those traditional paths are no longer open.

For these young men, joining a group of fighters in a righteous cause is a path to recognition as an adult and establishing themselves as heroes in the eyes of their community. A young man without a woman in his life becomes anxious and aggressive. As fighters, they may be given a wife, they may just take a wife, or they may just rape women as they see fit. Terrorism has disrupted many traditional social customs, but at the same time, it also presents another path. Some people turn to terrorism because of their ambivalence toward authority, their disdain for convention, and their emotional detachment from the consequences of their actions or simply defective insight. Many potential recruits are prone to destructiveness, with a devotion to violent subculture norms and weapons fetishes, group dynamics, or religion. In the last few years, we have seen them travel from country to country, from fight to fight, learning their war craft as they go. These traveling fighters have now congregated and morphed into ISIS, the Islamic State. Many terrorist groups have come to recognize these personality differences, or defects, in their new recruits and have learned how to best exploit these individual "talents." Some recruits are religious zealots willing to martyr themselves for the cause. Some recruits are veteran fighters. Some only wish to provide logistical assistance. Others with possible psychopathic tendencies or psychological deficiencies may serve well as suicide bombers. But interestingly enough, there is no clear proof that psychological maladies are the main cause of terrorists acting the way they do.

Jerrold Post's studies (2007) involved respected forensic and clinical psychiatrists, cultural anthropologists, social workers, and journalists interviewing hundreds of jailed domestic and international terrorists from a diversity of terrorist groups around the world. These included organizers, supporters, longtime fighters, homegrown terrorists, and (failed) suicide bombers.

In his book, he concludes the following:

Terrorists are not depressed, severely emotionally
disturbed, or crazed fanatics. It is not individual
psychopathology, but group, organizational, and
social psychology, with a particular emphasis
on "collective identity," that provides the most
powerful lens through which to understand terrorist
psychology and behavior . . . this collective identity
is established extremely early, so that from childhood
on, "hatred is bred in the bone." The importance
of collective identity and the processes of forming
and transforming collective identities cannot be
overemphasized. (p. 8)

There is a widespread assumption in the lay
community that groups and individuals who kill
innocent victims to accomplish their political goals
must be crazed fanatics. Surely no psychologically
"normal" individual could perpetrate wanton violence
against innocent women and children.

In fact, those of us who have studied terrorist
psychology have concluded that most terrorists are
"normal" in the sense of not suffering from psychotic
disorders. (p. 3)

After each terrorist attack against a country not within a
recognized theater of war and committed by citizens of that country,
discussions begin about homegrown terrorism. Prevailing theories
often identify disenfranchised youths with social or behavioral
difficulties or mental deficiencies who have found terrorist propaganda
websites as their alternate source of social conscience and direction.
These fighters may decide to commit some act within their own
country or travel to the actual war theater. Not only are these foreign
fighters valuable as propaganda tools but they are also educated and
social media–savvy. More importantly, they are extremely useful for
their linguistic abilities (especially in English), their knowledge of

their home country's legal and civil rights laws, their knowledge of their home country's transportation infrastructure, and their ability to move around freely. Their understanding of hostage psychology is obvious, as they have significantly improved and adapted their hostage handling to thwart any humanizing efforts. It is obvious they have made excellent use of dehumanizing tactics most likely learned from higher studies, Guantanamo Bay, and the Internet.

LEADERSHIP AND RECRUITMENT

Jerrold Post's assessment of leadership is particularity instructive today in light of the recent phenomenon of international citizens traveling to join ISIS. Islam's failure to grow and evolve over the last 1,400 years is a direct result of being mired in its own strict adherence to religious dogma. It is a victim of its own resistance to change. However, its recent military and propaganda successes are directly due to the influence of these educated international recruits.

The role of the leader is crucial in drawing together alienated, frustrated individuals into a coherent organization. The leader provides a "sense-making" unifying message that conveys a religious, political or ideological justification to their disparate followers. (Post 2007, 8) I believe that Post's research is equally applicable to why people join cults. With only a few thousand people to recruit from, a charismatic leader can always attract sufficient numbers of followers—a collective of people with similar political, religious, or social ideals who will follow and obey him. A recent North American example of a charismatic leader with a group of dedicated followers is the Branch Davidians of Waco, Texas, led by David Koresh (Breault and King 1993). Living in a protected compound, Koresh forced marriages, rapes, and beatings and enforced bizarre rules for behavior such as a strict diet, enduring his day-long prayer meetings, and training in weaponry. "I am the son of God," said David Koresh (Breault and King 1993).

In March of 1995, in Tokyo, Japan, a cult called Aum Shinrikyo, formed by leader Shoko Asahara, set off five separate sarin gas attacks in the Tokyo subway system. These attacks killed twelve people and injured fifty others. Asahara had earlier written a book in which he declared himself as Christ and promised his followers spiritual powers.

Is a terrorist group recruited and organized any differently from a cult? I don't think so—it's only a difference of scale. But historically, cults have preferred to keep to themselves.

If we look back a few years to the 1960s and '70s, it was "hip" to "drop out," essentially "escape the establishment" and "do your own thing." This often involved living in social communes with few rules and plenty of self-love. Curiously enough, this coincided with the times of global antiwar protests. During the 1960s and '70s, cult recruitment, communal living, or a sociopolitical movement were very much dependent on a charismatic leader who would take his message on the road, speaking face to face to groups of like-minded people, who would gather and participate in nonviolent social protests called sit-ins or love-ins. These people were proud of their open-mindedness and were willing to try anything new. Interestingly enough, these cults always included a religious or spiritual component.

Today, with access to the Internet, a charismatic leader can safely recruit from hundreds of millions of potential followers. The charismatic leader has been replaced by slick advertising with a message and a lifestyle. Terrorist Web pages have spectacular photographs and videos accompanied by upbeat music and religious chants selling a message, offering inclusion and a lifestyle. This is no different from how young car buyers are lured with television commercials. Are young buyers attracted to a vehicle's performance and handling or to the adventures that can be had with a car full of smiling, happy friends? It's both. They can choose the message or the lifestyle. The terrorists know their websites have to offer both the message and the lifestyle. You can be the fighter, or you can be one of their happy friends.

Discussions of how or why these people are converted is beyond the scope and purpose of this book except to advise the reader, the traveler, and the potential hostage that coming into contact with these people is becoming more likely every day. This contact may be as close as the internet, or on a foreign street as one who may approach you under some friendly guise or scam or as one of your captors who may be giving you his righteous speech about why you have been abducted. As your captors, they may be more difficult to deal with in some ways but easier in others. As the reader will learn, understanding your captors is extremely important to your survival.

I believe that ISIS is an old-world cause in wait of new-world leadership.

CHAPTER 3
PREDEPLOYMENT TRAINING

Predeployment courses are offered by a number of security companies around the world. However, predeployment training—which involves putting a smelly burlap bag over the student's head, taking him for a drive into the woods or dumping him inside an abandoned warehouse, then yelling at him, intimidating him with gunfire, death threats, or sexual violence—makes good theater, but it does not fit with the nature of this book. (Many of these burlap bag–training techniques have been updated and now include more security and scenario training.) If that kind of predeployment training scares the student into realizing he must better prepare himself in a number of different areas, then it has been partially successful. The survival strategies offered in this book are more behavior- and psychology-based and have been used successfully by surviving hostages. However, the best hostage-survival strategy in the world is still to avoid being abducted in the first place.

Every released hostage I have interviewed, every hostage I have heard lecture, and every hostage case study I have researched acknowledges the same persistent and distressing burden—how their captivity is negatively affecting their families and loved ones back home.

In the early stages of their captivity, hostages wonder how their family is handling the news of their captivity. As the days wear on, they broaden their thinking to include all that can go wrong at home, all that was not done before they left, and what effect their inaction and procrastination are having on various family members. As time goes by, they begin to worry if their family even knows they are a hostage or if the family thinks they are long since dead and have made the decision to move on with their lives. Hostages have lots of time—time to worry about their family's finances, time to worry about their family's health, time to blame themselves for the pain they are causing, and time to be depressed. How does spending all this time to worry about things back home serve the hostage? It doesn't . . . it makes everything worse.

If the hostage takers inform the hostage that a financial ransom demand has been made to the family, one the hostage knows full well the family cannot possibly meet, this only adds to the feelings of guilt and shame. The depressing scenarios a hostage can come up with are endless.

It is a common negotiation tactic by hostage takers to wait weeks or even months before making contact in an effort to build extreme anxiety within the family, thereby increasing the likelihood of the family paying a large ransom demand relatively quickly. From personal experience, I can attest that the stresses upon the family during this time are extraordinary as they try to make very important decisions under incredible emotional pressure and with little or no information.

Before long, a hostage's worry about family becomes a constant burden and invades his every thought. These thoughts are with him every morning when he awakens, all day long and before he sleeps at night. If not countered by appropriate survival strategies, these worries will soon consume the hostage's every free thought and will eventually drain him of valuable mental and physical strength. If not checked, they will soon affect his will to live.

> The first five days were the toughest . . . I just could not get my mind to rest, to stop or slow down even if only for a few hours. I could not quit analyzing probabilities and options and endlessly producing largely unhappy end-game scripts . . . dark thoughts would churn endlessly through my head. (Fowler 2011, 161–162)[4]

---

4   For decades, Robert R. Fowler was a dominant force in Canadian foreign affairs. In one heart-stopping minute, all of that changed. On December 14,

Early in the ordeal, the hostage starts to wonder how his family heard the news. Was it from his manager? Was it his coworkers? Did they hear it on the morning news, or was it a late-night knock on the door by the police? The hostage begins to wonder how it all played out at home. Who got called first? Who got called next? How did they react? This is particularly troubling to hostages with elderly or ill family members. In time, hostages begin to imagine the many terrible ways this is playing out at home. They, of course, blame themselves. The memories play out as they recall the words of safety and caution family members gave them before heading out on this trip; they remember how they might have dismissed the concerns of safety with a joke or a laugh. All hostages admit that even after a relatively short time in captivity, this worry about family became oppressive. When there are hours, days, and weeks on end with little to do except worry about what grief they have caused, the sense of guilt and shame can become all-consuming.

> How would she [Mary] and our girls handle the news? In
> short—would they be okay? Would friends immediately
> rally round? Would Mary and the girls forgive me for
> putting them through such torment? I was terrified, sad
> and desperate, and in no little discomfort. (Fowler 2011, 16)

If these are the thoughts of hostages who survived, it is reasonable to assume they were the thoughts of those who did not survive—they died knowing they could have done more to benefit their family; they could have said important things to those they loved. They could have made things right with friends and estranged relatives. They

---

2008, Fowler, acting as the UN secretary-general's special envoy to Niger, was kidnapped by al-Qaeda, becoming the highest-ranked UN official ever held captive. Along with his colleague Louis Guay, Fowler lived, slept, and ate with his captors for five months in the open desert. He gained rare first-hand insight into the motivations of the world's most-feared terrorist group. Fowler's capture, release, and subsequent media appearances have helped shed new light on foreign policy and security issues as we enter the second decade on the War on Terror.

died knowing they had the chance to do the right thing but didn't. Families of those who never return live on, wishing so many things had been done prior to the person's departure.

These overwhelming feelings of guilt and regret preoccupy the thoughts of the hostage and contribute to bouts of deep depression and a crushing sense of grief and remorse, and soon, thoughts of suicide begin to creep in. These persistent and intrusive thoughts interrupt clear thinking, cloud good judgment, and take away from valuable time the hostage could better use to focus on improving his own situation. If these thoughts are left unchecked, they adversely affect the hostage's will to live.

As a hostage, in order to survive, you must stop worrying and start thinking. *What is done is done. What is not done is not done.* You're here; you're a hostage. You must come to the realization that the past is over and done with and the sooner the better. It is a waste of your time to dwell on what you should have said or done or what you would have done differently if you had your time back. Nothing you can wish for will change anything now. It's time to recognize your situation for what it is and think about how to survive and return home safely.

A hostage should consider his situation is akin to his falling down a well. He can sit on the bottom of the well and continue to blame himself and wait for help that may never come, or he can begin to construct options of what he can do to get himself out. If your remorse and regret turn into determination and resolve, you have turned the corner and are now on the right path.

I can assure the reader that the family will also go through periods of misery and despair as they struggle to deal with stressors of their own. What drives this family to misery and despair . . . not knowing? Not knowing if their loved one was taken hostage and is being held for ransom; not knowing if they have been abducted, beaten, and left to die; not knowing if they have been raped and tortured and lie near death somewhere on the other side of the world. The family will experience these painful visions every day and every night. This everyday pain is similar to the pain felt by the families of missing children, the pain of not knowing, the pain of always wondering and imagining too many terrible scenarios.

Today's worldwide communication technologies offer a dependable voice, live video, e-mail, text, and chat to the point where families and friends with traveling loved ones have come to expect regular contact with anyone, virtually anywhere. The traveler can provide a play-by-play of their daily activities, and the family can, in turn, express their endearing love and encouragement. This regular contact fosters a sense of calm and a false sense of security on both sides. But when the traveler is taken hostage, the break in communications is abrupt and absolute. This communications withdrawal alone magnifies the totality and the shock of the event to both the hostage and their family. We often hear a family lament, "I knew there was something wrong when he/she didn't call."

Just as the hostage sits and wonders what their family is going through, the family sits and wonders what the hostage is going through. The family feels helpless; the hostage feels helpless.

> His [Jessica's husband] imagination was his worst enemy during those early days and nights, as it is for anyone who waits in fear and concern for word of a disappeared loved one. He tried not to picture the terrible things he already knew about the fates of some of the region's captives . . .

> The persistence of misery was fierce. Erik [Jessica's husband] was unable to turn off the thoughts of Jessica's torture, rape, murder—any of the most vile possibilities. (Buchanan, Jessica 2014, 102, 104)

During these early days and weeks, family members do not cope well and have frequent arguments and angry outbursts borne of frustration over what should be done and who should do it. Many arguments focus on who should make decisions or how the family will make decisions. Who will be the main contact with the police? Who will negotiate? Who will speak to the media? The family comes to realize at some point that their decisions may literally be life-and-death decisions . . . and they're not ready to make them.

Family members do not have the clarity of thought required to make necessary financial decisions. Some families may appoint a lawyer or ask a family elder to take on this task; some may hire an adviser or seek direction from a police family liaison officer (FLO), chapter 4. Depending upon the family dynamics and finances, the family must continue to go to work and may decide to hire a consultant to assume the police-liaison role. Considering the number of phone calls and the constant need to coordinate family decisions against the daily obligations of families with busy corporate executives, business owners, or at-home parents, many families eventually require a police-liaison consultant.

Proper predeployment training and following the suggestions provided during that training have a significant positive impact on the mental and physical health of the hostage. Just as importantly, an honest discussion with family members and sound financial planning prior to travel make the ordeal more manageable. Many hostages don't realize how difficult it is for the family to make informed financial decisions while being distraught about the many life-and-death decisions they are faced with during this ordeal. When hostages are released and return home, all too soon, they have to deal with the many decisions their families made without their direction and input. As marriage counselors will attest, most family arguments are about finances, even during good times. When hostages return home after many months or even years in captivity and isolation, they are far from a rational, nonjudgmental frame of mind.

Family members who have witnessed disbursements of estate monies or properties through a will can attest how some family members reacted in situations involving only a very few dollars or a set of dishes, arguing at length about who should be the executor and who deserved to be a beneficiary. The resulting bad feelings last a lifetime. A hostage taking is no different; relationships are strained, and most are never the same again. Without proper preplanning, the release and homecoming of a hostage can be even more traumatic than the hostage taking itself.

PREDEPLOYMENT PLANNING

Predeployment planning, for the purposes of this book, involves three main entities: the traveler himself, the traveler's employer, and the traveler's family. Each entity has a very important role to play, both separately and collectively. The most important aspect of planning for all three is financial planning.

FINANCIAL PLANNING

Some aspects of financial planning are solely the responsibility of the employer, some are the responsibility of both the employer and the employee, and some are the responsibility of the employee and his family.

The importance of sound financial planning prior to departure cannot be overstated. Good communication, legal support, and understanding between the employer, the traveler, and the family are extremely important.

THE EMPLOYEE AND THE FAMILY— FINANCIAL PLANNING

Travelers with financial and familial obligations must take measures to ensure their loved ones are properly provided for in case of a prolonged absence. This list is not exhaustive, as every situation is unique, but here are some important considerations:

- Can your spouse renegotiate your home mortgage or your apartment rental agreement without your signature?
- Can your spouse relicense the family car and negotiate vehicle and house insurance without your signature?
- Who will deal with monthly bills, bank accounts, or stock market sales, and who will exercise your stock options and other retirement strategies?
- Who can legally continue with your retirement planning with the bank, a financial institution, or your employer? Who even knows what to do?
- Who has the passwords to your online trading accounts and the knowledge to act?
- Can your spouse renew your credit card without your signature?

Do not cancel a hostage's corporate or personal credit cards without speaking with the police. I recommend that a senior corporate financial officer, with the approval and assistance of the police, request that all credit cards remain valid, although with a much lower approved-spending limit of, say, $100. If the card remains valid, there is a strong likelihood that the hostage takers will use it and continue to use it without considerable financial loss to the company. This usage will be tracked by the credit card company, thereby providing police with an opportunity to track and identify the card's users and possibly obtain a photograph and handwriting sample. A $100 purchase is a small price to pay for such a valuable investigative lead.

- Can your spouse renew your family's health insurance?
- Can your spouse continue to pay residential taxes? Submit income tax?
- Who can renew your cell phone contract?
- As terrorist groups become more IT-savvy, a hostage's online banking, money transfer, and online shopping access must be severely restricted but not cancelled.

Similar to earlier advice with respect to credit cards, do not automatically cancel a hostage's cell phone without checking with the police—again, for tracking purposes.

In October 2008, Melissa Fung was abducted in Afghanistan and held for twenty-eight days in a hole dug under a vacant house. One of her captors took the SIM card out of her cell phone and installed it in his cell phone. He thought he could now make free phone calls; he was wrong. Each time a call was made in or out of the hostage taker's phone, the cell phone company recognized it as a call in or out of Melissa's phone. Soon, military personnel were tapping on the floor of the vacant house, looking for the secret entrance. Eventually, these phone calls identified the hostage takers in Afghanistan plus those who were conducting the negotiations out of Pakistan. Tracking those phone calls led to the arrest of her abductors and was directly responsible for her release. (Fung 2011)[5]

- Can your spouse sign your children into schools? Some schools require both parents' signatures for admission?
- Are your will and your spouse's will up to date? Of significant importance is the custody and financial support of children in the case of the death of a parent.

When you consider that hostages may be kept for many months or even years and their families back home continue to be exposed to the everyday perils of traffic collisions, in-home accidents, injuries,

---

[5] In October 2008, Mellissa Fung, a long-time reporter for CBC's *The National*, was leaving a refugee camp outside of Kabul. Suddenly, she was grabbed by armed men claiming to be Taliban, stabbed, stuffed into the back of a car, and driven off into the desert. When the group finally reached a village in the middle of nowhere, her kidnappers pushed her towards a hole in the ground. For twenty-eight days, Mellissa Fung lived in that hole, which was barely big enough to stand up or lie down in, nursing her injuries, praying, writing in her notebook, and as a veteran journalist, interrogating her own captors.

medical emergencies, and health problems, a will that outlines both parents' wishes is extremely important.

All travelers, married, single, divorced, or in any relationship that may be considered common-law with even the slightest chance of financial or social implications, should have a will so that others may act responsibly in their stead.

Just for a moment, consider the implications of a single parent taken hostage. How does this affect any existing child-custody issues? Do they fall to the estranged parent, the godparents, or the grandparents? If a divorce or separation was less than harmonious and custody was an issue, the other parent may reopen the question. If the parent with custody remarries and is now absent, maybe even dead, how does this affect custody? If the breakup left hard feelings on either side, it will be almost impossible for those who were once family members to sit down and rationally discuss the future. Can anyone but the hostage really comprehend the mental distress felt by a hostage whose family situation has even a few of these complications?

The way to resolve many of these questions is to obtain power of attorney. Power of attorney will allow a named person or persons to act on your behalf in all legal, financial, and medical matters. Powers of attorney can be held in abeyance for a period of time and acted upon only with concurrence of a lawyer or a judge, or they can be acted upon immediately by the spouse and remain in effect for years or indefinitely.

Always seek appropriate legal advice on issues such as power of attorney, wills, or medical care before departure. The military's SOPs have this well in hand.

As a hostage sits in confinement on the other side of the world, not knowing if each day will be his last, there is comfort in knowing that he left his family with fond memories intact and his loved ones being cared for.

Two weeks prior to Judith and David Tebbutt traveling on vacation to East Africa, David said, "Jude—if anything happens, you'll be OK."

I mean, the holiday in Africa, you know? If anything
were to happen—I just want you to know you'll be
OK. If I died now I'd be happy because I know you
and Ollie [their son] are going to be looked after.
And I know you'd get through it, you wouldn't be
frightened. (Tebbutt, Judith, 10)

David Tebbutt did die. He died fighting off their kidnappers.
Judith was taken hostage and held for ransom for 192 days.

As outlined earlier in this book, a hostage who is not stewing
in depression, ruminating over all the problems he has caused his
loved ones, and blaming himself for their pain can apply his mental
capacities to strategies that will improve his day-to-day living
conditions, reduce the likelihood or the frequency of beatings, and
increase his chances of returning home safely.

EMPLOYER/EMPLOYEE PLANNING—DUTY OF CARE

The employer must assure the traveler and his family that it has
the necessary administrative and operational policies in place to
ensure all travel plans and accommodations are made with the safety
of the employee in mind. The employer must make it clear to the
employee and his family that, should the employee be taken hostage
or suffer serious bodily harm, the employer will act immediately
and responsibly. Also, the employer must satisfy the employee that
during his absence/captivity, his family will be attended to with all
due regard to their legal, financial, and emotional needs. It is not
uncommon for families to require the intervention and guidance of
psychologists or psychiatrists during prolonged hostage situations.

During one prolonged hostage situation involving a relatively
large extended family, I was contacted by a family member who asked
me to "*PLEASE*" provide some immediate intervention because "*the
family is tearing itself apart.*"

Many international corporations have Duty of Care policies and best practices in place that speak directly to their corporate responsibilities and liabilities with respect to their employees. Duty of Care can be found in a country's constitution (Fourth Amendment in the USA) or in its civil and criminal statutes. This duty of care goes beyond medical and dental coverage and speaks to differences in care for short-term business and long-term business assignments. For many employers, duty of care also mandates kidnap insurance coverage. For most federal, provincial, and state departments, these policies are mandatory, constantly updated, and made available to all employees for their review. Discussion of these policies with senior corporate personnel, human resources, and the employer's legal department should be part of any predeployment training. It is essential that an employee and his family fully understand the employer's corporate responsibilities and have the confidence that the employer will carry out those responsibilities.

Corporate social responsibility (CSR) and duty of care have come to also include responsibility for employees traveling on vacation. The United Nations (UN) has made it clear that an employer has the same responsibilities to an employee, whether that employee is at home or abroad. As stated earlier, when it comes to how an employer handles personal emergencies involving its employees, the company's actions are closely scrutinized by all other employees of that company.

As an aside, the UN's CSR also directs all employees to act in the same legal and ethical manner when working and traveling to other countries, as it requires them to act at home. This position directly relates to the use of bribes and other incentives that encourage corruption.

One complication to corporate duty of care is that this responsibility may be defined—and therefore limited—by shareholders, or it may form a legal component of the corporate charter. For this reason and many others, the company's legal personnel must attend, participate in, or directly assist with predeployment training.

A significant factor of corporate duty of care is that the employer should be aware and conversant with the political, financial, social, medical, criminal, and terrorist situation of any country to which it sends employees. This information should be mandatory on the predeployment training curriculum. Again, your state department, external affairs, foreign office, embassy, and consulates are an up-to-date source. These government department websites should be checked periodically for any updates to relevant travel warnings and travel alerts for regions of interest.

Employees and vacation travelers must educate themselves on particular and even peculiar criminal and religious laws. Criminal laws prohibiting the possession of recreational drugs or the possession of a weapon, such as a simple pocket knife, or certain religious or pornographic pictures may land you in jail. Consumption or possession of alcohol—even worse, the trafficking of alcohol—can be a very serious criminal offense. Also, consider the hazards of purchasing illegal animal skins or parts thereof made into clothing or into illegal leather products. *Do not* take the vendor's word on whether an item is legal or not.

In many countries in the Middle East and beyond, it may be illegal to photograph government buildings, police stations, military equipment, or aircraft. It may be illegal to even photograph a soldier on the street. Taking these types of photographs can easily label you as a spy. As such, in many countries, spies do not have the right or access to civilian courts. They do not receive fair treatment, or even warrant a phone call to their embassy or consulate. They may just disappear.

The United States National Counterterrorism Center's counterterrorism calendar for 2015 identifies every terrorist group in the world, including photographs of their leaders; it explains their philosophies and allegiances and even shows their flag. Also, very importantly, it lays out a calendar of the group's activities in the regions in which they are active. The calendar also has important information on chemical, biological, radiological, and nuclear (CBRN) dangers, including descriptions of these agents, physical symptoms of exposure to them, and first aid. Such information is a must for any employee traveling into an unstable region, especially for the first time. Regardless of your citizenship and reason for travel, the US State Department travel advisories and worldwide cautions are an excellent source of predeployment information and travel warnings.

There are many security companies who offer excellent custom travel and security reports for virtually any city in any country around the world. These reports provide in-depth detail of the political, economic, social, criminal, health, and terrorist climate as well as personal profiles and photographs of relevant leaders, activists, and terrorist modus operandi. They can provide recommendations on in-country travel and time lines and secure accommodations and security protection. These security companies are often founded and run by retired police, military, and intelligence officers who maintain personal business relationships with colleagues resident in those countries.

This duty of care also extends to NGO relationships. However, most NGOs have significantly more experience in dealing with employees/volunteers working in hazardous regions than international corporations. They routinely have emergency evacuation procedures in place, along with experienced security personnel whose responsibility is to ensure the safe transportation and evacuation of every employee and volunteer. Those who are self-employed or unemployed and traveling into dangerous regions must rely on their foreign embassies and personnel for assistance.

Here are some guidelines on employer-related considerations:

- The employee/hostage must know that his pay will be either directly deposited in the proper account or delivered to his family. I recommend direct deposit over having the spouse take a check to the bank every few weeks and possibly face difficulties with requiring the proper signatures or having to suffer the embarrassment of explaining the situation to countless bank tellers.

- The employee must be confident that he has full job security and that all pay entitlements, increments, and perks associated with that position will be maintained. It would be insensitive indeed to have the employer inform the hostage's spouse that the company car in the driveway must be returned, thereby leaving the spouse without transportation.

  This also goes for any housing or vehicle subsidies. It would be wise for a company's policy to direct that a senior human resources staff be identified as a direct financial contact for the spouse.

- The employee must be confident that the months or years of captivity will not adversely affect his seniority or promotional opportunities. An employee returning home after many months as a hostage will want to work in a stable social environment, conducting familiar tasks. He cannot view his absence as a penalty or feel that somehow it was his fault and he is being punished.

- The employee and his family must have confidence that the employer health benefits will help cover the costs of psychological intervention for the returning hostage and his family. It is not unusual for family members to require assistance in coping with the constant stressors they experience during the hostage taking as well as health complications after the return of the hostage. In the case of large extended families, frequent personal and conference calls may not resolve many of the issues a family experiences, and personal travel for face-to-face family meetings may be required. The company must be willing to assist with these expenses. Corporate health plans may not cover all the medical and psychological treatments that the hostage survivor requires. The employer or the federal government must be willing to help cover these expenses.

- The employee and his family must be confident that the employer will maintain a clear path of honest communications with the employee's spouse. Employer policy should state that a senior executive be designated as the contact person for the spouse. This ensures that up-to-date and accurate information is available to the spouse and family and that this senior executive has the authority to quickly handle requests by the spouse and respond in a timely manner.

- The employee and his family must be confident that the employer will maintain absolute privacy with respect to any and all criminal investigations and hostage negotiations. This relates to the abduction particulars and all financial, legal, and social family matters.

- An important suggestion for high-risk or frequent travelers is to make arrangements with a local flower shop to have flowers delivered to your spouse on future anniversaries and birthdays, etc. This can be arranged beforehand by either the traveler or the employer. If the employee returns on schedule from his travels, these arrangements can easily be cancelled. The positive impact this will have on the spouse and family members of a hostage cannot be overstated.

A significant positive mental factor in determining a hostage's survival is having a high level of confidence in his family's financial and social survival back home.

MANAGEMENT FALLOUT

The employer must realize that the media will jump at the chance to interview the spouse of any hostage, and if the employer has not treated the family well or has gone back on any of its earlier promises, the spouse can make this headline news. This will affect employee morale and the employer's reputation.

Employers may fail to realize that the family has many friends within the organization and if the family is not treated well, that information will soon be well known throughout the organization, both at home and internationally. When other employees hear these rumors, they begin to distrust all employer policies regarding employee treatment. I use the term *rumors* here because an international hostage situation has a natural tendency to generate all kinds of discussions among employees. Not all information that is passed along is accurate; much of it is conjecture, hypothesis, or opinion.

At the beginning of the hostage taking, a company's best media strategy is to say very little and refer the media to the police. The employer's only comments about the employee should be positive and emphasize its love and respect for the family and their community. The employer should state that its purpose for being in the particular country is for humanitarian purposes, through business partnerships that will directly benefit the people of that country. (Refer to hostage interrogations later on in this book, which stresses that company press releases and a hostage's statements must always agree.)

At the end of a hostage event, employers may be approached by the media for a statement. The employer may wish to provide a press release that is polite and informative but sensitive to an ongoing police investigation and with full consideration for the privacy of the family. The release should be scrutinized by the FLO and the family.

An employer can spend many months or even years working hard to bring an employee home safe and sound, but if it doesn't treat the family well along the way, the family will likely expose the employer to the media. All of its hard work will be lost amid the disenchantment cries of the family. An employer might win esteem in the boardroom but lose all respect and admiration in the court of public opinion.

CHAPTER 4
THE FAMILY LIAISON OFFICER (FLO)

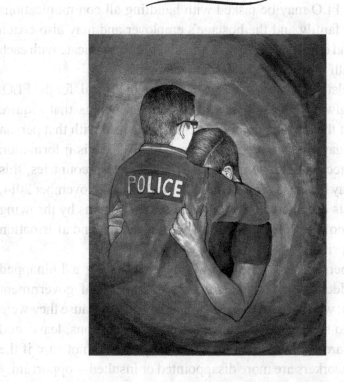

Most large police services, having learned from handling previous hostage takings or operating under a federal mandate, have trained hostage negotiators who serve the investigation as an FLO. In the UK, they are often referred to as the *communications officer,* and other countries have different names. It is the responsibility of the FLO to make contact with the family as soon as possible and to inform and prepare the family for what may lie ahead. Some countries do an excellent job of establishing solid and trusting communications between enforcement agencies, FLOs, and the families. Sadly, others I have worked with do not.

The role of the FLO is critically important to every facet of the hostage taking. This person should be a trained negotiator who understands the negotiation process and the role of other international police forces; he must understand what political pressures may be involved and what opportunities or frustrations these may present. The FLO must understand the role of the criminal investigators at home and abroad. The FLO may be tasked with handling all communications between the family and the hostage's employer and may also coach the family and employer on how to effectively communicate with each other and with the local and international media.

Media relations experience is valuable, if not critical, for the FLO. There will always be personal or professional details that require sensitivity. If the hostage or any other hostages held with that person are lesbian, gay, bisexual, or transsexual (LGBT), this information must be protected because in many Middle Eastern countries, this fact alone may be cause for execution. As recently as November 2014, ISIS terrorists executed suspected homosexual persons by throwing them from rooftops—again, spectacle, propaganda, and affirmation of religious principles.

I have personally witnessed discussions among a kidnapped person's saddened coworkers upon the departure of government investigators, who seemed to have stopped by only because they were ordered to do so. They ask a few perfunctory questions, leave, and are never heard from again. When this happens, I'm not sure if the hostage's coworkers are more disappointed or insulted—opportunity and information are lost. Confidence and support are lost.

One of the first tasks of the FLO is to construct a physical and psychological profile of the hostage. Negotiators must be aware of any medical conditions that may affect the hostage in both the short and long term. They need to understand the hostage's personality and how the person is likely to handle stress, extended confinement, and physical abuse. This research requires delicate discussions with a variety of family members and may also involve discussions with work colleagues.

Family of the Heart

Regardless of whether the hostage's country, state, or province recognizes same-sex marriages or unions, it is the hostage's perspective and opinion that matters. FLOs, employers and governments must respect that opinion. Regardless of the terminology used—*partner, spouse, wife, husband,* or *significant other*—this is the person the hostage recognizes as *family.* To treat the person otherwise would be a legal and social injustice to the hostage, the fallout from which may have untold consequences.

A word to the hostage's employer, government, and any other organization that may become involved with the hostage's family affairs: it is imperative to clarify the definition of family. How that term is defined in these situations is entirely up to the hostage. It is only the hostage's perception that matters; in this context, family is the family of the heart.

A personal example is pertinent here. During my debriefing of a released female hostage, she told me how her employer did not recognize her same-sex union and routinely did not involve her partner in family communications or provide situational updates. When I later spoke with both of them together, they expressed not only their anger and frustration but their disappointment and sadness to the point of tears. Whether this was a failure of the employer's human resources policies or a failure on the part of the police liaison practices, to the hostage and her partner, it appeared to be directly related to their sexual orientation.

Any time a hostage's family recounts, to the point of tears, their experience of how badly they were treated, it means that something went horribly wrong. If the family recounts this experience with these same emotions in front of the media, the press will exploit this and begin to wonder what else went horribly wrong.

EXTENDED FAMILIES AND CHILDREN

Keeping family members aware and up to date sounds easier than it is in practice. A family, for the purpose and obligations of the FLO, is more than just the hostage's spouse, children, and parents. A hostage's family includes the siblings, the brothers-in-law and sisters-in-law, and sometimes, grandparents and cousins. Of course, there can be stepfathers and stepmothers as well. Including extended family is important because their actions and opinions have a direct and profound impact on the day-to-day mental health and well-being of the immediate family. If the FLO does not directly answer the questions of the extended family, they will put the questions to the immediate family. This not only puts even greater pressure on the immediate family, but also accuracy and timeliness will most certainly suffer and this will eventually lead to family discord.

It is imperative for the FLO to consider all children in the immediate family when updating the family and when they are making decisions. Anyone who has brought up preteens and teenagers knows that even though they may lack the decision-making skills or the maturity to understand the complexities of the situation, they want to be included. Of course, the decision to include them lies with the parent; however, the long-game situation is often made easier if the children hear the news directly from the FLO and are able to ask their own questions. This factor alone can make a significant difference in the continuing parent–child relationship, especially if the parent hostage does not return. Children of a deceased hostage cannot be left to wonder for years, or for the rest of their lives, what decisions were made and by whom, based on what information and circumstances and if everything that could have been done was done. Another tough decision to be made by the hostage's spouse.

When it comes time to make important decisions with respect to hostage issues, who gets the final say? Is it the hostage's mother and father, or is it the spouse or partner? One can only imagine the tensions this uncertainty may cause.

In some cultures, the extended family may have a community member or cultural leader designated as the family's disciplinarian, and sometimes, that person is also the appointed decision maker for the family. Sometimes this works in your favor, and sometimes it works against you; sometimes religion or political convictions become confounding factors in family decision-making.

I was involved in one situation where friends, family, and political ideals came together and a number of vigils turned into quasi-political events. These events were covered by the local media, picked up by the international media, and then watched by the kidnappers. The kidnappers were not impressed by some of the comments made by the protesters, and of course, the hostage was deemed guilty by association.

Family, friends, and employers back home must consider the biased view of most hostage takers. What may seem obvious to everyone as a rally in support for the hostage may appear to the hostage takers as a protest against their religious or political ideals. Improperly done, political opinions expressed by family and friends can undermine the entire media effort. Even well-thought-out media releases are often taken out of context by the hostage takers, so the rule here is, fewer is often better. Negotiators and FLOs are constantly juggling family situations, federal politics, religion, corporate activities, and the mental and physical well-being of the hostage against the political and religious beliefs of an unknown group of religious and criminal extremists in a foreign country. It's not easy, but it's what we do. But when well-meaning friends, family, or corporate interests attempt to run a parallel investigation and negotiation, it seriously jeopardizes the hostage's safety. And should the hostage die, by any means, the state quickly becomes the focus of the blame. That said, however, the state is not infallible either.

FAMILY COMMUNICATIONS

During prolonged hostage situations, which many of them are these days, it is not enough for FLOs to phone family members daily; they may have to travel and meet with a core of family members every few months. A family needs to meet with the FLO at least once and, preferably, early in the process. This is imperative if they are to become familiar with each other, to put a face to the names and build a sense of trust. The family desperately needs to be able to look the FLO straight in the eye and ask tough questions; the FLO desperately needs to be able to look the family straight in the eye and give them tough answers.

As with any information-passing mechanism involving people, information can be lost, omitted, or embellished as it passes from one family member to another. When one family member finds out that another family member has more information or different information, this creates problems. Anger, jealousy, and contempt are only a few emotions that come to mind. For this reason alone, the FLO must contact each family member personally and pass on the same information to each one. Often, this means answering many of the same questions over and over again. Conference calling or video conferencing is the best way to effectively accomplish this, as it is the best means to update all participants simultaneously.

I recommend the use of landlines for these calls, as Internet-based communications still suffer from voice and technical dropouts, and they are not secure. I can attest that when you have a conference call involving ten to fifteen concerned family members, clear and dependable communications are mandatory. If your Internet voice connection is lost, it takes several minutes to get everyone back online and conferenced. This significantly complicates matters when timing, sensitivity, and decision-making are paramount, and they always are.

These conference calls provide an opportunity for all family members to ask questions of the FLO and of each other. They also provide the immediate family with recourse when extended family members later ask them a question that they obviously want to bring up and rehash; the family member can remind that person that the issue was brought up and answered by the FLO in the conference call or the issue was discussed during the conference call and a course of action was agreed upon.

Of course, these conference calls are valuable to the FLO as well. The FLO can make assessments of the many personalities involved and identify hierarchical struggles or sibling rivalries that may impact upon the decision-making requirements of the family. The FLO can often identify and diffuse any counterproductive issues before they become a problem.

The FLO role is even more critical when a hostage taking or ransom demand includes a number of hostages from various countries. The FLO must confirm with all other FLOs that all national, corporate, and family media strategies are aligned so that one hostage does not appear to be any more or less important, more or less valuable, or more or less innocent or guilty than another.

As the FLO begins to familiarize the family with what is likely to happen at the various stages of the hostage taking, the family is better able to make clear and informed decisions. The FLO often meets with the senior executives, human resources, and legal representatives of the hostage's employer and advises them on how best to communicate with family members; the FLO also advises them on the best corporate decisions to help the family, assist the investigation, and satisfy the media. The FLO assists the family with developing proof-of-life questions (see chapter 5, "Employer/Employee Planning") and keeping negotiators, the employer, and federal officials apprised of how the family is holding up. The FLO may also have to organize professional family and personal counselors for family members, as problems are bound to arise.

Because the FLO is in constant communication with police negotiators, the FLO often has information regarding a hostage taker's latest demands or a soon-to-be-released video. The FLO always informs the family about impending media coverage, another hostage family's media release, or a hostage video release. This ensures that the family is not traumatized by a surprise news report. The FLO is the one who asks the family to study the video and provide any information or relevant clues to the investigation. The FLO communicates with any foreign FLOs, sharing investigative information and media strategies.

I recall one family member who, after many months of a hostage taking, said, "I don't have to worry about watching the television news or listening to the radio for the latest information because I know Larry will call me." This confidence and peace of mind is extremely important to family members, as it reduces their level of anxiety and allows them to get on with their lives.

Media strategies are even more important when multiple hostages, multiple governments, and multiple employers are involved. It is imperative that media releases are discussed with members of all the families, with all the governments and all negotiators to ensure that media strategies focus on the release of all hostages. Although media interaction is necessary, media overexposure can be detrimental to the safety of any and all hostages. When it comes to hostage negotiations, hostage families and governments must be seen to be speaking with one voice and a consistent message.

The FLO is often responsible for planning video and conference calls between families and between government officials and the families. It is common that even the highest levels of government will seek the FLO's opinion on matters such as the best time for the family to receive a phone call.

The role of the FLO cannot be understated; however, it is not without its difficulties. When a police officer takes on the role of media liaison, almost immediately, many police officers are apprehensive as they fear the media liaison officer is providing confidential information to the media; at the same time, the media believe that the police liaison officer is withholding information the media are entitled to. Also, police negotiators and investigators are hesitant about telling the FLO everything as they are concerned the FLO may pass on information to the family that they shouldn't.

During the investigation, FLOs walk a fine line indeed, but without their knowledge of hostage negotiation principles, their investigative experience, and communication skills, the negotiation and investigative processes would stumble, and their relationship and service to the families and, in turn, to the hostage, would be dismal.

The role of the FLO is often not fully recognized until the investigation is complete and is being debriefed. It is during these debriefings that less experienced police officers and government officials begin to realize how significant the FLO's knowledge of negotiation practices, interpersonal skills, and sensitivity for the family's feelings and frustrations positively contributed to the outcome. The FLO is the hub of the information wheel; the FLO knows what is going on in most every aspect of the investigation, nationally and internationally—the negotiations, the family situation, and the worldwide media. The FLO's job is made all the more challenging by the need to know what information is important to whom and what information cannot be provided to anyone. The FLO becomes everyone's confidant.

Even in cases where the hostage situation does not turn out as well as all would have hoped, the FLO's open and honest communications, combined with empathy and compassion for the family, go a long way toward helping the family deal with the outcome.

Many governments have learned the hard way that without trained and dedicated FLOs, the government can involve all the assets it wishes but still lose admiration and sought-after esteemed public opinion if the family is not fully considered or not treated with the respect it deserves.

The following is an excerpt from appendix 5, which appeared shortly after the parents of Kayla Mueller released her letter to the media and the general public. President Obama's associated TV comments very closely reflected Kayla's parents' concerns.

> The Obama administration is considering the creation of a "fusion cell" of law enforcement, intelligence and other officials to better coordinate its response to hostage situations. Its mission would be to focus exclusively on developing strategies to recover American captives being held overseas.

> The proposal is described in a letter sent to the families of American hostages and is one of several ideas the administration is considering as it gets closer to concluding its review of hostage policies. That review was launched in December amid frustration at the government's response from families of American hostages, some of whom were held and later killed by the Islamic State and other terrorist groups. (Goldman 2015)

Critical incident commanders coordinating police tactical and negotiation teams during barricaded persons and at-home hostage events must include FLOs in their command team to act as liaisons with family members. This is an excellent training opportunity for FLOs and follows important community-based policing initiatives.

CORPORATE PRIVACY AND CORPORATE INTERFERENCE

The hostage's employer must ensure that any and all internal and external communications with respect to the hostage taking are kept secure and on a need-to-know basis. A hostage does not need to return to his workplace and find that his entire ordeal, including any of the more interesting or embarrassing details, is common knowledge and a regular watercooler topic.

A final word on employer privacy, communications with the family, and employer relationships with the FLO. Multinational corporations usually have offices in the same country, or even the same city where the hostage was abducted. There is always the temptation for the employer to unofficially conduct its own investigation of the abduction by exercising company and employee network contacts.

Often what happens is that unscrupulous con men approach employees or business contacts with information or direct assistance "for sale." These offers of assistance are always tempting for the employer, as they feel obliged to help. However, these activities may compromise the police investigation in a number of ways.

First, these con men begin to ask around the neighborhoods, looking to buy some proof of contact with the hostage, such as buying a piece of his clothing or identification. When the hostage takers hear of this, they will most certainly throw it in the face of the police negotiators, accusing them of failing to negotiate in good faith.

Second, the actions of these con men may spook the holders of the hostage and cause them to move the hostage to another location. If the police have identified the location of the hostage and are not yet prepared to carry out a rescue, this can compromise any existing or even future rescue plans.

Third, if the hostage takers are relative newcomers, this may cause them to become nervous and kill the hostage.

Fourth, as the employer engages in this activity, rumors get back to the family members through their company contacts, and they naturally become anxious and hopeful that real progress is being made, only to be let down and saddened when the company "contact" comes up empty-handed, over and over again. This roller coaster of emotions takes a huge toll on families and does more harm than good. The practice of con men approaching the hostage's employer is a well-known opportunity to make a fast buck, and it is often too tempting for the employer to pass up. Overall, it is not helpful to the investigation, to the negotiations, or to the family. Taken to the extreme, corporate activity or influence may be criminal obstruction.

I have personally been involved in cases where corporate involvement was so rampant that family members were calling me to confirm information they had heard through the company about who the police negotiators were meeting with later that day and the next. This undermines the family's confidence in the police negotiations as they begin to think that the company is working more leads than the police. It also puts the FLO in a difficult position wherein he doesn't want to insult the employer and its well-meaning efforts in the eyes of the family. These situations now require sensitive discussions between the employer's senior executives and the FLO.

CHAPTER 5
TRAVEL AND SECURITY

INTERNATIONAL CORPORATE TRAVEL

Employers sending employees anywhere in the world have a legal responsibility to ensure that all travel arrangements, accommodations, and in-country transportation and security services are carried out by reputable companies and personnel. Organizations with years of international experience have developed lists of preferred accommodations, ground transportation, and security professionals in almost every country in which they carry out their business. New organizations would be well advised to take advantage of business contacts and benefit from organizations that have acquired this relevant experience and these trusted security contacts. Sharing these contact lists and discussing particular security concerns provides newcomers with customized and detailed travel advisories.

New organizations and even individual citizens traveling abroad are wise to follow their country's travel advisories. These are available online from a number of government sites. Your foreign embassies and consulates can provide names of trusted national businesses plus a more localized security report, including lists of recommended hotels and security companies.

I shake my head in amazement at news reports of adventurous but naive travelers who express their surprise about being abducted while hiking along the remote borders of warring countries. Being abducted, tortured, and sexually abused is not the kind of travel story they wanted to bring back home—assuming they make it home at all. Terrorist groups in these areas or even fledgling terrorist or criminal groups who haven't decided just yet whether to abduct a Westerner or not and then come across these travelers by accident must laugh at their good fortune as their hostages literally walk right up to them.

CORPORATE SOCIAL RESPONSIBILITY

For many international companies, travel is the modern workplace. They have no choice but to send employees to international sites in order to maintain a level of oversight. International business requires international travel.

Corporations have a legal and moral responsibility to conduct themselves at home and abroad in a socially responsible manner. In the interest of the physical and mental well-being of their employees and their families, corporations must familiarize themselves with the guiding principles of CSR and the UN Global Compact. Surprisingly, as many corporate security officers will attest, many large international companies often discount the possibility of one of their employees being taken hostage, citing, "It hasn't happened yet," and of course, security costs money.

In 2000, Professor John Ruggie, the UN special representative on transnational corporations and other business enterprises, released the draft "Guiding Principles for Business and Human Rights: Implementing the United Nations 'Protect, Respect and Remedy' Framework." The framework evolved from Ruggie's work on the connections between business and human rights. He argues that corporations have a responsibility to respect human rights, and in discharging this responsibility, corporations need to engage in due diligence (United Nations 2000).

This due diligence includes an awareness of the impact or influence that a corporation's activities may have on the financial and social lives of citizens both at home and abroad. This influence goes a long way to determine how employees will be treated in foreign countries. If their presence is welcome, the likelihood of their being abducted is lessened as the general population will be more concerned with their well-being and general safety. A group that kidnaps an employee of a company favored by the general population may quickly find itself out of favor, which is a significant security risk to its continued operations.

The United Nations Global Compact (2000) is a call to companies everywhere to voluntarily align their operations and strategies with ten universally accepted principles in the areas of human rights, labor, environment, and anti-corruption and to take action in support of UN goals and issues. The UN Global Compact is a leadership platform for the development, implementation, and disclosure of responsible corporate policies and practices. It is the world's largest voluntary corporate sustainability initiative, with over 12,000 signatories from business and key stakeholder groups based in 145 countries. A company that aligns itself with these strategies and the principles of social responsibility will be favorably accepted internationally. And should one of its employees be abducted, they stand a better chance of resident political support, including legal and military cooperation, in efforts to secure the hostage's release.

Predeployment training should always include familiarizing the employee with the corporate social and human rights principles within the country in which the employee will be traveling, should the employee be taken hostage and need to defend the corporation's activities to the hostage takers. If a hostage is familiar with how his company's activities are benefiting the social, political, environmental, and even religious values of the country, he stands a better chance of being seen as a friend, or at least as less of an enemy.

EMPLOYER/EMPLOYEE PLANNING

Employers have a duty of care under their CSR to ensure that their employees travel in safety and to properly respond to any medical emergency or natural disaster.

The following are steps you and your employer can take to prepare in the case of abduction:

- The employer or the employee should hold DNA samples to provide to the local and federal police assisting with the investigation and negotiations. These can be as simple as collecting hair clippings when you get a haircut. You may also consider retaining a copy of your fingerprints. If you do not wish to alarm your family by informing them that you are collecting DNA information (as some family members may see this as a fatalistic practice), you can collect these items and have them held by your employer or a close friend.

- The employer and the family should know the identity and contact information of your family doctor and dentist in order to assist the police negotiations and investigation.

- The employer and the family principals should have a prepared proof-of-life document. A proof-of-life document includes questions that only those close to you would know the answers to, in case of abduction. Proof-of-life questions are used by negotiators to confirm that the hostage is actually who the captors say he is and that the hostage is indeed alive. The proof-of-life answers should be simple and known only to you and very few others. They should not be available from the Internet or any social media sites; it serves no purpose whatsoever if the hostage takers can find the answers on the hostage's Facebook or Twitter page. Here are some sample questions to consider, including:

  a. What was the name of your first dog or cat?
  b. What is the nickname your kids gave your pickup truck?
  c. What is your favorite local restaurant?
  d. What is your favorite TV show?
  e. Who is your favorite TV actor?
  f. What was your childhood nickname?
  g. Where did you buy your black cowboy hat?
  h. What was the year, make, and model of your first car?
  i. What is your favorite homemade dessert?
  j. What was the name of your first boat?

Negotiators may also ask for a proof-of-life photo. These are often photos of the hostage holding up a reputable newspaper that clearly shows the date.

You, your spouse, and your employer should also consider generating a list of captivity hints that you can embed into phone calls or written correspondence. Here are a few examples:

"Under the weather"—I'm being held underground.
"I like the desserts"—I'm being held in the open desert.
"Built-in issues"—I'm being held in a cave.
"It's cramped"—I'm being held in the city.
"It's not too cramped"—I'm being held in a small village.
"It's lonely"—I'm being held alone, no other hostages.
"It's not too lonely"—I'm being held with one or more hostages.

- You should be aware of your employer's negotiation policies and family management practices. Has your employer retained the services of a recognized international hostage negotiation or crisis management company? Knowing that your employer has competent plans to handle hostage situations will provide you with some peace of mind. However, you do not need to know every detail of how negotiations would be carried out.
- You should know about your employer's corporate life insurance policies. Will the policy be voided if you travel to certain countries or regions? Will the policy be honored if there is an ongoing war?
- You should travel with only corporate credit cards, but if you are taken hostage, your employer should not automatically cancel the credit cards. This way, your usage can be tracked.

This topic was mentioned earlier in chapter 3, but it warrants repeating here. Your corporate or personal credit cards shouldn't be canceled without first discussing this with the police. I recommend that a senior corporate financial officer, with the approval of the police, request that all credit cards remain valid but with a much lower approved spending limit, say, $100. If the card remains valid, there is a strong likelihood that the hostage takers will use it and continue to use it without considerable financial loss to the employer. This usage will, of course, be tracked by the credit card company, thereby providing the police with an opportunity to identify the card's users and possibly obtain a photograph and a handwriting sample.

TRAVEL—DELIGHT AND DANGER

Travel is exciting. Almost everyone enjoys traveling, seeing new places, tasting new food, enjoying new cultures, or simply relaxing. Travel can often be compared to sports—exciting and exhilarating— but they have their own inherent dangers.

Skydiving is an adrenaline rush. Scuba diving explores a world many have never seen; hot-air balloon rides are quiet and peaceful. However, an experienced skydiver knows what safeguards to look for when choosing to dive at an unfamiliar club or airport, regardless of whether it's at home or away. An experienced scuba diver can recognize scuba equipment that hasn't been properly maintained. Even if you've never been on a hot-air balloon ride, you have a pretty good idea about what a safe balloon should look like. Through experience, all skydivers, scuba divers, and balloon riders have learned what to look for and what to look out for. Comparing new situations against a template of previous training and experience is what keeps them safe.

It is exciting to travel to a foreign country, but if your experience in this new cultural environment is low, that places you at risk. It takes time to become familiar with what is normal in this new environment, and until you are better at it, you must be more cautious than usual. Yes, it's a new country and maybe a new city—there are new people and a new language—but that doesn't mean you don't have the necessary skills and experience to take care of yourself. Growing up, maybe you lived in a few different towns. Maybe you changed schools a few times, made new friends, and learned, maybe the hard way, the differences between good people and bad people. Whether you realize it or not, you have developed a template for survival skills. These skills may seem a little rusty, but they come into play more often than you may think.

In his book, *The Gift of Fear* (1997), Gavin De Becker refers to these acquired skills through experience as "pre-incident indicators." He describes them as one's intuition, hunches, gut feelings, suspicions, or apprehensions. We can all remember times when we were introduced to a person and we had a feeling that something just wasn't right. We have all found ourselves in social circumstances with other people when things just didn't seem right, even seemed dangerous. If asked why we felt this way, we might not be able to explain ourselves, but subconsciously, our years of experience from interacting with people of all ages and in many different circumstances told us something just didn't feel quite right. Was it because the person came across as just weird or creepy? We don't know, but we do know one thing—we will avoid that person in the future. Was it the people we were with, the time of night, or that we were in a bad part of town? Maybe, but our instincts have added up the facts of the situation and led us to decide that we shouldn't be there. These are the social and situational templates we have learned; these are the pre-incident indicators we have come to trust.

These indicators are the basic fundamentals of behavior-based detection, which is in use worldwide in airports, train stations, and subways to identify suspicious travelers. Behavior detection has been used extensively for years by the Israelis, who are likely the most experienced in the world. In the United States, this Screening of Passengers by Observational Techniques (SPOT) program is supported and encouraged by the DHS.

High-level drug dealers often have a trusted female friend present when they meet a potential drug buyer for the first time. This is because women are much more familiar with men approaching them and trying to convince them of their background stories while trying to hide their true intentions. These drug dealers have come to trust those female "instincts" and often accept their judgment without question.

∽

When traveling, you will meet persons from other cultures, and you may experience those same nagging feelings of suspicion and doubt. Trust those feelings. Customs and language aside, you will automatically and subconsciously read strangers' facial expressions, hear the intonation in their speech, and read their body language. If these are the traits of people you have learned not to trust back home, then listen to these same suspicions when you're away.

Many who travel to countries whose merchants proudly proclaim that tourists should bargain over prices, as it is part of their culture, will attest that the merchants are very practiced at grossly inflating the prices for tourists; they routinely overstate the quality, craftsmanship, and authenticity of their products. It has been my professional police experience that many of these people are so adept at, so comfortable, and so habituated with lying that their nontruthful responses to polygraph (lie detector) questions do not register as strongly as persons from other cultures. The lesson is that many strangers who initially appear outwardly friendly and genuine are practiced in deception. It takes tourists some time to tune their senses and adjust their risk template or pre-incident indicators to these people. Until then, travelers must be more cautious than usual.

> No dishonor attaches to such primary transactions as
> selling short weight, deceiving anyone about quality,
> quantity or kind of goods, cheating at gambling, and
> bearing false witness. The doer of these things is
> merely quicker off the mark than the next fellow;
> owing him nothing, he is not to be blamed for taking
> what he can. (Pryce-Jones 1989, p. 38)

I have personally posed the question regarding the ethics of false and deceptive bargaining to foreign shopkeepers with whom I had established a rapport. They replied that there was absolutely nothing wrong with inflating the price and the authenticity of an item, thereby making more money from the tourist than they would by selling the item to the locals. They felt that this showed that they were just

80

smarter than the tourists and had simply *tricked* them out of their money. Again, interpretation is everything. No shame, no remorse, no guilt. More on this later.

One particular greeting I have learned to be wary of is "Hello, my friend!" The first thing this greeting tells you is that this person is familiar and comfortable approaching foreigners and is also likely to be charming and persuasive. This greeting attempts to suggest a history of a trusted and familiar relationship. Often, the person's second line will be "Where are you from?" He will present his best first guess based upon your physical features or the hotel you're staying at as "Canada, America, English?" Whatever your reply, he will respond, "I love Canadians/Americans/English." Around the world, the overuse of *my friend* causes me to be a little more than suspicious.

As a traveler to a new area, you are a soft target. This means you are unprotected, unaware, and yet predictable. You are likely to do stupid things like take a walk at night in an unknown neighborhood; you sometimes want to get off the beaten path or get away from the tourist traps, and you are far too trusting of strangers. For most criminals and kidnappers, this makes it almost too easy.

HOTEL AND TRAVEL SECURITY

You are traveling to a foreign country. Your employer is sending you on a business trip, or maybe you will be working for an international agency that has an established presence in a foreign country, or maybe you're just going on a family vacation. Regardless, you will be outside of your home country and outside of what is familiar to you.

The Internet is full of travel sites and security companies offering suggestions on how to keep yourself and your family safe during both domestic and international travel; often, suggestions are applicable to both. Many of the following recommendations are similar to what you can find on these sites, and some of them are my own.

The terrorist attack at a popular international hotel in July 2008 in Mumbai, India, and again in November 2015 at another five-star hotel in Mali, Africa, highlight what is likely to become an evolving worldwide security threat—that is, the opportunity to attack foreigners where they gather.

As mentioned earlier, you or your employer should be booking your travel arrangements, hotel accommodations, and transportation with reliable companies—this is a no-brainer. Your predeployment planning should include awareness of relevant government travel advisories; these government advisories are updated regularly by government staff living and working in those countries. They provide an overview of local and regional crime trends, disease outbreaks, and vaccination requirements, as well as an overview of possible political turmoil and, very importantly, labor strikes that may affect your travel plans.

Your company should contact the nearest embassy or consulate to the city you intend to visit and ask them for their hotel and transportation recommendations. When subsequent reservations are made, quoting your embassy or consulate's recommendation, many hotels will book you into a preferred corporate or international room. In the more remote locations, these preferred rooms will often have more functioning light bulbs, an upgraded television, improved sanitary conditions and serviced by the more senior housekeeping personnel.

With the advent of social media, today's traveler should make use of the numerous hotel and transportation sites, with the associated apps, which offer a wide variety of reviews; many include up-to-date travel precautions and helpful suggestions.

Your employer and your family should have a duplicate copy of your travel arrangements, flight numbers, hotel contact information, and names and addresses of business contacts you will be meeting, as well as a photocopy of your passport. If you have not previously traveled to that country or city, international hotel chains that are familiar with the safety requirements of business travelers are a good source for security information.

High-risk cities have reliable and experienced security companies that offer trained drivers, secure vehicles, and security personnel or bodyguards for hire. These personnel know the more dangerous parts of the city; they know the local scams and provide the traveler with suggestions on what to wear and what not to do.

These security companies can recommend reliable tour guides and escort travelers to the local places of interest. This is of particular importance when you are traveling on business with your spouse and family. They won't want to sit around the hotel all day; they will want to see the sights while you're working. These professional services are a small price to pay for the safekeeping and confidence they provide you and your family.

Interestingly enough, these security personnel are familiar with the local thieves and scam artists just as much as the thieves and scammers are familiar with them. Often, just having one of these security personnel with you is enough to deter thieves, scammers, and hostage takers.

Here are some common security company and government recommendations for staying safe while traveling, plus some of my own:

- Travel with others; there is safety in numbers. If you are traveling on business with colleagues, travel together at the foreign location as often as possible. Considering you all should have similar predeployment training, you can look out for one another. From a logistical perspective, it is more difficult for strangers to identify a specific target, and the hostage taker's vehicle likely cannot hold more than one hostage. In the event of a physical confrontation, you will help defend one another and you are all witnesses to any abduction attempt.
- Beware of false meetings/interviews. Some con men may discover your identity from a business card or just local knowledge that certain international companies or tourists

frequent certain hotels. These people may approach you and tell you that they are in a similar business. They may say they are looking to invest in your company and might invite you to meet their senior personnel.

- Use only company- or hotel-recommended transport or taxis. Never hail a taxi from outside of the hotel property. This is a favorite pick-up spot for unlicensed cabs that are more likely to run up the meter or take you to a deserted area and rob you. Don't allow an unknown driver to use his cell phone during travel. This warning is not only to prevent the driver from being distracted, but it ensures he cannot relay any information to his friends.
- In case someone is watching your hotel and recording your arrival and departure times, make it difficult for the person to collect the necessary information. Don't be shy about ducking down in your seat when your vehicle departs the hotel. If they can't get enough information about your travels to formulate their abduction plans, they will look elsewhere.
- Even when using reliable transportation, instruct the driver to vary the routes and pickup times so as not to be predictable.
- Beware of drivers chatting you up. Some bona fide taxis are "rented" after hours by friends looking to make a fast buck or for gathering information (intelligence) on hotel guests. For drivers who may be gathering information (planning a hostage taking), in order to identify a potential hostage target, a common tactic is to ask questions like "How long are you in town?", "Are you working on that big project?", or "Do you have to drive there every day?" This will often lead the driver to suggest he become your daily driver, offering a reduced fee and dependable service.

It is widely accepted that terrorist groups planning an attack can gather over 70 percent of the information they need from the Internet. Of course, many international companies like to put the names and photographs of their senior executives on the company websites, plus the address and photographs of the company's buildings. Don't give potential hostage takers the remaining necessary background information they need to identify you as a valuable commodity, and don't provide the tactical information they need to abduct you. Don't be embarrassed that the driver may think you are rude if you don't answer his questions; they get that every day, and you can always lie and say, "I'm leaving today."

The practice of taxi drivers chatting you up is not just a threat while traveling in a foreign country. When traveling in North America, I have personally experienced taxi drivers asking obvious intelligence-mining questions when I've taken taxis from airports to government buildings. This happens more often than you might think. Pay attention next time and see if you can recognize a taxi driver trying to gather intelligence on your activities. Play along—it's good practice.

- When you open the door of a taxi, look to confirm that the rear door has inside window handles and working door handles. If it doesn't, just walk away.
- Always lock your door after entering any vehicle. This will provide a level of protection from robberies when the vehicle stops in traffic, at red lights, and so on.
- If you must use an unfamiliar taxi and driver, pause before getting into the vehicle and take a picture of the driver with your cell phone. When the driver asks why you are taking his picture, tell him you are sending it to your *police* friend or your office. In case you are robbed or anything bad happens to you, the police will have his picture. If he replies, "No picture, no picture," you simply reply, "OK, no taxi!"
- If you do use a hailed taxi, take a photograph of the driver plus his taxi license and tell him you are sending the pictures to your company *police* in case of problems.
- If your driver stops and another passenger jumps in, jump out. If you can't jump out, take that person's picture and inform him that you are sending it to the police. Also, anytime your

driver stops to pick up a friend or a second fare, look for ways to safely escape the vehicle.

- Do not go outside of the geographical boundaries and curfew times suggested by your national travel advisories or your hotel.
- Always have some of your hotel's business cards with you. If you get lost or need a taxi, your hotel's business card will have the name, address, and telephone number, likely in English and in the language of the country you are visiting. This will greatly assist any person or taxi driver in helping you get back to your hotel. If you find yourself in a restaurant unexpectedly late, show the card and ask the restaurant to call your hotel, and have the hotel send a trusted taxi to pick you up at the restaurant rather than hailing an unknown taxi from in front of the restaurant. Too many unscrupulous taxi drivers or even fake taxis frequent restaurants late at night, preying upon stranded or intoxicated foreign patrons.
- Do not be predictable with your hotel departure times, your routes, or your restaurants.
- Do not be easily recognizable; change your appearance with different clothing and hats. Do not wear a distinctive hat or jacket day after day, as this makes you too easy to follow in a crowd and an easy descriptor to pass on to other surveillants.
- Watch for surveillance outside of your hotel and your business locations. Take photos of suspicious persons hanging around outside your hotel or your business. The ones that turn away when you raise your camera are the ones to be afraid of. Be seen to be cautious. When untrustworthy persons realize you are suspicious of their intentions, they are likely to try elsewhere.
- Activate the GPS locator on your cell phone and also for your photos. If possible, set an emergency button on your cell phone.
- Depending on where you are traveling, consider the use of emergency locator beacons. Emergency locators have built-in GPS beacons that integrate with satellite telephone systems, providing pole-to-pole coverage. Most are the size of a package of cigarettes, only weigh 7–8 ounces, cost about $300, and have an accuracy of 100 meters or less.

Many experienced mountain climbers and backcountry trekkers carry these locators as they cannot rely on cell phone coverage for reception during emergencies. They are inexpensive and simple to operate. They can be programmed to relay automatic location, speed, and heading updates and can even be pinged. Some provide two-way communications with rescue personnel and offer worldwide e-mail service. They are small enough to carry on your belt like a cell phone or in your pocket. They can be activated when walking, in your hotel room, or in a vehicle. If you're abducted, several minutes or several hours may pass between the time you push the emergency button and when your abductors search you and eventually find it. When they do, this may provide a huge incentive for them to release you immediately. Emergency locators should be a strong consideration for people traveling into rural areas. A number of emergency locators such as SPOT and DeLorme's inReach can be sourced on the Internet.

- Leave your primary cell phone and laptop with hotel security or lock them in your room safe. Carry a secondary cell phone with only a few basic phone contacts.

- Use a doorstop in your hotel room. Just a simple wedge of wood or a rubber doorstop will protect you from anyone trying to use a pass key or even their shoulder to get into your room. Don't forget to have one for the adjoining door as well. If you don't have a regular doorstop with you, in an emergency, you can shove a hotel room towel under the door. You can use a hairbrush handle to jam the towel under the door from the inside. Be sure to leave the remainder of the towel folded into a wedge or as a roll on the inside of the door so that as the door is pushed from the outside, it forces more of the inside part of the towel under the door. You may find that a wet towel is denser than a dry towel, and it is also less likely to slide on most surfaces. Leaving the hairbrush inside the towel under the door will provide extra wedging resistance. Also, a woman's high-heeled shoe, a sandal, or flip-flops may do well as a doorstop.

- When traveling to areas known for their abundance of crawling insects, throw a pet flea collar into the bottom of your suitcase and then into your hotel room drawer as this will often dissuade the invasion of many local insects. Also, pull your socks over the tops of your shoes when they are not in use in order to seal them off from scorpions, ants and other critters.
- Many electronics shops or security shops sell small battery-powered portable motion-sensitive alarms that hang by a cable or loop around the doorknob on the inside of your hotel room door that will trigger when your doorknob is jiggled or turned. There are portable infrared motion-sensing alarms as well.
- Runners are almost compulsive when it comes to their daily run. It is often a personal ritual that cannot be ignored. The body and the mind look forward to the feeling that only a good run can provide. However, when traveling, don't run outside unless you are absolutely positive of your safety, and who can be 100 percent positive? Run on an inside track or on a treadmill. Many runners will shudder at the thought of a treadmill, but if you are taken hostage and chained to a wall for three or four months, you won't be getting any exercise at all. Consider using the hotel pool for exercise.
- When walking or driving in foreign cities, don't distract yourself from paying attention to your safety by listening to music from your phone or other portable device. A distracted target makes it so much easier for your abductors.

The best survival strategy in the world is not to be abducted in the first place.

COUNTERSURVEILLANCE

Countersurveillance is the art of applying a variety of techniques and tactics designed to detect, deter, and avoid persons who may be attempting to gain intelligence about you.

Keeping in mind your situational template and De Becker's pre-incident indicators—essentially recognizing potential threats by comparing them to your past experiences and listening to your intuition, feelings of anxiety, and instincts—let's apply countersurveillance tactics that will reduce your feelings of anxiety and situational dangers.

You're walking down a busy sidewalk in a foreign city, surrounded by two-way vehicle traffic and lots of hustle and bustle, and suddenly you feel nervous about the possibility that you're being followed. This brings to mind the scene of a potential kidnapping—yours. I've already advised you to pay attention to these feelings and not brush them off as silly or foolish. What can you do right this minute to reduce these fears? What can you do to regain your peace of mind and regain control over the situation? Countersurveillance.

- Walk on the sidewalk facing oncoming traffic. You must be able to see all vehicles approaching you. You must pay particular attention to any vehicles that might be moving more slowly than other traffic, with occupants who might be staring or looking at you longer than what is normal. You certainly don't want to be walking in the same direction as traffic, as this will prevent you from seeing vehicles that might be pacing you from behind.

- Move to the inside of the sidewalk. This will put you further from any vehicle traffic and put more pedestrians between you and vehicular traffic. It will also prevent you from becoming surrounded on all sides by abductors and may provide you with a doorway to duck into, a railing to hold on to, or some other type of physical anchor in case someone tries to pull you away.

- With your cell phone set to camera, quickly turn around and take two or three quick photos of everyone walking behind you from about three to twelve meters (ten to forty feet). Make sure your flash goes off so your picture taking is obvious to everyone behind you. Just as when taking a picture of people in front of your hotel, the people who turn away from your camera are the ones to watch out for. You can repeat this once or twice. If you're too nervous to turn around, you can put your phone over your shoulder and again take two or three photos. If you are being followed, this should spook most amateur surveillants who will break off the surveillance. Their report to the rest of the group will be that you know you're being followed, you know exactly who is following you, and you have photographs of them as well. These photos should be geotagged.

- When you come to a busy corner of the sidewalk, turn the corner, stop in about three meters (ten feet), turn around, and see who comes around the corner. Amateur surveillants will come around the corner, stare directly at you, and look confused about what to do. They will often make a little stutter step and turn back around the corner or decide to continue walking around you. Whatever they do, it will look obvious to you, and they, in turn, will know you're on to them.
- You can also use this tactic when you walk into a shop. Stop, turn around, and see who comes in after you or leaves the shop after you.

Amateur surveillants might even get to the corner and not walk completely around the corner but do a peek-a-boo. Of course, this will be obvious as well, and they will know they've been seen. If you happen to have taken photographs of them prior to turning the corner, they will realize that you have now positively identified them. They will report all of this to whoever ordered the surveillance, and they should wisely make the decision to select another target.

If you recognize that you are being followed, it's time for you to reconsider your visit entirely. If someone wants to kidnap you, your choice should be obvious—leave. Do not choose adventure over security.

INSIDE HELP

Even with all these travel tips, travelers should also be aware that sometimes kidnapping groups have inside help and it's not always obvious. This help may come from hotel employees who know when you will arrive and when you will depart. They know your room number, when you are expecting a taxi, and when you are traveling for meetings. This kind of insider information is extremely valuable, as it saves kidnappers considerable planning time and it's very accurate. Travelers should be on the lookout for hotel employees who may be trying just a little too hard to be friendly outside of what seems like normal behavior to encourage a better tip. Cleaning your room and wanting fresh towels are normal actions, but wanting to know about what you are doing today and at what time is not normal. Just like the more-than-curious taxi driver who's looking to compile intelligence, mentioned earlier, learn to spot these people.

Hotel employees are not the only ones who might be passing on intelligence. It can be office employees, groundskeepers, or maintenance personnel. This is true at home or abroad.

Many released hostages who felt they were never at risk and believed their travel plans were known to only a trusted few continue to ask themselves the question, "How did they know?"

> Later, they would tell me they'd been watching the hotel. They knew we were there. They didn't know who exactly they'd catch, but they were aware there were foreigners at the hotel . . . Most assuredly, there was cash promised to somebody—a driver, a hotel employee, a guard—in exchange for word of where the foreigners were headed that day. Somebody—we don't know who—sold us out. (Lindhout and Corbett 2013)[6]

---

[6] In August 2008, Amanda Lindhout, a fledgling television reporter, traveled to Somalia, "the most dangerous place on earth." On her fourth day, she was abducted by a group of masked men along a dusty road. Held hostage for 460 days, Amanda converts to Islam as survival tactic, receives "wife lessons" from one of her captors, and risks a daring escape. She survives on memory—every lush detail of the world she experienced in her life before captivity—and on strategy, fortitude, and hope. When she is most desperate, she visits a house in the sky, high above the woman kept in chains, in the dark, being tortured.

Any intruders to the facilities had to be forearmed with knowledge of when that lookout was down. They also had to know how to steer a path through sand dunes in the dark . . . they had to have precise understanding of local tides and the challenging coral reefs . . . the pirates who broke into our *banda* . . . came armed with all of that information. (Tebbutt, 302)

I learned that a former groundsman at Kiwayu by the name of Ali Babitu Kololo had appeared in court in Kenya the day before, charged with having led my kidnappers to the *banda* where David and I were staying on the night of 10 September. (Tebbutt, 300)

He was wearing one of the Mine Risk Education bracelets my NGO gives out to all the kids after they attend our classes on avoiding war munitions. I had to swallow hard to keep from gasping out loud while the thought hit me: *This boy was one of our students?* (Buchanan, 105)

We now knew for certain that the UN Special Envoy had not fallen into the hands of Al Qaeda simply as a result of an unhappy coincidence. We took bizarre comfort in the fact that our abduction was not the result of appallingly bad luck. (Fowler, 31)

Even when traveling at home, business travelers have become more security conscious. There are many news reports of guests planting covert video cameras in their hotel rooms that caught employees going through their computer and briefcases.

FIXERS

International news outlets regularly use people they call *fixers*. These are very reliable people with comprehensive local knowledge. They have access to translators, security vehicles, drivers and security staff and maintain an excellent network of contacts on both sides of the issue the media is covering. These fixers run a fine line every day, as they exercise their network of informants while maintaining contacts within local politics and local law enforcement, both savory and unsavory. It is difficult indeed for fixers to maintain an image of nonpartisanship, day in and day out, in troubled regions of the world. If a news reporter and cameraman are abducted or arrested, the fixer is often abducted or arrested as well. Without reliable contacts, a fixer's life is always in grave danger, as they are sometimes dispatched (killed) and not included in negotiations for the release of the news team.

Recognized international news personnel, although kidnapped from time to time, are not often held long—usually only a few days. This is mostly because the local terrorists, criminals, or corrupt officials don't want to evoke the ire of the media because the wrong media coverage can do their activities considerable harm.

PERSONAL ITEMS

- When traveling, carry a secondary cell phone with only the most necessary contacts on it. Leave your personal or primary cell phone at your hotel or office. Activate the GPS tracking function. As the latest cell phones become more attractive as a status symbol, carrying one, especially in questionable surroundings, increases the risk of being robbed.

  Carrying a secondary phone reduces the social and financial impact if you are robbed or taken hostage. Also, if your secondary phone is lost or stolen, you can still contact family and friends and carry on business with your primary phone back at the hotel. If you carry your primary phone and it is stolen, your personal contact list could end up in the hands of Internet con men. In the event you are taken hostage, you also don't want hostage takers to know all the companies and their personnel you deal with, in case some of these businesses don't meet the hostage taker's approval. Also, you don't want the hostage takers to start calling every one of your contacts, threatening to kill you and asking for ransom money.

- Wear a cheap watch, something financially unattractive and of no sentimental value. This is to avoid attracting the attention of thieves. Also, if you are taken hostage, you are not likely to ever see your watch, wedding ring, or other jewelry again. When you consider that in some parts of the world, even a relatively inexpensive watch can pay a thief's rent for months, robbing you is tempting indeed.
- Your travel laptop computer should contain only friendly information or business articles with respect to the business you are conducting and—accuracy and truth not necessarily a factor—no jokes, risqué photos, or anything that may be construed as offensive.
- Your Facebook, Twitter, LinkedIn, or any other professional or personal social media sites should be heavily vetted to remove any items that can be used against you as a hostage, especially any references to prior military or police service or government affiliations of any kind. One of the most frequent accusations by hostage takers is that you are a spy. This designation gives them all manner of justification to beat you, as your true purpose has been exposed and you are now firmly identified and treated as their enemy.
- Your wallet and computer should contain photos of any family, including children. You want to be seen as a loving family man.
- Carry a traveling wallet (minimal loss if robbed or stolen) with only one active credit card and numerous false credit cards. Populate a traveling wallet with your expired driver's

license and expired credit cards but with one valid credit card so you can still purchase items. This wallet should contain many small denominations of paper currency so it looks legitimate. If you are robbed, the thief may take a quick look inside, be satisfied with what he sees, and leave. That said, many thieves have come to expect this and will also ask for your "hidden" money.

- Carry photocopies of your passport, driver's license, medical information, and prescriptions in a waterproof bag. Resealable sandwich or freezer storage bags are excellent for this purpose. In many countries, con men posing as plainclothes police officers may ask for your passport. If you provide them with your real passport, they will take it and run. If they are real police officers, a photocopy will be sufficient for identification purposes.

If taken hostage, you should be able to spell the names of your prescriptions; a photocopy will be helpful.

TRAVEL WARNINGS

The following are samples of travel warnings you can expect to find on many government websites. This one is from the United States Department of State on January 9, 2015.

WORLDWIDE CAUTION
On September 22, 2014, the United States and regional partners commenced military action against the Islamic State of Iraq and the Levant (ISIL), a designated terrorist organization in Syria and Iraq. In response to the airstrikes, ISIL called on supporters to attack foreigners wherever they are. Authorities believe there is an increased likelihood of reprisal attacks against U.S., Western and coalition partner interests throughout the world, especially in the Middle East, North Africa, Europe, and Asia.

MIDDLE EAST and NORTH AFRICA
There is an increased threat of terrorism from groups such as ISL, al-Nusrah, as well as other extremists whose tactics include use of suicide bombers, kidnappings, use of small and heavy arms, and improvised explosive devices (IEDs). Since the start of the uprising against Syrian President Bashar al-Assad's regime in March 2011, the United States has received reports of numerous foreigners kidnapped in Syria, many of whom are still in captivity. The majority of the victims are journalists and aid workers. U.S. citizens and other Westerners have been murdered by ISIL in Syria. (United States Department of State 2015)

WORLDWIDE TRAVEL ALERT
A few days after the terrorist attacks in Beirut, Paris, and Mali, on November 22, 2015, the United States government issued a worldwide travel alert for its citizens. It cited the likelihood of "increased terrorist attacks" were possible "in multiple regions." The alert would be in effect for three months until February 24, 2016.

Chapter 6
Stages of a Hostage Taking—
Planning and Abduction

As mentioned in the introduction, most government travel sites and security companies describe four stages of a hostage taking; I describe five, as I include planning. I believe that today's travelers want to understand how to travel more safely, be proactive and self-aware, and not just remember security lists. Therefore, by understanding why kidnappers kidnap in the first place and what information they require to carry it off, what logistics they must consider, and how the actual grab or snatch takes place, travelers can better understand and interpret their environment and then adapt their behaviors accordingly.

The Planning Stage

The first stage of a hostage taking, the planning, is pretty much in the hands of the hostage takers. The more travelers know about how their abductors must go about planning an abduction, the more they will understand why they need to take the precautions outlined previously. To the traveler who is now a hostage, knowing what planning *should* have been carried out, as compared with what planning *was* carried out, is also an indicator, a first step in making an informed assessment about the experience and skill sets of the abductors.

Being able to assess the group's capabilities and experience level and recognizing the social makeup of your abductors is an important start to developing survival strategies.

Understanding the purpose of your abduction and knowing the history of abductions carried out by this group prepares you for what may lie ahead; you are then better able to select and apply specific strategies that will improve your day-to-day treatment and your chances of an early release. Knowing what may lie ahead also removes some of the mystery and, with it, some of the fear. When you have this kind of information, you begin to take back some control over your life.

Some hostage takers take the time to do a proper amount of planning; some do a little, and some do very little. The amount of planning depends on their abilities and experience; then again, some abductions are just opportunistic.

Opportunistic abductors are often inexperienced. They are more likely to get the wrong target, have improper transport, and have poor holding facilities and poor financing. This type of abduction is more dangerous, as the hostage takers wouldn't have had time to practice their roles, and they will be more aggressive and violent. Opportunistic abductions lead to more mistakes. The hostage takers often take the wrong person and end up with a hostage who cannot pay the ransom or one who is not as valuable as they were hoping for. Without the proper facilities and financing, a hostage will probably be in more uncomfortable surroundings and be guarded by inexperienced persons who are likely to act out of fear and panic.

A hostage who can recognize inexperienced hostage takers is at an advantage. Inexperienced hostage takers are not as likely to hold their hostages for long periods of time. The abductors soon realize that the care and feeding of a hostage must be properly coordinated. Reliable armed guards must be identified and a schedule set; meals must be prepared on site or brought in. The hostage must be secured and kept in some sort of confinement—a small room, a closet, a cave— somewhere. The hostage must have bathroom facilities—usually just a bucket, but it has to be emptied or everyone, guards included, will become uncomfortable. Although they captured the person, hostage takers are always afraid of the person breaking out of his confinement and killing the guards in the process. Most hostage takers are wary of the self-defense skills and escape abilities of Westerners.

The longer a hostage is held, the more nervous the inexperienced captors are likely to become. They are nervous about what clues they may have left behind during the abduction, who might have recognized them, and what the authorities already know. Hostage takers, like criminals, get very paranoid.

The hostage who knows what planning and skill sets are required to abduct someone can gain valuable information. More information will be forthcoming when the leader of the group gives his speech detailing why you were taken. This ability to learn from the abductors is much like the way an audience can tell if a presenter is relatively new to public speaking or more experienced. If the leader is overly nervous, anxious, and fidgety and appears to be more afraid of you than you are of him, this indicates that the abductors are likely newcomers to hostage taking.

Inexperienced hostage takers are more eager to get negotiations started, get their money, and get it over with. They are much like newcomers to buying and selling real estate who want to buy easily, sell quickly, take their money, and be done with it. And they are like day traders in the stock market who want to buy stocks, hold them just long enough to make a respectable profit, and then move on to the next deal. Newcomers to hostage taking do not want to keep hostages for long; the willingness to do so comes only with experience.

Deficiencies in one or more of the planning details can cause significant problems for the hostage takers at any stage of a hostage taking. It can be bungled from the start, and the hostage gets away or is killed, or a member of the group can be injured or arrested. They can run into a road block or a routine enforcement action, or the hostage location may be located before they collect any ransom monies. The hostage may escape, or one of their own may inform on them for a reward. As mentioned earlier, criminals are known to plan the robbery well but not the getaway.

ABDUCTION

> The attack begins as if an umpire has just blown a
> starting whistle. A large car roars up beside us and
> careens to a stop, splashing mud all over our windows.
> Men with AK-47s encircle our car, pounding on the
> doors, shouting over each other in Somali. Their
> behavior is ferocious.
>
> My heart goes straight to my throat. Adrenaline sends
> a jolt of fear from head to toe. The terror feels like
> heat, like we are suddenly being roasted alive inside
> the car.
>
> My brain is seizing up from trying to process this. I
> hear a little version of my own voice in the back of my
> skull chanting: *This is really bad this is really bad this
> is really bad,* and for some reason I can't get myself
> to stop. (Buchanan 2014, p. 8)

It takes only a few seconds, but the abduction can be the most
dangerous time for a hostage. Many hostages have been shot, stabbed,
or beaten during their abduction. Hostage takers are keenly aware that
they must overcome a target by force, coercion, or intimidation. They
know they must surprise the target, thereby overcoming the target's
basic instinct to resist and fight back. A target must be overwhelmed
by the sheer number of attackers and forced into a vehicle before
he can mentally register what's happening; sometimes a target is
approached and threatened with a gun or a knife as the abduction
vehicle pulls alongside, again in the hope that the target will follow
instructions before he realizes what is happening and begins to resist.
Once inside the vehicle, the target is threatened by being shown
the gun or knife in a much more direct manner, and the threat is
reinforced by physical intimidation such as punching, kicking, and
yelling further threats. Once inside the vehicle, targets may have their
eyes and mouth covered with a sack or tape, and they are forced onto

the floor or other uncomfortable and out-of-sight position. The target is now a hostage.

The decision to fight or not is hotly debated. If you don't fight, you will certainly be taken hostage; if you do fight, there is a chance of serious injury. Only the target can make this decision at the time, given his ability to resist and fight back, the overwhelming odds against him, and the type of weapon being used against him. This same argument is at the forefront of all sexual assault discussions: should the female victim fight back or not?

Police officers, military personnel, and martial arts enthusiasts will react more quickly than civilians because they have had training and practice in responding quickly to physical threats with maximum and effective force. Those not so trained should be prepared to yell and scream loudly, move their feet, and flail their arms wildly so that their arms are difficult to catch and hold on to and then start running before they actually have the time to think about it. This too requires a level of mental awareness and physical readiness.

During periods of high stress, cognitive capacities become narrowed. This is a fight-flight-or-freeze situation, and freeze is not an option. Protesting while being led to a waiting vehicle and asking, "What are you doing?", "What do you want?", or "Where are you taking me?" is freezing. It is useless and a stupid waste of time. Do you think these people want to debate with you on the sidewalk? You must pick fight or flight *now* and commit to it completely. The next few seconds may define the rest of your life. If you decide to fight, then fight. You must be ferocious and not afraid to cause injury and pain to your attackers. They will be surprised and startled for an instant and therefore likely to hesitate. This may provide you with the one or two seconds you need to break free, run, and escape.

Although your attackers are likely to be armed in some fashion, this is more for intimidation than to deliberately inflict injury. They have come to kidnap you, not kill you. This will give you an edge because your would-be abductors will not have formed the intent to kill you; all their planning would be lost.

If you are grabbed in any manner, yell at the top of your voice, "Police! Police!" Yelling serves a number of internal and external uses. It will startle your attackers and provide you with one or two more seconds to react. It will trigger your body to produce adrenaline; this will tense your abdominal muscles as well as a number of large upper and lower body muscles. This immediate extra physical strength in your arms, shoulders, and legs might be just what you need to break away from your attackers.

Psychologically, when a target hears himself yell, it serves as a trigger that commands every muscle in the body and every mental function to react and defend the body from attack. Psychological training for elite athletes focuses on the mental visualization of exactly what the body will do when the athlete hears the bell, buzzer, or starting pistol. Yelling informs your body that this is indeed a "fight-or-flight" life-threatening situation that requires its immediate and complete reaction. "It's time to do what we have to do."

If you have paid attention to your pre-incident indicators and realized that whatever you are doing or wherever you are doing it has put you in dangerous circumstances, you have begun to prepare yourself mentally. Your body has been tipped off to react to the sound of yourself yelling. This will be your bell, your buzzer, or your starting pistol. In preparation of the yell, mentally go through a drill of what you will do should anything happen. Along with this realization comes a heightened situational awareness. You will begin to visually search for threats, listen for threats, quicken your step, assume a straighter posture, and consciously think about how to either remove yourself from this situation or dramatically improve the situation.

Yelling will also attract attention from people in the immediate area. This might cause someone to come to your aid by also yelling at your attackers or by physically helping to pull you away from your attackers. Yelling is also likely to produce witnesses who might recognize the attackers or get a description of them or their vehicle. If the attackers are successful in abducting you and they believe your yelling did, in fact, attract witnesses, they might suddenly view this as a higher-risk situation than they'd anticipated and quickly dump you out of their vehicle.

Back at home, in similar physical situations that are much less threatening, yelling, pulling away, and running when someone grabs you by the arm might seem silly, but that same reaction here and now might be the appropriate response to someone grabbing your arm—and it might save your life. An overreaction to a startle response is not always a bad thing. It may sound trite, but many a hostage has admitted that if he had known he was going to be taken hostage, he would have fought harder.

Released hostages describe their abduction as happening so quickly they didn't have time to think or react. A hostage's common first response once inside the vehicle is to verbally protest this treatment, to verbally defend himself, and to argue that his purpose in this place is peaceful and nonthreatening. This protest will be answered by a kick or a punch. At this point, escape is unlikely. Any struggling by the hostage is useless because he is outnumbered, outweighed, and outgunned. Any physical struggle from here on is futile and will be met with overwhelming force and pain. At this point, the abductors don't give a damn if they have the right target or not—they have a hostage, they are full of adrenaline, and they just want to get out of the area.

Released hostages report that the abduction and transport is the most terrifying event of their lives. "I've never forgotten it. Terror, helplessness, anguish. One human being bearing witness to the last seconds of another" (Loney 2011, 13).

"Any victim taken by force is subjected to a complicated group of insults to his or her humanity. Your freedom, well-being, mental state, physical state—they all suddenly mean next to nothing" (Buchanan, 83).

The reader may be interested to know that confessed hostage takers have also acknowledged that the abduction of a hostage is the most terrifying time of their lives. This is valuable information for a potential hostage, who can take advantage of his hostage takers' fears and react in a manner that might startle them into making a hasty decision to quit the abduction, turn, and run.

Injuries during abductions are common but not lethal. Just as the hostage is suddenly filled with adrenaline and all the nervous muscle energy that comes with it, the abductors may have been sitting for hours waiting for the right opportunity, and they too are filled with pent-up anxiety, fear, apprehension, and now adrenaline.

If the hostage takers have ingested drugs to bolster their courage, this only adds to the danger and their unpredictability. The loss of bladder control is not unusual during times of heightened fear or even following such an incredible event, when the body commits to sudden and complete relaxation. I have had some of the toughest and burliest criminals "wet" themselves and even defecate in their pants in the backseat of my police car. Abduction can be that frightening.

Abductors who carry a handgun in one hand while grabbing and scuffling with the target with the other hand can accidentally fire the weapon. This is called sympathetic muscle response—if you hold a gun in one hand and make a fist with the other empty hand, the fingers on the hand with the gun will squeeze as well. The harder or more quickly you squeeze the fingers of the empty hand, the more likely your other hand will be to squeeze the trigger. Police officers and military personnel are trained to hold a rifle or a pistol with their finger outside of the trigger guard until they are prepared to fire the weapon. Abductors who carry a knife will often use their knife hand to help grab or push the target into the vehicle, and sometimes they accidently stab the target in the process. Abductors without a formal weapon will often use their fists and feet as they attempt to force, squeeze, or jam the target into the vehicle as quickly as possible. Abductors have a tendency to use excessive force. The longer it takes the abduction team to get a target into a vehicle, the greater the chances of a hostage escaping, other persons coming to the person's aid, or abductors being identified.

During the abduction and transport, considering the confusion and time constraints, the hostage might not be completely searched. This may provide the hostage with an opportunity to activate an emergency locator device.

RURAL ABDUCTIONS

Some hostages are taken in towns or cities, where target intelligence gathering, surveillance, and eventual abduction might go unnoticed amid the hustle and bustle of crowds. Many hostages are taken in more rural areas, where abductors surround the target's vehicle with other vehicles or create a road obstruction in order to get the target's vehicle to stop without force.

During my first day on a particular United Nations mission, I was leading a cross-country convoy of twelve brand-new four-wheel-drive UN vehicles filled with water and supplies when we came to a halt behind about six civilian vehicles blocked by a very large tree directly across the road. To my right, I noticed a small footpath beside the road that led into the jungle. I got out of my vehicle and followed the path for about one hundred yards and then made my own path from there as I tromped through the jungle and came out on the other side of the tree that blocked the road. I climbed over the tree, walked back to my vehicle, and told my local driver to move over. I put the vehicle in four-wheel drive and followed my path into the jungle, around the felled tree, and back onto the road on the other side. I radioed the other drivers to do the same. In less than ten minutes, we were on our way. A few days later, as I was explaining to UN officials how I had damaged my brand-new Land Rover (seems I had knocked down a couple of trees), they laughed and told me that blocking the road with a tree is a common tactic by guerillas to stop traffic, attack and plunder the vehicles, then rob the people in the convoy. I wish they had pointed out that little fact in premission training.

That day, I came as close as I ever wanted to becoming a hostage. I have since wondered, if I had stood around any longer or spent too much time weighing all the other options and not acted immediately and decisively, how that day might have turned out much differently. It can be that simple.

In such rural situations, the abductors jump out of their vehicles and point rifles at the target's vehicle, start yelling, and order everyone out. This is, of course, accompanied by threats of violence, possibly punctuated by gunfire. Rural abductions provide the abductors with more time to properly identify everyone in the target vehicles, search their vehicles for tracking devices or weapons, and physically search all the occupants for cell phones and any other devices.

Rural abductions are usually less physically violent than urban ones, as there is often not the urgency to grab the target and quickly force him into another vehicle and leave immediately. Abductors will also have the time to search the vehicle and remove laptop computers, tablets, and any other electronic or communication devices. Depending upon who the hostages are and whether tracking devices are suspected in the vehicle and if logistics dictate, the abductors may expropriate the target's vehicle to help transport their hostages.

In rural areas, a target's vehicle can be seen a long way off, and abductors will not have to jump into their positions as quickly as they might in urban situations. Rural abductors plan the abduction in an area they are familiar with because they know the roads into and out of the area; they are also known in the area and therefore less likely to attract attention. In rural areas, police vehicles can also be seen a long way off, so abductions can often proceed without unnecessary urgency.

In Africa and in much of the Middle East, most towns and villages have only one major road between them. Therefore, if a hostage target is known to travel between one town and another on a regular basis, it is only a matter of time until he comes down that road and into the clutches of his abductors. This makes hostage planning much easier as now only the timing needs to be set.

Communications logistics for rural abductions are easier, as one or two cell phones are all that may be required to advise teams about target movements. As kidnappers become more experienced and technically savvy, they have begun to recognize the value of using satellite phones over regular cellular phones—satellite phones provide reliable worldwide coverage and are less likely to be intercepted. Rural abductions are less likely to suffer from unexpected interruptions and unforeseen events and are likely to have fewer, if any, witnesses.

In abduction situations, an experienced driver can make the difference between abduction and escape. Trained security drivers will take immediate countermeasures, such as driving around or driving through an attempted abduction.

After you have been abducted, it is helpful to know some of the details about your captors' planning so you can put together an assessment, a kind of report card on how experienced the captor group might be. The amount of planning and the details of the planning necessary to complete a successful abduction would depend upon several factors:

- *The mental capacity of the hostage takers.* Does this group exhibit the level of intelligence and the experience necessary to undertake such a project? It might seem to them like a good idea and they might have heard stories of other groups that have taken hostages, but can this group actually carry out a hostage taking themselves? How hard can it be, right?

- *Target selection.* Did the group appear to have done a proper background workup? Did the group have a photograph of the potential hostage? Did they know who they were abducting with respect to the hostage's financial worth? Was the group aware of the social and community repercussions of abducting this particular target? Will the abduction of this hostage bring a swift and intense police investigation? Will the abduction cause a social backlash from the local civilian population that will cause security concerns and risk detection?

- *Target surveillance.* Does the group have the know-how to collect the kind of information required to carry out this abduction successfully, or is it obvious they had inside information? They would have needed to know when and how the target traveled. What was the route? Did he travel alone? What personal security did the target have? Could this security be overcome? When would be the best time and what would be the best location to attempt the abduction? What could go wrong?

- *Vehicle logistics.* Did they have a suitable vehicle for transport? Did they have a vehicle large enough to carry all the would-be abductors plus a hostage stuffed into the vehicle in a less-than-optimum traveling position? Did the vehicle require the trunk to carry the hostage, or would the group need another compartment?

- *Weapons and equipment.* Did the group have available long guns, pistols, or knives, or did they just have overwhelming numbers to physically overcome and secure the target? Did the group require radios or cell phones for communications? Did they need handcuffs, tie wraps, a blindfold, or tape?

- *Confinement logistics.* Does the group have access to nearby secure temporary or permanent confinement facilities? Do they have the means to adapt to a secondary plan for multiple hostages? Do they have a secondary location if they have to move the hostage(s) on short notice?
- *Finances.* Does the group have the finances to pay for the confinement property, meals for the hostage(s), and guards and negotiators for weeks or months?
- *Negotiations.* Does the group have an experienced negotiator? Do they have the necessary contact information to begin negotiations? Do they have a secure method of communication?

As mentioned earlier, proper travel arrangements, secure accommodations, reliable transport, knowledge of the social and political situations in the area, and your ability to recognize dangerous people and places go a long way to thwart those who may be attempting to identify you as a possible target and eventual hostage.

CHAPTER 7
STAGES OF A HOSTAGE TAKING—
TRANSPORT AND CONFINEMENT

Hostage transport can often be as dangerous as the abduction. Your abductors must run the gauntlet of discovery or enforcement. Until they get to a safe location, they are at risk of detection, arrest, or even death. The hostage is always in danger of injury and death, sometimes deliberate and sometimes accidental. Transport may be your last opportunity for escape.

TRANSPORT

Transport from the abduction site to a confinement site might take only a few minutes, a few hours, or several days. The longer it takes, the more time the abductors have to calm down and begin to review the precautions they have taken and go over any kind of checklist. Have they forgotten anything?

The hostage can expect to be repeatedly warned to remain concealed and be quiet or be killed. The hostage can expect this warning to be repeated prior to the vehicle approaching any sort of enforcement checkpoint or enforcement vehicle, when in heavy civilian vehicle traffic, or when pedestrians are in close proximity, as those are the times there is a danger the hostage may be seen or heard. The hostage can expect to hear nervous chatter or even celebration among his captors at this point as they begin to realize they have successfully taken a person hostage—they have their prize.

The hostage will likely be blindfolded very soon after the abduction so that he can't identify any of the abductors or any landmarks that might give him an idea of where he is headed and might eventually be confined. If a hostage can't identify his abductors and doesn't know where he is going, he is less likely to make a successful escape and provide the police with sufficient information and detail to make arrests.

During transports, hostages should observe and collect as much information as possible. Even blindfolded, hostages must use their other senses. What can they hear, what can they smell, what did they feel on the road, and does anything give them a sense of which direction they are traveling and for how long? Did they drive over any bridges? Did they drive off the road for any portion? Although this will be covered later, if you are planning to escape or if the opportunity suddenly presents itself, having some idea of where you are and what direction to travel is valuable, if not mandatory.

If you are confined in the trunk of a vehicle, try to kick out the vehicle's taillights and stick your foot or hand out of the hole to attract attention. Newer North American vehicles are required to have a luminescent plastic handle on the inside of the trunk that will open the trunk lid. If you can locate one, use it at the appropriate time and safely exit the trunk and the vehicle. There's not much chance of that happening in the scenarios I describe, but if you're in a different scenario, it is something to keep in mind.

In the case of a rural abduction, it is not likely that a hostage will have a short drive to a nearby town or village. These villages would be a logical first stop by local authorities to question occupants and carry out a house-to-house search. It is more likely that a rurally abducted hostage would be driven a long distance to a more secure location and not likely back into a large city. If you are blindfolded or have a bag over your head, you might still be able to determine which direction you are traveling. If all you can see is sunlight, and it is late afternoon or sundown, if the sun is coming in through the left side of the vehicle, you are traveling north. If the sun is coming in through the right side of the vehicle, you are traveling south. If it is early in the day, the sun will be coming up in the east, etc.

RETRANSPORT

Hostages can expect to be moved from one location to another without notice. Some holding facilities might only be temporary, or the hostage may be moved in case the abductors think the police may be getting too close.

In order to keep hostages quiet and ensure they obey instructions during transport, the abductors will threaten physical harm or tell the hostages they are being released. If a hostage believes he is going to be released, he won't want to do anything that might interfere with those plans. Of course, this is often a ruse, but it works very well for the abductors. If the hostage is sold or resold, he will be transported again and again with the same rules enforced.

Transport can be lying down on the backseat or floor of a vehicle, in the trunk, or in the back of a truck or inside a bag or a box. Hostage survivor Terry Waite, who was kidnapped in 1987 and held for 1,763 days, was transported from place to place inside a large fridge. In December 2008, Robert Fowler, a Canadian diplomat working as the UN secretary-general's special envoy to Niger, and his colleague Louis Guay were kidnapped and transported for three days (56 hours of driving time), traveling over 1,000 kilometers across the barrens of the Sahara Desert and then held for 130 days; their travel was arduous, both mentally and physically.

> About every ten seconds we would bounce in such a manner that . . . we smashed our heads on the roof or slammed our faces into the dashboard . . . My face smacked into the dashboard with such sufficient force I partially lost consciousness. (Fowler 2011, 14)

During transport, hostages are most always blindfolded, gagged, tied, handcuffed, or tie-wrapped. Abductors realize they are exposed and therefore more vulnerable to arrest during transport, and there is always the risk the hostage may try to escape should the opportunity arise.

If multiple hostages are being held and all must be relocated, they may be moved one at a time or all at once in order to limit the risk of detection. This decision depends on the availability of suitable vehicles or is as dictated by other factors such as time of day or the number of drivers and guards available. The less time the abductors spend in public shuffling hostages, the less chance there is of being detected and the safer they are.

There is also the chance that a hostage may be sold or given up by the original abductors to another group, and transport and confinement will start all over again. This second group will be more experienced than the first, and the hostage can therefore expect different treatment. If a hostage is sold or given up to another group, time served with the initial group will probably not be a factor in determining how long the second group may hold him. He will also have to start all over again in assessing the group as a whole and the group as a collection of individuals and applying his survival strategies from the beginning.

CONFINEMENT

The hostage confinement stage is likely the cruelest mental and physical treatment a person will ever experience. Confinement is the most significant stage of a hostage's ordeal. Confinement will be dangerous, brutal, and frightening, and sometimes, it will be fatal. Confinement can be days, months, or even years. The confinement location might be a hole in the ground, or it might be a cave or a closet or a boat; it could be in the wide-open desert or in the dense jungle. Confinement locations and treatment depend upon the number of hostages, their nationalities, and the sex and/or religion of the hostages. Confinement can be anywhere. One thing is for certain: this is not going to be like visiting your relatives, where you have the luxury of a guest bedroom with an en suite. It is more likely to be dark and dank and smell terrible.

The remainder of this chapter will deal with a variety of issues particular to early confinement; the later chapters will deal with strategies particular to extended confinement.

cm

This book's earlier outlining of travel and safety precautions could be referred to as *travel and safety strategies*. However, the core purpose of this book is to present a selection of physical, behavioral, and mental hostage survival strategies that have been proven to be successful in the past by a variety of hostages held by a diversity of groups for any number of reasons and for varying lengths of time.

Only a very few hostages I have worked with, researched, or interviewed had training on travel and safety strategies; even fewer had any hostage survival training whatsoever. Many hostages survived by adapting their existing communication and social skills with their will to live; sometimes they survived solely on their will to live. This was sometimes a deliberate and conscious act, and sometimes, survivors fell into these behaviors more or less automatically.

The strategies I present are based upon years of solid psychological and behavior-based studies. These studies were initially the result of after-the-fact investigations of how soldiers and civilians were treated and had survived for years in either Japanese or German World War II prisoner-of-war (POW) camps. Included also in these studies were the prisoners of the Korean War, political prisoners of the recent Apartheid in South Africa, and political prisoners in South America and criminal prisoners many other countries. The results of these studies became the basis for instructions to American soldiers going into the Vietnam War. As that war progressed and reports of the treatment of Vietnam POWs became known, the American military updated its training. When the war ended, the stories from released American POWs from the infamous Hanoi Hilton, citing years of torture, malnourishment, social isolation, and brutal interrogations, provided the incentive and motivation for the military's scientists to study the success stories of how hostages survived.

While on UN peacekeeping duties in Western and North Africa and Southeast Asia, I spoke with hundreds of refugees, civilians, and internally displaced persons who had been oppressed for twenty years and more, and I routinely visited refugee camps holding tens of thousands of people. Many had been victims of brutal physical and sexual assaults, both outside and inside of prisons, and many had been witness to family members being raped or killed before their eyes inside their own homes. One woman showed me the stains of her husband's blood still on the wall and on the floor of their home; she had watched her husband's murder, buried him, and then cleaned up as best as she could. Another man showed me the jagged scar diagonally across his chest where he and a number of prisoners had been set upon with machetes and left to die in the jungle. My UN officers found village wells filled with headless bodies. What was most concerning was that 90 percent of these assaults and murders were carried out directly by, or under the supervision of, uniformed military personnel and police officers. I began to recognize the demeanor and behavior by civilians toward UN personnel, especially the police and military, as symptomatic of PTSD. This was obviously brought on by physical and psychological torture, and who could blame them? I also came to realize, in their eyes, we were just another uniform; we were just another occupying force.

Most of my early academic research into torture comes from publications that included interviews with tortured prisoners in a variety of South American countries, such as Argentina and Chile, during the reign of Augusto Pinochet. During his reign, eighty thousand people were interned, and thirty thousand were tortured (United States Institute of Peace 1993; Metin (1992); Conroy (2000); and Basoglu (1992); Allodi and Cowgill (1982). These publications also identified the different physical and mental tortures endured by POWs in Japanese camps as compared with the type and number of tortured POWs in German camps.

Their conclusion, with which I agree, was that confinement alone, even without physical abuse, is a form of psychological torture that often leads to PTSD. "From their study is generated a 'torture syndrome' which is characterized by psychosomatic, affective, behavioral and intellectual abnormalities" (p. 111). These effects range from headaches and nightmares to anxiety disorders, depression, and phobias to irritability, aggressiveness, sexual dysfunction, and suicidal ideation. My research into torture also brought me to recognize three major conclusions on how personal torture, witnessed torture, and torture guilt can affect hostages. These conclusions are described in detail in chapter 11, "Torture."

REALITY—RESOLVE

At some point after you have been kidnapped, bagged, dragged, and driven to your first holding area, it will be time for your reality check. Your first reality check will usually happen only after you've had a few minutes to mentally process what has happened over the last few minutes or hours.

Initially, your brain will start by processing just the basic facts: *I've been taken off the street or I've been taken from my bed. I've been taken hostage. I'm a hostage. I've been kidnapped.* Then a sense of realization sets in as your brain tries to make sense of what this means for you in the coming minutes, hours, and days. Your thoughts will begin to jump around in erratic flashes of interrogations, beatings, and starvation.

You will begin to realize the pain and suffering that will now be experienced by your family; you chastise yourself for not taking the safety precautions you know you should have taken, and you see flashes of the many ways you just might die.

As time permits, you begin to consider all these truths and certainties in greater detail, and you begin to realize just how serious your situation is and how close to death you may actually be. As reality sets in . . . you cry. You cry, sob, and verbally chastise yourself for being so stupid, for being so blind, for being so smug and cocky about other people's feelings and only thinking of yourself. This early reality stage will continue until after your first interrogation. We'll pick up on the topic of reality and resolve after that.

HOSTAGE TREATMENT

The two dominant and all-inclusive factors that determine how you are treated as a hostage by Islamists/jihadists are *taqiyya* and *halal*. *Taqiyya* is the Koran's permission to lie and mislead any infidel in order to achieve the goals of Islamic jihad, while safeguarding the user's ethics and honoring and protecting him from religious or personal shame. *Halal* is another term often used by jihadists that permits the use of any object, usually referring to food or drink, but also, very importantly, it permits any and all actions that are not otherwise specifically forbidden in the Koran. This pretty much leaves the door wide open for your captors to do with you as and when they wish and to say or promise you anything as long as they can justify it in furtherance of their jihad. Their actions carry no personal shame, no religious sin, no dishonor. How convenient. Everything your captors say to you—everything they might promise—must always be taken in the context of *taqiyya* and h*alal*.

Unless you have confirmed reports of how a fixed set of captors treated similar hostages under similar confinement conditions and circumstances, you cannot accurately predict how the next hostage will be treated.

There are a host of factors that come in to play during confinement that will determine how well a hostage might be treated and how long a hostage might be held. Most of these factors are dependent on the reasons for taking the hostage in the first place—terrorism or political leverage, financial gain, or as human shields. The most important influencing factors are the experience of the captors, their degree of commitment to their cause, their psychological makeup, how well they are financed, and the relative security of the confinement location.

Some Islamist religious groups have stolen every item of value from a hostage, and other captors from religious groups in the same area will preach to the hostage that their religion forbids theft and will treat the hostage's possessions with respect, returning everything at the time of release. When Robert Fowler and Louis Guay received a Christmas package through "channels," their captors brought the unopened box to them and said, "These things . . . they are not for us."

Fowler writes, "Here were these vicious desert warriors, dedicated to the path of bloody, no-holds-barred jihad, planning martyr operations against civilians and particularly targeting aid and humanitarian workers—but they did not steal cookies" (Fowler 2011, p. 191).

Some captors have treated female hostages with the respect dictated by their religion, and others of the same religion have sexually abused hostages routinely and in every way imaginable. Some captors have a propensity for violence and take out their anger and frustration on the hostage; others do not.

This is just a polite way of explaining that some captors enjoy taking hostages because they are mean, sadistic, possibly psychopathic sons of bitches that enjoy beating someone into a pile of blubbering meat. They do it because they like it, and they do it because they can. ISIS is one of those groups. See appendix 1 for statements of two released Spanish citizens held by ISIS. If you are being held by one of these guys, make no mistake—you are in for a long, hard ride.

Some terrorist leaders knowingly permit their guards to abuse hostages from time to time as a perk or reward for their service. They are told, "Just don't kill them." Being a guard in a lonely outpost is not seen as a very rewarding or prestigious position for a dedicated and enthusiastic fighter. Bored guards will sometimes beat hostages or stage false hostage executions for their own entertainment. Hostages who attempt to escape are always punished. Attempted escapes shame and embarrass the guards, plus the guards are often punished by the group's leader as well. Humiliated guards will take away any privileges a hostage may have "earned" during his stay. These privileges would have been hard-won and, once lost, are never returned.

When a leader has plans to include a hostage in a video or present him to visitors in a negotiated visit, the hostage may be told he is being released. They will offer him the opportunity for a shower and a shave. This is indeed a treat for the hostage and hard to resist. Of course, this is not intended for the hostage's benefit at all but serves only as propaganda that the group is treating the hostage well. A hostage will be left filthy and unshaven if the plan is to send a photograph to the family, as this appearance suggests pain and suffering, thereby encouraging a ransom payment.

Sometimes treatment can be a matter of hostage status. Hostages who are politicians, especially foreign politicians, are likely to be better treated, unless that country is seen as responsible for deaths of civilians and fighters. Senior executives of international corporations are often better treated than people in traditional blue-collar trades, and as can be expected, enemy soldiers are poorly treated. Journalists are often accused of being a spy and berated for their "false" stories and skewed reporting. These are only generalities; as stated earlier, there is no sure way of predicting who will be treated in what manner and for how long. There is also the fact that some hostages are kidnapped solely for execution.

During his confinement, the hostage will be subject to a range of physical abuses, starting with interrogations, bindings, and beatings, from physical torture and sexual abuse to neglect and near starvation. The hostage will be subject to the many mental abuses of lies and threats against the hostage's family, excruciating boredom, social deprivation, hopelessness and depression, thoughts of suicide, the intimidations of false executions, and the fear of death.

The permutations and combinations of hostage confinement and treatment are pretty much endless, and any predictions of hostage treatment are only a best guess.

As I proceed to sketch out the treatment a hostage may suffer at each stage of confinement, I will describe the level of physical and mental abuse and the appropriate hostage survival strategy for each. In my scenarios, the hostage is subjected to physical beatings and a range of psychological tortures. This is intended as a best example to illustrate to the reader the relevance and practicality of each strategy. Many hostages go through their entire confinement without any physical abuse whatsoever, save malnourishment and isolation; other hostages are seriously beaten and/or sexually assaulted time and time again. If the treatment a hostage receives is less than I describe, then he is the better for it. That said, many of these hostage survival strategies are imperative, regardless of the harshness of the treatment.

A hostage might be abducted initially for one reason, and then the intentions of the kidnappers can change and the treatment of the hostage will change along with it. A hostage's nationality might not have been an important factor in the beginning, but as external or internal politics change over the period of the confinement, so might the captor's attitude toward the hostage change.

There have also been hostage situations in which a change in terrorist leadership produced a change in hostage treatment, both good and bad. Just as in business, new leaders will want to employ different practices that will impress their bosses and their subordinates, especially if they think previous leaders were too soft or failed to achieve prescribed and expected goals.

The hostage survival strategies that I describe speak particularly to recent hostage takings, from the 1980s till the time of this book's publication, in the Middle East, by religious extremists and organized crime groups. That said, all these strategies are applicable to any hostage situation, whether it is by a criminal psychopath, a sexual predator, or a captor suffering from a mental illness—basically, anyone held anywhere against his will.

Before presenting the physical, behavioral, and mental survival strategies a hostage needs to survive, there must first be context. The reader must first understand what physical and mental treatment he is likely to sustain if ever taken hostage and under what circumstances because from here on, your emotional strength will be tested as it has never been tested before.

INTERROGATION

If the interrogator is not immediately present at the confinement location, the hostage will be searched, shackled, or tied and possibly beaten before the interrogator's arrival. Again, amateurs may not always thoroughly search the hostage. If the interrogator is present at the location, it is more likely the hostage will be strip-searched in his presence; all jewelry and watches will be taken. This strip search serves many purposes: firstly, to ensure that the hostage is not carrying any weapons or electronic devices; secondly, to demonstrate to the hostage that the interrogator and his assembly are in charge without having to say a word; thirdly, as a means to demean and humiliate the hostage by conducting the strip search in front of strangers. This puts the interrogator in a position of advantage, as he can now reward good behavior and bargain the hostage's clothes in return for the correct answers. Negotiations have begun.

Sherwood (1986) identifies a number of torture tactics used by captors on captives. One is "immediate post-capture interrogation," which tends to be more forceful and thereby is geared more towards "indoctrination and reeducation."

In the earlier years of Middle East hostage taking in Iraq and Afghanistan, hostage takers were inexperienced and paranoid when taking Westerners hostage. I debriefed one particular hostage who reported that his captors thought he had radio transmitters embedded in his tooth fillings. They also had no idea what the credit cards in his wallet were. When they released him, after months of brutal beatings and a ransom paid, they gave him back his wallet with all its contents. To his relief, they did not remove his fillings. Since that period, hostage takers on the whole are more experienced, but this kind of naïveté may still be found.

Canadian journalist Scott Taylor was kidnapped in 2004 by Iraqi mujahedeen who believed the military challenge coin found in his wallet was a "tracking disk."

Jessica Buchanan recognized her captors "had holes in their knowledge." Her captors had lived most of their life near a very small Somali town without electricity and whose tiny remote airport had no landing lights. Hence, they had seen planes take off and land only during the day.

They had concluded from observation that planes did not operate at night. Pilots are only human, and see in the dark no better than they do. But they appeared not to have heard of infrared night vision cameras or unmanned drones that can stay aloft for many hours, day or night, and even see you clearly in the darkest of night and under thick cloud cover." (Buchanan 121)

A hostage must look for these clues.

Because of their lack of technical knowledge, Jessica's captors ensured that she and her co-hostage, Paul Thristed, remained concealed under trees during the daytime hours. However, after sunset, they were permitted to walk around the camp freely and were actually required to sleep out in the open, under the stars, as it were. Jessica and Paul were later rescued at this very same campsite by U.S. SEAL Team Six at night and, of course, with the aid of night-vision equipment. Although it has not been admitted by the US government or the SEAL team themselves, it is reasonable to assume that significant tactical intelligence was gathered by unmanned drones and/or satellites.

First and foremost, the hostage takers will need to confirm who they have abducted—is this person the correct target? Hostage takers will examine your wallet and all personal items. This will be done prior to bringing you face to face with the prime interrogator. Experienced interrogators will examine your identification, your cell phone, and your laptop prior to the first interrogation. This will give the interrogator time to prepare a number of questions and accusations. Experienced interrogators will let you sit, likely still bound and gagged, for a while before the interrogation. This gives you plenty of time to realize the gravity of your situation as the fear about what lies ahead begins to sink in. The interrogator wants you to feel vulnerable and afraid.

Having been arrested many times when I worked as a police undercover operator and, subsequently, having spent many hours lying on a plastic mattress in a barren jail cell, sometimes alone and sometimes with other prisoners, I can assure you that a prisoner has plenty of time to think about what is going to happen.

Hostage takers will check your cell phone and likely dismantle it to turn off any GPS or tracking functions. Hostage takers are becoming more technologically aware, but they may also be technologically naive or paranoid.

They will check your computer and cell phone to verify who you are and to confirm any suspicions of your allegiance. They will look for any pictures, information, articles, or e-mails that might be used to accuse you of anything against their religious or political ideology. Ensure that any articles on your computer match your story and your government, your company, and your family's upcoming press releases. Nowadays, the more technically savvy interrogator will check your Facebook page and Twitter accounts to read what you really say to your friends as compared with the stories you're telling him now. If these stories don't match, you have lost your credibility early. This is not a good foundation on which to start your interrogation and captivity.

If you are the victim of an opportunistic abduction, your interrogator will have to establish your identify, your history, your occupation, and your purpose for being where you are. An opportunistic abduction is pretty much potluck, as the hostage takers have virtually no idea who they have until they ask you questions and you decide to give them answers. You can expect that only after establishing your identity can they even begin to consider how long they will continue to hold you and why—political leverage, ransom, or as a human shield—and then use some arbitrary formula and agree on your estimated value.

In cases of opportunistic abductions and until they can confirm your identity and verify your story, your abductors will likely accuse you of being a spy. Again, this label provides them with the justification to treat you harshly and threaten you with death. Accusing a hostage of being a spy is often their fallback position when they have no information about the person's true identity or purpose for being in their country. This happens more often in cases where foreigners are abducted and explain they are backcountry hiking and simply appreciating the beautiful landscape and the vibrant culture or they are merely a fan of ancient architecture. To the uneducated Bedouin effectively living as a social recluse, these reasons sound absurd and are therefore suspect.

CHAPTER 8
BEHAVIORAL STRATEGIES
FOR SURVIVAL

Behavioral strategies are activities specific to your day-to-day conduct—how you present yourself every day to your captors, how you reflect your mood to your captors, and how you want your captors to see you and form a favorable impression of you. The behavioral strategies in this chapter are subtle, yet they are very powerful. They are designed to positively influence your captors and thereby improve your living conditions and the likelihood of your survival. These strategies are to be applied every day for the duration of your confinement.

I will use the term *captors* when referring to your abductors collectively or the group confining you; I will use the term *guard* when referring to those individuals within your captor group who have been assigned, for the most part, to the day-to-day responsibilities of care and feeding of the hostages.

It is vital for a hostage being interrogated and, later, when living among his kidnappers, to always consider their vocabulary and terminology from the terrorist's perspective. Recall in earlier chapters the difficulty of UN states to agree on a definition of *terrorist*. When hostages find themselves face to face with their kidnappers, definitions or terminology such as *terrorism* versus *freedom fighter*, *war* versus *occupation*, *good* versus *evil*, and *fault* versus *innocence* change with perspective. Again, one slip of the tongue can set religious fundamentalists off on a verbal tirade or evoke an immediate physical retribution.

During your earliest interactions, even during your abduction and transportation to what may now be your first real interrogation, pay attention to their terminology. Throughout your ordeal, from

125

interrogation, through confinement, and when applying all your survival strategies, you must always consider their perspective. Use the same terminology and the same references they use and how these relate to their situation and why they have kidnapped you.

Just as military personnel, civilian trekkers, campers or hunters who take survival training learn, first you take physical inventory, next you set a goal and then you establish a plan to achieve that goal, so too must a hostage.

HUMANIZE

The first hostage survival strategy you must understand and apply to your situation is to humanize yourself to your captors. The interrogation is your first opportunity to humanize yourself to your captors, and you must continue to do so every day for the duration of your captivity. This strategy is the most important survival strategy of all.

To *humanize* is to cultivate, to improve, and to civilize. The term *protocol* refers to the rules for modification—the rules for correct behavior or accepted practices. Much of this chapter is dedicated to survival protocols that relate directly to this humanizing strategy. As the hostage, you must establish your identity, be recognized as more than just a hostage, get your captors to realize or accept your true purpose, and garner their respect through your religion, your manners, and your day-to-day behavior.

This humanizing strategy is not necessarily a list of what to do or what not to do as much as it is a philosophy—a philosophy of applying one's knowledge of human behaviors to influence the behaviors of another. We do this every day. Some of us have better social skills than others; some have better communication skills, better logic, and better planning skills or more experience at influencing others. However, it is incumbent on each hostage to use his skills and experience to positively influence his guards and, collectively, his captors, to improve the chances for his survival and release. The hostage must know what strategies have proven effective and successful and apply his particular skill sets to those strategies.

The reader will recognize a number of protocol components woven among the survival strategies in this book. As a hostage, your first struggle, your first survival protocol, is to humanize, to gain—or sometimes regain—your identity.

First of all, let's get something out of the way. For many years, as soon as anyone mentions hostage takers and hostages, someone always brings up Stockholm syndrome, often referred to in psychological circles as the hostage identification syndrome. It is rare, and I believe it is given far too much consideration, but the media love it. Here is some background:

> In 1973, two men entered the Kreditbanken bank in Stockholm, Sweden, intending to rob it. When police entered the bank, the robbers shot them, and a hostage situation ensued. For six days, the robbers held four people at gunpoint, locked in a bank vault, sometimes strapped with explosives and other times forced to put nooses around their own necks. When the police tried to rescue the hostages, the hostages fought them off, defending their captors and blaming the police. Later on, one of the freed hostages set up a fund to cover the hostage takers' legal defense fees. Thus "Stockholm syndrome" was born, and psychologists everywhere had a name for this classic captor-prisoner phenomenon.
>
> In order for Stockholm syndrome to occur in any given situation, at least three traits must be present: 1. A severely uneven power relationship in which the captor dictates what the prisoner can and cannot do. 2. The threat of death or physical injury to the prisoner at the hands of the captor. 3. A self-preservation instinct on the part of the prisoner.
>
> Included in these traits are the prisoner's belief (correct or incorrect, it doesn't matter) that he or she

cannot escape, which means that survival must occur within the rules set by the all-powerful captor; and the prisoner's isolation from people not being held by the captors, which prohibits any outside view of the captors from infringing on the psychological processes that lead to Stockholm syndrome. (Layton 2015)

One truism of the Stockholm syndrome is that the longer a hostage is held the more likely the hostage will develop negative feelings towards authorities. This is due to the fact that the hostage becomes impatient as to why they haven't been rescued.

The London syndrome is the exact opposite of the Stockholm syndrome. During the 1980 siege of the Iranian embassy in London, England, terrorists took twenty-six people hostage. A single hostage was killed and thrown out of the window onto the street, in effect initiating the tactical assault that ended the crisis. The ensuing investigation found that the dead hostage had continually intimidated and provoked the hostage takers, and therefore they killed him.

Obviously, there is plenty of room for hostages to operate between the parameters of these two syndromes. This is where my survival strategies lie. The challenge for hostages is to identify the opportunities for survival within their particular situation and adapt their behavior accordingly. Such "syndrome" feelings and reactions to an extremely stressful event are understandable; it is the level of commitment I question. In the heat of the moment, these are typical responses, but they generally decrease after a short period of time. It is common for reactions to vary from one individual to another.

According to research, hostage survivors often develop an unconscious bond to their captors and experience grief if their captors are harmed. They may also feel guilty for developing a bond. This is typically referred to as the Stockholm syndrome. Hostage survivors may also have feelings of guilt for surviving while others did not. It is important for survivors to recognize that these are usual human reactions to being held captive. (Speckhard, Tabrina, Krasnov, and Mufel 2005)

Showing human sympathy or empathy toward one's captor does not necessarily mean the hostage is going to pick up a weapon and fight alongside his captor. I believe real Stockholm syndrome means a hostage has gone completely over to the captor's side, essentially joining the criminal or the terrorist organization, and will fight with them to the death. It is literally changing a person's lifelong personality, changing his religious beliefs, his concept of right and wrong, and his belief in the rule of law. In brief, hostages find themselves in a psychological pressure cooker with someone who threatens to kill them. So in order to save themselves, the hostages sympathize with the criminal against all others.

Certainly, there is an anticipatory anxiety because captors control all the physical resources for sustaining life and the immediate control over life and death itself. However, I agree with Layton (2015) that the actions of the hostages in the Swedish bank robbery were more a factor of the strengths and weaknesses of the personalities of the actors than a predictable behavior. The hostages viewed small acts of kindness as huge kindnesses. The hostages were not aware of much of their hostage takers' criminal past, so there was a tendency to want to believe. If Stockholm syndrome was as common as many purport it to be, then thousands of POWs would have joined the opposing army and fought against their own homeland; thousands of people, of various religions, held in concentration camps during the Second World War would have joined the German army, and convicts in today's jails would become prison guards.

It is my opinion that the Stockholm syndrome card has been played far too many times by too many self-described experts in hostage negotiation. That being said, hostages, in this book's scenarios, are likely to express some milder traits of the Stockholm syndrome such as negative feelings towards the authorities, whom they may see as partially responsible for their situation or for having failed to rescue them.

Many of the survival strategies in the scenarios in this book, in particular those that relate directly to humanizing, are designed to accomplish the complete opposite. **They are designed to assist the hostage with influencing the hostage taker, to manipulate the hostage taker—a paradigm shift in the Stockholm syndrome.** It is embedding personal behavioral strategies into your day-to-day activities plus embedding interpersonal behavior strategies into your interactions with your guards and captors in order to positively influence them. Later, mental strategies will deal directly with your own positive mental focus and psychological well-being.

Your overall safety, your day-to-day treatment and the likelihood of your eventual release all depend on your captors recognizing that you are a person—a person with an identity. They must appreciate you as a human being with a name, with a family and loved ones, and appreciate that you have feelings. Your captors must identify with you in as many ways as possible. You have a family, children, and parents. You have brothers and sisters. You have friends, and you try to make more friends every day. You enjoy living. You enjoy feeling sunshine on your face. They must come to accept you as having the same kinds of feelings of joy and sadness they too have experienced. You are flesh and blood; you get hungry and you get sad, just like they do. They must realize you are trying to make the world a better place to live . . . just like they are. And as such, you merit better treatment, even respect.

We all understand that during negotiations, both sides must have something of value that the other side wants, something to bargain with and something to trade. Your interrogator thinks he is holding all the cards and that you have nothing to bargain with. He's wrong. He wants your answers; he needs your compliance. He needs your help.

Here's the scenario. You've just been brought into a small room, bound and gagged, and you are sat down in a chair. In the room are three or four guards (everyone wants to watch) plus your interrogator; your gag is removed. As I mentioned earlier, your interrogator will very likely start off with his speech about who they are, what righteous and just cause they are fighting for, and why you have been selected as a hostage.

Regardless of the first question you are asked, you must reply with your name. For example, "My name is"—whatever, let's say—"Michael."

The name you give should be two syllables or more. If your name is David, don't say "My name is Dave," even if that is the name you normally go by. Similarly, if your name is Mike, use *Michael*. Shortened or one-syllable names don't have the same psychological personality and weight as multisyllable names like David or Michael. Short, one-syllable names are often used for dogs so that commands can be short and the dog's name can be spoken sternly and with emphasis. You don't want your captors to order you around using abrupt commands. You want them to speak to you with some level of recognition and respect.

If the interrogator does not start the next question with your name, your only reply is "My name is Michael" or just "Michael." This is reminiscent of the "Name, rank, and serial number" routine we are accustomed to in movies with POWs.

This might frustrate your interrogator, and you may get slapped around or punched, but it is imperative that he address you by name. You're likely going to get slapped around or punched anyway, so you might as well make it worth something. Remember, especially if he has followers in the room witnessing the interrogation, he wants to show them that he can get results. You answer only those questions in which he uses your name so that he is promptly rewarded. Keep your answers short so that he has to continually ask you to elaborate. When he begins to call you by name, you can feel good deep down inside because you've won your first small victory. You have begun to be humanized by your captors. You have established your identity.

You are accepted as a real person. This is a very important first step. You are negotiating.

Consider that for weeks or months, this group of people who planned to kidnap you have gathered intelligence on you and planned your abduction, and who knows what demeaning labels or insulting names they may have been calling you? Having them now refer to you by your real name is a huge step. When they begin using your real name when speaking among themselves, that is an even greater step.

After the first few questions, begin to reply using his name. If you don't know it, ask for it; everyone likes to hear the sound of his own name. When you begin to use each other's name as you ask and answer questions, the exchange begins to sound less like an interrogation and more like a conversation between two people—exactly.

If he asks questions about your background, you answer with humanity-based replies, such as "I am married, like you are [looking at his followers]. I have children, just like you do, and you . . ." again addressing him and his followers, some of whom will likely be your guards for the coming weeks and months ahead.

It is very important that you apply this same strategy toward your interaction with the guards. They too must become accustomed to calling you by your proper name. Later on, when you are sitting in your cell or your tiny room and your guards demand that you stand up or carry out your toilet bucket, you must resist or refuse to do so until they call you by name. It is likely that the first few times, they might give you a beating and drag you out of the room, but soon they will find that this becomes too much trouble for them. They don't want to have to fight with you each time they ask you to do something, so hopefully, one by one, they will begin to call you by name—another small victory for you. Also, don't forget to begin calling them by name when they call you by name.

You must humanize yourself to your guards. They will be bringing you food and water every day, and if you have entered into a basic relationship with them, they may be inclined to bring you a blanket when you ask. Having your captors call you by name is an important first step, but don't overdo it as this will look patronizing and manipulative. Use your social sense, just like you would back home when meeting someone for the first time and want to develop a relationship. The major difference here is, you don't *want* to develop a relationship, but you *need* to develop a relationship.

> We determined as well that we would seek to conduct ourselves with dignity at all times and in all circumstances, and that we would be respectful, open, and correct in our dealings with our guards in the hope of encouraging them to treat us in the same manner. (Fowler 2011, 141)

Under no circumstances should you put up with your captors calling you by a name that is similar or identical to your company's name. Let's say, for example, you work for a company called Muchmore Oil or Muchmore Mining. You cannot have your captors calling you Muchmore Oil or Mr. Muchmore or Killer Muchmore. This is dehumanizing; this is not recognizing you as a person. This is allowing your captors to see you as the embodiment of everything they have come to hate about Muchmore Oil. Maybe Muchmore Mining has displaced farmers from their land or is responsible for an oil spill or a gas leak that has killed people or destroyed prime farmland. If the activities of Muchmore Oil have been even remotely responsible for any deaths in this country, in their eyes you have now become personally responsible for those deaths. It doesn't have to be a fact; it just has to be a rumor for them to consider you guilty. The more they can blame you for directly, the less they will blame themselves for your kidnapping and treatment. When they want someone to blame, they will blame you. You do not want to be held up as the focus of their hatred like some effigy carried aloft by protesters and then burned and trampled in the street.

So why is humanizing such an important strategy? Why do you need to have your captors see you as a human being? **Because it is more difficult to kill someone when you know the person's name and you recognize them as a human being.**

When you are humanized to your captors, it is difficult for them to make life-and-death decisions easily. It is more difficult to kill someone with whom you have built some kind of rapport or relationship. Livestock farmers understand this strategy very well. Livestock farmers will not permit their children to give newborn calves or piglets or even chickens a name because when it comes time to kill them, the children will become very upset and, often as not, beg their father not to kill the animals. The children will beg their father to find some other way the "pet" can be useful without having to be killed.

I remember taking my two young children to visit their grandfather, who had two large white ducks roaming around his suburban backyard. Being quite impressed by the presence of these ducks, one of my boys asked his grandfather, "What are their names?" to which my father replied, "Christmas and New Year's." Enough said.

Similarly, you don't want them to give you a name that is a number or a date. Like a death-row inmate, you don't want to sit around brooding about a specific day and a month you might be killed. (See appendix 1 on the Spanish hostages.)

If negotiations come to a point where your captors must decide whether to accept a ransom and release you or make an example out of you, you want their decision to go in your favor—your release. If your interrogator asks questions about your purpose in this country, your reply must be a practiced speech. "I am here to help your country," "I am here to help your wives and your children," "My company wants to help your leaders do a better job," "My company/country wants to help your doctors and hospitals," "My government was invited to help stop corruption."

At this point, it is very important to get your interrogator to agree that these are righteous acts; these are good deeds. These are helpful to him, his family, and his country. You must ask your interrogator directly and simply, "These are good things to do, right?" "These things will help you and your family, right?" Look at him directly and nod. Psychological studies in neuro-linguistic programming (NLP) confirm that when trying to influence someone's opinion, nodding will encourage your listener to nod as well. Your listener will adopt his own nodding as internal agreement even prior to any intellectual assessment. This nodding will reinforce your comments both physically and subconsciously. How can he not agree that these are all good things? How can anyone in the room not agree that these are all good things? When they begin to nod or, in some manner, soften their position on their accusations as to your intentions, they have begun to realize your purpose for being where you are and doing what you are doing. You are negotiating.

The case of Vincent Cocketel, a thirty-seven-year-old Frenchman working for the United Nations High Commission for Refugees (UNHCR) in Chechnya who was kidnapped in January 1998 and held hostage for 317 days, provides a glimpse of his confinement and survival and is an exceptional example of the benefits of humanizing yourself to your captors. The following excerpts are taken from his twenty-minute speech given at the Palais des Nations in Geneva on March 24, 2015.

> When in '96 I was sent by the United Nations High Commissioner for Refugees to the North Caucasus, I knew some of the risks. Five colleagues had been killed, three had been seriously injured, seven had already been taken hostage. So we were careful. We were using armored vehicles, decoy cars, changing patterns of travel, changing homes, all sorts of security measures.

> Yet on a cold winter night of January '98, it was my turn. . . . I was handcuffed, blindfolded, and forced to kneel, as the silencer of a gun pressed against my neck . . . Then a process of dehumanization started that day. I was no more than just a commodity.

> I was kept in an underground cellar, total darkness, for 23 hours and 45 minutes every day, and then the

guards would come, normally two. They would bring a big piece of bread, a bowl of soup, and a candle. That candle would burn for 15 minutes, 15 minutes of precious light, and then they would take it away, and I returned to darkness.

Isolation and darkness are particularly difficult to describe. How do you describe nothing? There are no words for the depths of loneliness I reached in that very thin border between sanity and madness . . . One part of your brain wants you to resist, to shout, to cry, and the other part of the brain orders you to shut up and just go through it. It's a constant internal debate; there is no one to arbitrate.

I was interrogated for 11 days by a guy called Ruslan. The routine was always the same: a bit more light, 45 minutes. He would come down to the cellar, he would ask the guards to tie me on the chair, and he would turn on the music loud. And then he would yell questions. He would scream. He would beat me. I'll spare you the details. There are many questions I could not understand, and there are some questions I did not want to understand. The length of the interrogation was the duration of the tape: 15 songs, 45 minutes. I would always long for the last song.

On one day, one night in that cellar, I don't know what it was, I heard a child crying above my head, a boy, maybe two or three years old. Footsteps, confusion, people running. So when Ruslan came the day after, before he put the first question to me, I asked him, "How is your son today? Is he feeling better?" Ruslan was taken by surprise. He was furious that the guards may have leaked some details about his private life. I kept talking about NGOs supplying medicines to local

clinics that may help his son to get better. And we
talked about education, we talked about families. He
talked to me about his children. I talked to him about
my daughters. And then he'd talk about guns, about
cars, about women, and I had to talk about guns, about
cars, about women. And we talked until the last song
on the tape. Ruslan was the most brutal man I ever
met. He did not touch me anymore. He did not ask
any other questions. I was no longer just a commodity.

Mr. Cocketel was rescued on December 12, 1998, by Russian
commandoes. Three terrorists were killed and two commandoes
were injured (http://news.bbc.co.uk/2/hi/europe/233746.stm).

His videotaped speech and transcript are available through a
number of websites, one of which is http://www.krmagazine.
com/2015/03/24/video-vincent-cochetel and http://www.ted.com.

My argument for employing a humanizing strategy toward one's
captors must be tempered with the caveat that humanizing itself
is subjective and may not always work on every captor. As I have
said earlier, your captor group is a likely to be made up of religious
extremists, political fanatics, experienced kidnappers, or just plain
criminals; throw in male chauvinism and the frailties of human
emotion or mental imbalance, and you have a dangerous cocktail.
Jessica Buchanan experienced this initially but was able to overcome
their contempt.

The men didn't show any signs to indicate that
anything about our common captivity humanized me
in their eyes. Naturally, in such company the term
"humanized" would be literal. As a woman and a
foreigner, full human status was not mine to claim.
(Buchanan, Jessica and Landemalm, Erik, *Impossible
Odds* 2014, 153)

Later on during her captivity, Jessica took over the task (out of
sheer laziness of her captors) of making the morning tea and baking

the morning bread in the ashes of the campfire. She believes this also provided her some protection from sexual advances from the group of ten to nineteen male captors as they began to see her in somewhat of a mothering role. Jessica had humanized herself in spite of her captors' chauvinism and social constructs.

Judith Tebbutt was also successful in humanizing herself to her captors. Even though her filthy room had no windows, no fresh air, was always searing and sweaty in the heat of the day, and was full of crawling, biting insects, "The men always took their shoes off on entering the room, as if it were a mosque. This was meaningful." (Tebbutt, Judith, *A Long Walk Home* 2013, 84)

PASSIVE COMPLIANCE

This is your everyday demeanor as a hostage. Don't show enthusiasm when asked to carry out some menial task, and take your time doing what you're told.

Do what you are told, but do not do it eagerly. Figuratively speaking, drag your feet.

We can all remember how, as a child or teenager, we reacted when asked to clean up our room, take out the garbage, mow the lawn, or turn off the television and do our homework. We sulked and did what we were told, but we did it begrudgingly. It showed in our body language, and it showed in our voice and our demeanor. Let's face it—you're a hostage and you're not going to be excited or eager to do anything you're told, but reflecting on the psychological strategies outlined earlier, you must learn to walk a thin line when it comes to your behavior. Calculate what you must do to gain favorable treatment from your captors, but do it in a manner that does not make you appear weak or unworthy. Do not show favor nor outright contempt. Keep a poker face while you think and plan.

"Sit down and shut up." This statement is nothing new to us. We remember our school years when we had to act differently for different teachers. We evaluated every teacher's personality; we learned their rules, and we learned where their line was drawn about our behavior in class. We learned what we could get away with and what we could not. Sometimes we learned this lesson the hard way, but we learned how to calculate and adapt our behavior depending upon the circumstances, the personalities, and the penalties involved.

As we left school and entered the workforce, we applied what we learned along the way. We learned what we could and could not do, how often we could call in sick, and how often we could show up late for work. We had learned how to get along in the schoolyard; we learned how to be friends with some people and how to stay away from others. Then we applied what we had learned in the schoolyard to the workplace and to our everyday lives. We learned to read and understand human emotions—our own and those of others. We adapted our behavior according to the circumstances.

Being a hostage is no different. Your ability to read and understand people will be crucial to your survival. Who is the weakest of your guards? Who is the strongest? Who might be more susceptible to your humanizing effort? Who might be less susceptible? What have you noticed in their eyes or in their facial expressions and tone of voice? What in the hesitation of a guard might give you clues into his personality? It's critical to recognize these things—it might save your life.

Overall, your very survival depends upon your ability to balance your emotions, as this will improve your safety. Are you happy about being a hostage? Certainly not. Would you like to kill each one of your captors, especially those who have beaten or sexually assaulted you? Of course you would. But you're in a situation where you must control your frustrations and emotions to improve your safety. I'm not suggesting you should never show your frustrations and true emotions, but the decision to do so must be calculated. You must consider the most likely outcome if you do. What are you trying to achieve?

There are times when it will be necessary to show your anger because you must draw the line regarding your treatment; not to show emotions in those circumstances would be counterproductive.

If you are hungry and cold, make a fuss and ask for more food and blankets. If you are being treated harshly, make it known to those in authority that this is not acceptable. It's OK to get angry at your captors. They expect you to be unhappy and angry, so show this through passive compliance and calculated emotions. This is normal behavior.

As in any relationship, your emotions and communications must be timed and calculated in order to encourage a specific outcome.

You have only your intellect with which to influence your treatment and your release. You have your day-to-day behavior, your application of emotions, your knowledge of social relationships, your experience of reciprocity between people, and your communication skills. Use these skills to select and apply survival strategies at the right time, in the right place and toward the right individuals. Be smart, but be cautious, and don't be seen as manipulative.

Don't overdo passive and don't overdo compliant.

If you are too eager to comply, you will be seen as a weak person and be given very little respect. Remember, these people see themselves as fighting soldiers; they bolster themselves and their fellow soldiers every day about being strong and committed to the cause. They are proud to fight and proud to die. Among Jihadists, cowardice is viewed with contempt. Show a little defiance. If you are seen to be passive, patronizing, and a fake, you are more likely to be beaten or abused, picked upon, underfed, and bullied—kicked like a dog. (In the Arab world, there is nothing lower than a dog.)

On the other hand, don't be confrontational or offensive, as you may endure beatings as a means to bring you into line or to show you who's boss.

You must evaluate your captor's patience, hatred, tolerance, curiosity, fear, experience, and dedication, keeping in mind the reason you were taken hostage, and then calculate which strategies will serve you best, when, and with whom. Then walk that tightrope every day.

The hostage who causes the most problems, insults his captors, slanders their religious beliefs, or does not earn their respect may be the first to die. Remember how to live in the middle ground between the Stockholm Syndrome and the London Syndrome.

> "I had to get along with them, I couldn't waste every day confronting them, rebuking them, remonstrating with them. It wouldn't do me any good, not emotionally nor in terms of my material well-being. I had to be methodical, businesslike, ensure that there were pirates I could deal with, to whom I could make requests, so I could obtain whatever small conveniences were allowed me" (Tebbutt, p. 136).

> "The pirates had a settled patriarchal view of the world, and here I felt the pragmatic choice was to play up to that" (Tebbutt, p. 148).

RELIGION

In my example scenarios and in almost every other hostage abduction and confinement circumstance, religion is vitally important. To the reader, this might sound trivial, meaningless, or even stupid for overstating the obvious because religious ideology is often to blame for a hostage being in this situation in the first place. But it's not the hostage taker's religion to which I refer—it's yours.

Middle Eastern hostage takers are religious fanatics; as such, they believe all Westerners are heathens, nonbelievers, and godless infidels—*kafirs*. Your captors believe they are followers of the most devout religion—the one true and only religion, the religion that should be accepted by everyone, everywhere in the world.

Your captors, Islamist extremists of one sort or another, have assembled and sworn allegiance to this group in defense of their religious homeland, their religious beliefs, and their religious future. They pray five times a day or more, and they refer to Allah, the Prophet

Muhammad, or God in almost every single conversation they have every day, day in and day out, all year long. Almost every sentence they utter includes the words *insha allah*, which means "God willing." It would be similar to us saying *"with any luck"*. When they attend daily prayers, they are often preached to by religious leaders who incite them to follow passages in the Koran—passages and scriptures that oblige them to cleanse the world of godless, nonbelieving heathens. Muslims believe that the Koran's words are the authentic and literal words of the prophet, not just history's parables or gospels set in story form for easy understanding. When these extremists blow up a tank, blow up a truck, fire a gun, or blow themselves up in a suicide attack, they thank God. They don't yell "Take that!" or "Yee-haw!" They say *"Allahu Akbar* [God is great]" or "Praise be to God." Everything they say and do is based upon religion. Yelling *Allahu Akbar* justifies what they have just done is solely in the name of religion and immediately absolves them of any guilt, criminality, or wrongdoing.

As you begin to establish a rapport with your guards and you have proved to them that you are understanding and respectful of their religion, you may wish to include *insha allah* in your conversations. But be extremely careful not to use this too soon or too often as you risk being seen as patronizing—or worse, mocking their religion. Sparingly is the rule here.

Your captors may not feel you are worthy of uttering any Arabic words or any religious terminology whatsoever. In all things religious, be very cautious about what to say, when and to whom.

Throughout history, countless millions of people have been tortured and killed in the name of religion, in the name of God. Many religions and many governments are guilty; the Islamists are just the most recent.

Whether you are religious, agnostic, or an atheist, as a hostage, you are now going to need to be devoutly religious—devoutly religious every day, all day long. You must not only be *seen* to be religious, but you must be *heard* to be religious as well. This is just as relevant to a young girl kidnapped off her own street in her own hometown as it is for a hostage held by religious fanatics anywhere in the world. I recall a story told by an American POW in Vietnam who shared a cell with another POW, an admitted atheist. When this atheist POW returned to his cell after one particular torture session, he told his roommate, "During my torture I converted to religion." His friend asked, "Which religion?" To which he replied, "All of them." Humor aside, in his case, conversion to religion gave him spiritual and psychological strength—real or otherwise, it makes no difference. As the old saying goes, "There are no atheists in a foxhole."

In my scenario, the hostage uses religion to convert his guards and abductors—convert and convince his abductors to believe in him and to believe he is a God-fearing, God-loving man. This is part of his plan to humanize himself to his captors, survive, and return home safely.

If you do not already do so, you must begin to say prayers *out loud* over meals. You must pray *out loud* in the morning, pray in the evening, thank God for your family, pray for your release, even pray for your hostage takers, and then tell them you prayed for them. Pray when they're looking, and pray even when they're not looking. Again, your mission is to convince your captors that you deserve to be treated well and that you deserve to live.

When you believe you might be taken from your cell for interrogation or taken for a beating or for execution, drop to your knees and begin to pray aloud. As your guard unlocks your door and opens it, what does he see? He sees a religiously devout person praying to his god, just like he does. Respect for religion fosters respect. If he hesitates for a moment and permits you to finish your prayers, you will know you have achieved some level of recognition and respect from him and gained a little influence over him. You can test whether your guards have been influenced by your religious devotion by holding up your hand to him, signaling you have not yet finished your prayer. If he allows you a few seconds to finish praying before taking you from your cell, you have made an impression. Your religious actions have resonated with his religious actions, whether he realizes it or not. Again, don't overdo it.

Muslims are specifically ordered in the Koran to show tolerance to the faith and the beliefs of Jews and Christians—"People of the Book"—and permit them to practice their faith.

> There are some among the People of the Book who believe in God and what is revealed to them. They are humble before God and do not trade God's revelations for a small price. They will receive their reward from their Lord. God's reckoning is swift. (Koran 3:199)

Let's look at the situation from the hostage takers' perspective again. They have been taught that you are a nonbelieving, God-hating devil worshipper and you deserve to die; your kind must be wiped from the earth. Your captors vehemently believe their actions are protected, even mandated, by religion, and they will be rewarded for their service in this world and in the next. Now, all of a sudden, here is a Westerner who is devoutly religious. This Westerner kneels on the floor and says prayers during the day; he says prayers and even gives thanks to his God for his disgusting meal. He even prays for those who have kidnapped him and those who treat him so poorly—he even kneels and prays for me! Are these the actions of my enemy? Is this someone I am supposed to hate or kill without remorse? This hostage—this person before me—does not look like the kind of person I am supposed to hate.

A hostage taker, a kidnapper, a criminal who witnesses this sort of religious devotion will begin to have respect for his hostage. It doesn't matter if the hostage taker is a religious fanatic, a criminal, or some lonely and tormented soul who has kidnapped a young girl as a replacement for his mother, his spouse, or just for companionship; religious devotion earns respect everywhere.

The Koran repeatedly instructs its readers that God alone will judge the People of the Book—Jews, Christians, and Muslims—regarding "that in which they differ." This kind of knowledge about the Koran can assist the hostage to formulate his replies to questions and accusations regarding his purpose and character. For example, you might reply, "You may not believe me, but God believes me, and God alone will judge me." To your interrogator (the believer), positive religious references will strike a chord with him, whether he realizes it or not.

Your strategy here is to use religion as a tool. To your captors, religion is everything—it is their life; it is their death. Your religious devotion during captivity is everything—it could be your release; it could mean your life.

Again, look at what you as a hostage are trying to achieve. When it comes time for a decision to be made about whether you will be sacrificed as an example to the world or released in exchange for political prisoners or for a ransom, you want the decision to go in your favor—your release, your life.

YES!

You must encourage a two-way discussion as soon as you can rather than sit and remain the object of insults and accusations. Don't be afraid during your interrogations to ask questions. Be sure not to criticize or insult your interrogator or demean his motives. Ask questions that can only be answered by a *yes* reply. The easiest questions can be constructed from mirroring his opening statement. "You are fighting to make a better life for yourself and your family, *yes*?" Nod your head and wait for an answer. Remember neuro-linguistic programming (NLP). If he doesn't answer right away, repeat the question and wait.

It doesn't matter what questions you come up with; your strategy is to get him to say the word *yes*. Even if you have to ask him if you are pronouncing his name correctly, get him to say the word *yes*. Any statement the two of you can agree upon is a step toward a positive relationship. As his hostage, you have many steps ahead of you, and the earliest first steps account for the biggest impact.

You must downplay whatever accusations your interrogator announced to you in his opening speech. Sample answers for his questions should have been discussed during your predeployment training so that any press releases your employer or government provides will be similar to your answers. This preparation will also ensure that your answers match those of anyone else from your company taken captive—confirmation.

In all dealings with your captors, again try to look at the situation from their point of view. It is important to realize that they operate within a closed communications framework. Except for a few at the very top, your captors do not get their news from the CBC, CNN, or BBC. They do not have the luxury of listening to informed debates and making up their own minds. In times of crises, communications will most always be from the top down. Even on the remote chance that they have read a local newspaper, the information in that paper will be very biased, full of half-truths, falsehoods, and outright lies. The rest of their information about the West, about the "real" purpose of the occupation, the invasion, or even your presence is from rumors.

Many scientific studies have proven that the worst rumors travel faster, the worst rumors are believed, and rumors are embellished along the way. But we already knew that, right? Their newspapers and the rumors will be full of stories about Westerners having executed civilians and used poison gas on fighters and civilians; Westerners only want to indoctrinate their children and turn them against Islam. Westerners want to wipe out Islam and take over their lands. Be prepared for outlandish accusations.

Back in your predeployment planning, you should have prepared an "elevator speech" for such accusations. An elevator speech is usually about twenty seconds long. It is named as such because it represents the time you have between floors in the elevator at your office, when one day the door opens and the company president or CEO steps in and politely asks who you are. You can't be caught flat-footed, just standing there stammering and mumbling. You give him your elevator speech. Your elevator speech confidently introduces you and identifies your position within the organization; it highlights some of your achievements and expresses your aspirations within the company. If you miss your chance—if you miss this opportunity—you'll kick yourself for a long time.

If you have a prepared your "hostage elevator speech" for your initial interrogations, you will have the opportunity to establish your identity and your function within your company, your company's purpose in this country, the many achievements thus far, and the many beneficial projects (nodding) your company plans for the future. As the saying goes, you have only one chance to make a first impression. This is an opportunity to immediately impress your captors with all that you have done and all that you will do if being taken hostage doesn't change your company's or your country's magnificent and benevolent intentions. If there is the slightest doubt that they have kidnapped the wrong person, it may show itself here; if kidnapping you was Plan A, maybe they'll go with Plan B, a quick release. There is still time for them to save face.

Your answers should be short. Don't try to overexplain yourself, as it may appear as though you are trying to talk your way out of something or you are hiding something or being evasive. Stick to the short truth because you may have to repeat it many times over the following hours and days, so it must be easy to remember.

Never curse. Remember, these are religious people who believe you are a godless, evil person; don't prove them right by cursing. This will only provide them with an all-too-easy confirmation.

Regardless of your reason for being in this country, at this time, in this place, be aware that most hostages will be accused of being a spy. In countries where there is even the slightest suggestion of an occupation, anyone taking pictures can be accused of being a spy—again, fear and mistrust of the West. Often, when an interrogator accuses you of being a spy, this will tell you that your interrogator doesn't have much in the way of evidence to disprove your answers, and he's pretty much out of meaningful questions. Unless he has discovered information on your cell phone or your laptop that makes him suspicious or—heaven forbid—proves you wrong. If you are caught in a lie, it's a long way back to forming any kind of trusting relationship, if it's ever possible.

In August 2001, two American women, Dayna Curry and Heather Mercer, were arrested and jailed in Afghanistan for attempting to convert Afghan women to Christianity. They told their captors how they were only telling people how Jesus had changed their lives. Again, travelers must always remember they are living and working in a devoutly religious country and they must always be cautious. In Muslim countries, attempting to convert a Muslim is a capital offense, which means serious jail time or execution. This respect for religion goes beyond just Muslim countries. Recently, travelers have been arrested in foreign countries for showing tattoos of Buddha. A few months later, following 9/11, Curry and Mercer were rescued by American Special Forces (Curry and Mercer 2002).[7]

I believe the time of spreading religion to foreign lands is over.

If your interrogator asks why you were taking pictures of his people when walking down the street (chapter 5, "Countersurveillance") and where those pictures are on your cell phone, reply that your company has directed you to "send and delete." Tell him that if you don't regularly send pictures of your hotel and restaurants, they will bring you home. Let him ponder what your country's law enforcement will do with those pictures. A little fear about just how long your captors can safely hold you before they are discovered and you are rescued is a good thing. Kidnappers are always paranoid; use this knowledge.

Some studies on hostage treatment that focused particularly on the initial interrogations found that any new hostage who tried too hard to please the interrogator, thinking it may earn him an

---

[7] In 2001, Dayna Curry and Heather Mercer traveled to Afghanistan on a humanitarian mission. Within a few months, they were arrested by the ruling Taliban government for telling local people about Jesus. In the middle of their trial, the event of September 11, 2001 led to the international war on terrorism, with the Taliban as its primary target. In light of this, and fearing for their lives, they were rescued by the US Special Forces.

early release, was seen only as patronizing, weak, and cowardly. Patronizing men, especially, were seen as pathetic and undeserving of respect. Patronizing hostages were more often beaten out of contempt and shame.

Consider for a moment the psychological makeup and adversarial background of the people who now surround you. These are dedicated men and women who, possibly for years, believe they are fighting for a righteous cause, during which some of their friends or family may have died. During your first exposure to these captors, they will see you only as their direct enemy or view your captivity as an opportunity to punish their enemy; they will be judging you. They have attended many public protests, group meetings, and planning events where they have voiced hatred and espoused violence against you and what you represent. If you now come across to them as weak and pathetic, you are more likely to be treated poorly for the duration of your confinement. This is a first-impression opportunity, where resistance may be punished but integrity must always be shown.

Many hostages found that they were beaten the worst during the first few days of their confinement. If this happens to you, don't be surprised, but expect the physical punishment to be relatively short. As I mentioned, most of this treatment is a result of your captor's frustration, and it will pass.

THANK YOU!

Thanking your captors, your interrogator, and your guards is an important step in humanizing yourself to them.

Heaven knows there is absolutely nothing to thank these people for, but it must be done if you want to survive. Everyone likes to be thanked for something once in a while. Thanking someone shows your appreciation for some gesture or kindness that the person has shown you. When a stranger holds a door open for you, it is common courtesy to thank the person. We also thank someone in the hope that he will reciprocate or show another deserving person a similar favor in the future. Most of us expect to hear "thank you" when we act in a courteous fashion toward even a total stranger, and we feel jilted if we are not thanked.

While we're on the subject, it is important that the hostage learns how to say *please, thank you, good morning, more water*, etc. in the captor's language. By doing so, you are showing him that you are making an effort to communicate with him in a comfortable manner. You are also attempting to make yourself appear as less of a threat and less of a stranger. The object is to make him more comfortable and relaxed in your company, maybe even friendly. This is humanizing. If you wish to learn more of his language, he will see this as recognition of his culture and his background. Wishing to learn more about a person's history, language, and culture is a compliment and will garner respect.

As a hostage, you must always be thinking of how to continue to humanize yourself, to endear yourself to those who hold the power of life and death over you. When a guard leads you back to your cell or room and opens the door, let's face it, you're not capable of doing it yourself anyway, as you're likely handcuffed, but you say, "Thank you." The guard may not be amused initially, but he will be somewhat surprised, and he will remember what you said. Whether he admits it to himself now or later, as a person, he will appreciate being thanked. Thanking your abductor for putting you in a prison cell or locking you in a small room may sound ridiculous, but the object here is to ingratiate yourself to him, to show him you are a kind and friendly person and to hope that your kindness will be reciprocated. Is this self-serving? Certainly it is. Is it necessary? Of course it is. This is life and death. This is no time to rest on your pride or principles; it's a time to be humble and remember your goal—survival—to return home safely.

When your guards bring your disgusting and almost inedible meal, you thank them. As before, don't overdo it or it will most certainly look disingenuous and condescending. When we are shown kindness by another person, it is our human social conditioning, our herding instincts, our social conscience to want to repay that kindness. Sometime during your captivity, you might ask for a blanket or a book to read, and your kindness may be repaid. Even hardened terrorists were brought up with some level of social awareness and decency. Every mother teaches her children to say *please* and *thank you*. Treatment is likely to be harsh at first, but this is also likely to ease as you build rapport with your captors and they believe you are not an escape risk. As you both settle into a routine, you may become comfortable asking for favors or considerations, and they may become more inclined to agree to them.

BEING A HOST

In almost every culture around the world, it is customary to offer your guests food or refreshments. The Koran goes to great lengths to explain both obligatory and voluntary charity. "God will give the reward to those who give charity" (Koran 12:88). It has been my experience that for Muslims, offering guests food and refreshments is taken more seriously than it is for many non-Muslims, who do so more often out of courtesy or politeness.

As a prisoner, if you are visited in your cell by the leader or a senior member of your captor group or some other important person, make the simple gesture of standing up and greeting them and offering them the best seat in the house; this could be your dirty mattress or whatever you sleep on. Offer him a cookie if you happen to have one stashed away.

Standing up and greeting the leader is very important. In the Muslim religion, *as-salaam alaikum* is a common greeting which loosely means "May peace be upon you." The common reply is *wa-alaikum-salaam* which means "May peace also be upon you." (These spellings vary greatly depending upon the source, but the meanings are the same.) This greeting is common and widespread. Its usage can be compared to our common greeting of "Hi, how are you?" and the usual reply, "Fine, thanks. How are you?" Of course, the Muslim greeting is all about religion. Also, we would greet friends and work colleagues in this manner only once a day, and that's it. No need to greet them with a "Hi, how are you?" ten to fifteen times a day. This is the same for Muslims. However, variations with individuals will differ. Muslims make a big deal of proving to other Muslims that they are a "good Muslim," so some may use this rather-formal greeting more often. Pick up on these and other social nuances.

The importance in standing to greet the leader or the senior member when he enters your cell is to show him recognition. Same thing if the president of your company walks into your office; you stand up and greet them properly with a "Good day" and often with a handshake. You may not like the president (you may even hate the president), but you know you are obliged to show recognition and respect due to his position—the same for the leader of your band of terrorists. What you are conveying to the terrorist leader is that you recognize his position and his authority. This does not mean you like him in any fashion whatsoever; it is simply your recognition of his position. You mean it only as recognition, but he will take it as a sign of respect. Respect garners respect. This is humanizing. Next week when your guard goes to the leader and says you have asked for another blanket, you are more likely to be given another blanket.

Don't make a big deal of this, or you risk being seen as phony and deceitful. Even worse, your guest may think you are mocking his religion. The Koran (2:264 and 2:271) directs that the giving of charity is best done anonymously and without expectation of reward. As with saying "thank you," your gesture will be noticed, although not necessarily acknowledged.

Let's look at the opposite behavior. If the leader entered your cell and you remained lying on the floor—you didn't stand and you didn't greet him and you answered his questions with short grunts like a dog—how do you think you would be treated? Like a dog. You might smugly reflect on your actions and be proud of yourself that *you sure showed him* how much you hated him and hated having to be a hostage. But what did you gain from this? Nothing. Surviving is using your head to get out of the situation and return home. You lose nothing by standing and recognizing this man, and you gain everything. Use your head.

If two weeks down the road this leader has to make a decision to accept the ransom as it stands or to make an example out of this hostage, which of these two hostages is more likely to go home? Who showed whom? Your job is to survive.

Humanizing operates mostly on a subconscious level. These simple gestures are deliberately meant to resonate with your captor's religious beliefs and customs, whether they realize it or not.

BODY LANGUAGE

When you speak with your captors, maintain a nonthreatening physical posture and tone. If you are tall, try stooping slightly while keeping a few steps away so that you are not physically threatening and don't appear to tower over the other person. When you speak, use a low, soft tone of voice and do not hold sustained eye contact. You are seeking a balance. You don't want to appear overconfident, arrogant, or aloof, nor do you want to appear browbeaten or wimpy. You will have to adapt your body language and tone to fit the personalities you are faced with every day, just like at home, while continuing to apply the humanizing qualities your strategies require.

PERSONAL HYGIENE

Try to maintain personal hygiene; strive to maintain the appearance of being human. They don't want to have to smell you either. You can ask for water to wash your body and wash your clothes; ask for a comb for your hair. If you want to be seen as a human and treated like a human, you must do everything you can to look like a human. Many hostages have followed their captor's lead and used the frayed ends of small tree branches as a toothbrush.

During case studies with released female hostage survivors, I learned they were surprised when they were supplied with feminine hygiene products. Those that were not offered them used adsorbent pieces of cloth folded many times, which they washed out as required. Of course, these offerings of hygiene products depended on product availability, the decency and respect as required by religion notwithstanding. Females may also discover that because of the nutritional changes in both the quality and quantity of food they now receive, plus the impact of physical and mental stresses they now endure, their menstrual cycle will likely be out of sync or even absent, possibly for months.

As a male, you will begin to grow a beard. This is not a problem—probably all your captors will have a beard—but you can always ask for scissors to keep it trimmed and a comb to keep it presentable. If you look like a mangy dog, you may be treated like a mangy dog. If you can't get scissors—let's face it, they're sharp and dangerous—try grinding the whiskers between two small rocks. If you're lucky enough to be held with another hostage, take turns grooming each other's hair and beard with whatever tools you can find in your cell. Your efforts toward personal grooming will not go unnoticed by your captors.

Resolve to do as much as you can to look, feel, and act like a human being.

STRUCTURE

Try to establish some sense of structure to your day and to your confinement. Use a system to mark the days—a mark on the wall or the inside of the door. (Your captors rarely see the inside of the door.) Keeping track of the date, the days of the week, and the month will help maintain your psychological contact, your link and anchor with the world from which you were stolen. You can use this knowledge, this awareness, to mentally visualize and interact with your family and friends, celebrate holidays or just remember that today is soccer practice or it's a Sunday morning. Without links and anchors to the outside world, you may find yourself mentally adrift, without a sense of self or purpose. Being mentally adrift, you may lose sight of a future and begin to feel hopeless and helpless. Establish some sort of routine—walking and a long stretch routine. Then move on to a mental affirmation of what strategies you will continue applying—a mental confirmation of your will to live, loud morning prayers, a friendly verbal greeting to your fellow captives, and a friendly mental greeting to your family back home. Start your day with a focus on the positives.

The Koran directs imams (Muslim religious leaders) to "loudly call your people to prayer." This is why you hear prayers on loudspeakers from the mosque minarets. Don't be afraid to pray loudly so that your captors will hear you. Humanize.

CHAPTER 9
SITUATIONAL STRATEGIES
FOR SURVIVAL

The behavioral strategies identified in the earlier chapter are used by the hostage all day, every day for the duration of his confinement. The situational strategies outlined in this chapter are the here-and-now strategies which a hostage will use as and when required. They are used to limit, diminish or eliminate physical or psychological damage.

When faced with a situation of opportunity, the hostage will apply an appropriate strategy; when faced with a situation of physical danger, such as a variety of tortures described in chapter 11, the hostage will apply an appropriate mental or physical survival strategy. I mention this now because the next few chapters present a number of physical and mental challenges during which the reader must begin to apply what they have learned by recognizing when and where to apply which particular strategy. With passive compliance, there are times to be smart and there are times to play dumb.

The reader will, of course, recognize that there will always be an overlap of day-to-day behavioral strategies, situational or event strategies, and long-term strategies. Strategies are not always specific to a particular time or an event. They are like a mechanic's toolbox or a carpenter's tool apron, they must be readily available as and when required and used properly to get the job done.

DISCUSSING RELIGION

While on the topic of religion, let's look at some important behavioral protocols, some dos and don'ts when discussing religion with your captors. You may be surprised how often these captors—your guards—will wish to talk with you about their religion. Note, *their* religion, not your religion; they know of no other. They follow an uncompromising theology.

Firstly, it is important to understand that this will not be a discussion in the usual sense of the word. It will not be a debate or even an objective and informed examination of facts or events. It will not be a free and open analysis of duties or responsibilities; it will not be an educated conversation between two people, openly presenting facts and opinions. As mentioned earlier, they have been taught for years, possibly their entire lives, that all Westerners are godless infidels—worthless people. Now, curiously, here before them is a Westerner who loves God and appears to be everything they were told he was not.

Your predeployment training should have included some fundamental information about the country, its customs, and especially, its religion. Considering the number of news programs we are inundated with after a terrorist attack somewhere in the world, there are more and more panels of more and more experts who explain and discuss all the religious whys and wherefores of jihadists. We all have a better understanding of what goes on in the mind of the religious fanatic. But as a traveler who might just one day find himself literally face to face with one of these fanatics, you should have a better understanding of some of the most important discussion points. But first some ground rules.

> *During discussions about religion, politics, or culture,*
> *be understanding and do not be judgmental.*

Be understanding, and do not be judgmental. We can all agree that people's religious or political beliefs are strongly held and vehemently defended, but don't let that happen here. As in bars or pubs back home, promoting your opinions about religion or politics can turn ugly and violent pretty quickly. Some bars actually have rules about "no religion, no politics." We all know you can't hold a logical argument with a drunk anyway; it's best to just walk away. In a hostage situation, you can't just walk away, so tolerance, patience, and understanding are the key—*your* tolerance, *your* patience, and *your* understanding, not theirs. If you have ever had a religious discussion with someone who knew the Bible inside out, you know that whatever logical, scientific, or religious argument you bring, the other person will be able to cite a passage of scripture that proves him right and you wrong. It gets worse when they begin to act smug about it. It's at this point that things begin to get emotional.

You should know that Muslims believe that Allah and God are one and the same entity. Jesus and Muhammad were both prophets of God/Allah and were sent to earth to bring salvation to the masses through the teachings of religion. Jesus came hundreds of years before Muhammad, but Muhammad was the Last Prophet and will not be followed by another. Therefore, followers of Islam believe that the prophet's words and teachings can never be altered. There are many parallels between Christianity and Islam; being familiar with some of them would be an asset.

Example: Killing of innocent people is forbidden by the Koran. For this reason, we made it a law for the children of Israel that the killing of a person for reasons other than legal retaliation or for the stopping of corruption in the land is as great a sin as murdering all of mankind (Koran 5:32).

This same Sura is often interpreted to mean that the Prophet forbids the killing of captives or of anyone bound.

Example: The Koran rejects the notion that one human being can take on the burden of the sins of another. How then can a hostage be blamed, tortured, or killed because of who he may represent— Western influence, an oil company, or the transgressions of others?

Example: The Koran teaches that Jesus will return and do battle with Satan. Muslims and Christians share this belief.

> We believe in God and what He has revealed to us and to Abraham, Ishmael, Isaac, and their descendants and what was revealed to Moses, Jesus, and the prophets from their Lord. We make no distinction among them, and to God we have submitted ourselves (Koran 2:136).

All of this being said, as is the case in many religions, interpretation is everything. These many and varied interpretations are the basis for the secular violence among the numerous Muslim sects. How your captors interpret their religion will have a direct effect on your treatment and any religious discussions.

Catholics and Jews may be recognized as religious, just not of Islam. Robert Fowler says it well as he describes his discussions with a captor he named Omar One.

> Omar One wasn't at all interested in the differences between our Biblical parables and their Qur'anic parallels. His certainty was absolute. No other religion was of any import—on all pillars of faith. His version was right—completely and utterly—on all particulars of faith, and we and most Muslims for that matter were at best dramatically misguided ("Seventy-three of seventy-four sects were wrong," he would intone) and at worst screaming heretics. (Fowler 2011)

In a hostage situation, debating religion may do you more harm than good; *conversing* about religion is the better way to go—actually, the only way to go. Here's the difference. When you debate religion, each side states his beliefs and the logical or theological facts to support his position; the other side counters with his logical or theological facts and so on. In my hostage scenarios, you find yourself face to face with someone who has pledged his life on his holy book being the right and only book. His God is the only true God; his prophet is the last prophet, and no other will ever come again. Anyone who stands against his religion or even questions his religion must immediately be put to death.

> He [Omar Two] was one of the more enigmatic and interesting of our kidnappers—deeply, fanatically, religious, very much a Salafist mystic . . . Omar Two was interested in us, perhaps even intrigued, but he never, not for a moment, liked, admired, or befriended

us . . . At our first meeting he forbade us to use the classic Arabic greeting Salaam Aleikum (Peace be upon you, or God be with you), because as infidels, we were disqualified from invoking Allah in any context. He was both fascinated and appalled by what we represented. We were in his eyes inherently evil, literally godforsaken, and thus his implacable enemy. (Fowler 2011, 67, 68)

This person has the power of life and death over you; you do not want to argue with him over his religious beliefs. You do not want to try to convince him that his religion may be flawed or inflexible in some way or dare to suggest that his religion might be wrong. Remember, terminology is important here. The definition of *terrorism* is subjective. Ransom and tax are subjective. Right and wrong are subjective.

It is also important to understand that jihadists do not consider the killing of their enemy's civilians a crime. To them, there is no collateral damage. The civilians voted for their government, and their government wages war against their people and their religion; civilian taxes pay for the bombs and pay the soldiers that kill his family. As a hostage, you listen to his arguments and you say "I understand" or "That's interesting" or "I wasn't aware of that." Do not try to prove him wrong. Do not be judgmental; do not be confrontational. You learn to listen attentively to his arguments, sit passively, and nod your head when you know he is trying to make a point. Just as you do all day long as a hostage, you walk that line between your emotions and your behavior. You let him know that you appreciate his teachings and that you respect him and his religious beliefs. Again, you are humanizing yourself.

Not everyone can do this; not everyone can sit and listen attentively to someone else's opinions, sit passively, and nod his head in silent agreement. Senior executives and high-ranking military officers may find this difficult as they are not used to being empathic. Teachers are used to giving others their opinion, lecturing and preaching, as it were, and being the smartest person in the room. Politicians are used to arguing issues and winning opinions. But for any hostage being held by religious or political extremists, it's time to learn how to listen.

During his lectures about religion, he will bring up politics. His religion *is* his politics, plain and simple. Do not forget this. It is also very important to your situation to let him know that you realize that he, his family, his culture, and his religion are all victims of the violence in his country. You should be able to provide opinions and examples of how violence affects everyone, how it hurts families and children, how it affects husbands not being able to provide for their families and that children should not have to live in fear.

He will appreciate these kinds of statements from you. He will understand that you have awareness, sympathy, and understanding for his plight. *Seize the moment.* It's time for your elevator speech. Remind him of why you are here: to help his children's education, to help feed his family by helping farmers with better crops, to stop corruption, to stop the violence—the violence against him and the violence against *you.* Try to get across to him that everyone is trying to stop the violence, that violence hurts everyone, and that this includes the violence against *you.*

We all watch the news and hear the economic, political, and religious commentators discuss how violence impacts a particular region. Use this information to build discussion points in preparation for a possible face-to-face meeting with one of your more senior captors, possibly even the one in charge of your fate. Again, this is one of the things you should be doing during your long hours of captivity instead of sitting around feeling sorry for yourself. Just as you did prior to being brought in for interrogation, try to predict what you will be accused of and how you will answer. You must prepare answers to both religious and political accusations. Expect many of these accusations to be outlandish, almost ridiculous, so prepare short answers that are general in nature, and do not blame or accuse your captors in any way.

At this point, your kidnapper is likely to break into the earlier speech you heard when first introduced to the group that absolves them of any wrongdoing or acceptance of any fault. This just might be a sign that his conscience is coming to the surface and he needs to reaffirm his actions. You must learn to recognize these reaffirmations as evidence that your efforts to humanize are having an effect.

Religious Conversion

Islam teaches that if a believer (a Muslim, a present follower of Islam) converts a non-Muslim to Islam, that believer will receive extra credits when he meets Allah. The worse the non-Muslim or the infidel is prior to conversion, the more points, as it were, are awarded to the converter. So a hostage who finds himself in conversation about Islam with his captor, guard, or interrogator can expect to be asked to convert to Islam and be told that if he does convert, he will be released. This is a lie. He is allowed to lie because it is in the greater interest of Islam; he is allowed to rape you or sodomize you because it is in the greater interest of Islam.

Converting to Islam is covered again later in this chapter under the "Release Promises" section, and it is very relevant here as well.

Arguing Logic

As I mentioned earlier in this book, and specifically in previous sections of this chapter ("Religious Conversion and Discussing Religion"), certain humanizing strategies may not work on all your captors, but that is why I include a variety of strategies as options. There may be little hope of approaching some of your captors with some of these strategies or approaching any of your captors with any of these strategies, but you have to try. If religion is out, then reach into your toolbox of strategies and consider your options.

> Anything we believed, especially about religion but also about most anything else, they considered to be false, corrupt, and therefore not only unworthy of discussion but also intrinsically evil. Even talking about

such differences was likely to incur the wrath of their vengeful and famously jealous god. (Fowler 2011, 146)

Arguing logic may not be successful either, but you have to try. Terry Waite, an Anglican Church envoy of the Archbishop of Canterbury, was kidnapped in 1987 while acting as a negotiator for the release of hostages in Lebanon and held hostage for over four and a half years by the very same group he was negotiating with. He was often beaten; he spent most of his time chained to a radiator, suffered mock executions, and was transported from place to place inside a large fridge. One day during his captivity, he was having friendly discussions (humanizing) with one of his young guards. Waite asked if the guard's religion forbade stealing. The guard replied that it certainly did. When Waite pointed out that the hostage takers had stolen him from his family, the guard, puzzled, said he would bring this up with his senior officer. A few days later, when the young guard returned, Waite asked what his senior officer had said. The young guard replied, "He told me not to talk to you anymore." Obviously, Waite's attempt at logic and religion had struck a chord. The young guard realized he didn't have an answer, and the reply from his senior officer confirmed that he didn't have an answer either. Terry Waite had planted a seed of doubt.

When Waite was finally freed by his captors at the end of more than four years of captivity without political or financial ransom paid of any kind, they apologized to him and said that kidnapping him was wrong. What changed their minds? Waite does not know; he can only guess. Was it humanizing himself to his captors? Did his logic find fertile ground or did the politics of requiring a hostage change? Was it his faith? Was it a combination of all this and more? To this day he doesn't know, so neither do we, but he is free. What worked? Who really knows? What matters is that something worked.

After the immolation (burning) of the Jordanian pilot Lieutenant Muath al-Kasaesbeh by ISIS in February of 2015, ISIS allies questioned this act because such behavior was prohibited by the Koran. A number of pro-ISIS scholars debated the question and decided that "deterrence" is an objective permitted by the Koran in situations requiring "reciprocal action." It is difficult to argue logic when the rules change on a whim. It is also difficult to judge your progress when your captors spend very little time interacting with you. But a hostage's fight is never over; it will always be filled with setbacks and disappointment. The important thing to remember is to keep fighting the good fight; never give up. To give up is to give in. And remember, your family won't let you give in or ever give up.

OTHER OPPORTUNITIES

Always look for opportunities to interact with your guards and any other captors nearby. Consider that older guards may have the insight of the futility of war and may be sympathetic to your situation. Often the younger or lower-ranked members of your captor organization are very curious about the West and foreigners in general. Is everyone rich, does everyone have two SUVs, does everyone own two houses, and do you really eat your dead?

Often one or more of your guards will want to practice their English. This opportunity is a gift. Again, recognize the prospects for negotiation here—you have something he wants.

When you begin your English lessons, you will of course start with the various greetings between people, the usual hello and good-bye. More importantly, make sure to include the warm, customary greeting of shaking hands, eye contact, and a broad smile. Emphasize the shaking of hands at the beginning of a conversation and at the end of a conversation, when leaving the company of that person. This will provide you with an excellent opportunity to teach your guard how to greet you with a warm, friendly smile and physical contact. This sort of friendly physical contact also serves to subconsciously identify you as a welcoming person who is physically warm to the touch. Consider that your guards have rarely, if ever, had the opportunity to physically touch a foreigner. You need to influence them, to help them come to the conclusion that you are a real live person . . . just like they are.

Visitors to many Middle Eastern countries will surely have noticed the custom of shaking your hand and then putting that same right hand over their heart. This is a gesture emphasizing a warm and friendly greeting beyond the usual handshake. Be sure to include this in your lessons, as your guard will appreciate that you have taken notice of their customs. Take this opportunity to ask your guard about other customs too.

As your English lessons progress, your guard will not only begin to appreciate what you have taught him but he may also actually start considering you a friend and treating you as a friend. If he is a relatively new recruit, he may not be treated very well by the more seasoned kidnap personnel; he is likely given the more menial jobs and will look forward to your lessons as an opportunity to share some time with someone who will listen to him and treat him as a friend.

Be sure to include social greetings between males and females. As a youth, your guard is likely nervous about how to greet the opposite sex, but at the same time, he is anxious to learn about the opposite sex. This nervousness is amplified in many Middle Eastern countries because males and females are often separated along social and religious lines. Tell him he doesn't have to become a martyr to meet beautiful girls.

Your younger guards are likely to be more curious than your older guards. They may be curious about what it's really like to live where you live. They might ask about geography or what it's like to fly on an airplane. Indulge them.

As your friendship grows, your friend may smuggle in a piece of fruit or an extra helping of food without you even asking. Of course, you take this as a good sign that you are being recognized as a human being. You now may feel comfortable asking him for an extra blanket. Let's face it—you won't be fed any better than your captors, and if they need an extra blanket at night, your request for another blanket will look very reasonable to him and to his bosses.

With the older guards, your conversations may center on wives and family. If you had photos in your wallet, you could ask to have them back. Of course, your guards will have already looked at your pictures and will be familiar with the faces but not the individual backgrounds. When you receive the pictures, be excited and eager to describe them to your guards. This will provide you the opportunity to ask them about the ages and names of their children.

If any of your children have medical issues, be sure to mention this to your guard. Ask if anyone in his family has reoccurring medical problems. Are you looking for a little sympathy? Of course. But what you are really trying to accomplish is cultivating a sense of empathy through his recognition and awareness that you are a parent who is needed at home more urgently than he had previously thought. The guard may begin to recognize that your captivity impacts a young and sickly child and he is, to a degree, responsible for that.

You will, of course, be curious about what they are learning in school, and you can begin to ask about such things as school activities or sports and of course joke and share the usual laughs about homework. The more you can demonstrate that you have in common with your guards and other captors, the more they will see you as a human being with a family and with similar day-to-day challenges.

Often, and especially if you are being held in more a rural setting, guards' schedules may require that guards get time off to spend with their families. It is important to recognize when a guard has returned from these visits and remember to ask about his children by name.

There have been situations where hostages have been given a television as a way to overcome boredom. Many hostages have seen news programs about their own abduction and ongoing demands. These viewings are always rejuvenating and a source of renewed perseverance and hope. Of course the channels are few and the reception poor, but occasionally there might be a program that it's worth asking one of your guards to explain. Whether you really care or not is a moot point; what you are trying to do is show an interest in what is going on in his province or country. This may provide you with an opportunity to invite him to sit with you as you listen to his view of local and international politics. This kind of interaction breeds familiarity and forms an important part of your humanizing strategy.

Having said all of this, it is extremely important not to show any feelings of friendship toward one of your captors in the company of his colleagues. You cannot betray any sort of developing relationship that might cause any captor to suspect that one of their own may have betrayed his dedication to the group's cause. You must expect that a guard who has spent extra time in your company learning English or brought you an extra blanket has already had to defend himself and deny any suggestions or accusations of compromise or feelings toward the hostage; he likely had to explain that his actions were all part of the care and feeding of a prisoner. Any suspicions of compromise to a guard's loyalty will undoubtedly result in his removal from those duties. If this happens, you will have to begin all over again in an atmosphere of distrust and suspicion among all your captors.

> The believers must not establish (close) friendships
> with the unbelievers in preference to the faithful.
> Whoever does this has nothing to hope for from God.
> (Koran 3:28)

If the group believes you may have tried to influence or corrupt one of their own, you may be punished. In light of what your guards have been taught about building friendships with nonbelievers, your task is to develop a rapport, a level of respect, and recognition of human dignity that does not look like a friendship but has the potential rewards of a friendship. This is a delicate business.

It is very important for the reader to understand—and I would be doing you a grave disservice not to point out—that all these opportunities to humanize yourself to your guards and captors are totally dependent upon their interest and susceptibility. As a hostage, you can only do your best to try to engage your guards in conversation, make yourself available for language instruction, engage in discussion about religion, or show interest in their family life, but nothing may happen for many weeks or months—or ever. Again, so much of what you can do to improve your own comfort and survivability depends upon the personalities, the dedication, and the experience of your captors.

CLOTHING

After your abduction and transport, you will be searched—possibly strip-searched. Initially, your abductors will be looking for electronic devices and obvious weapons. Then depending on their experience, your clothing might be searched for hidden handcuff keys or hidden blades—anything you might use to escape. More experienced captors may take all your clothes and give you an orange jumpsuit, which will be your entire wardrobe for the duration of your stay. This is a common practice in Guantanamo. This clothing switch serves a number of purposes. If you had anything hidden in your clothes that they did not find, it would be gone. If you tried to escape, everyone who saw you would recognize you as a prisoner. Plus, the orange uniform dehumanizes you. Historically, the orange jumpsuit is not a good sign of what is to come. Many Middle Eastern religions abhor nudity; a possible strategy is to disrobe, discard the orange jumpsuit, and demand your own clothes back.

Depending on your situation and your judgement of how this humanizing strategy might work in your favor, you might want to dress in the same traditional clothes as your captors. If you are dressed alike, they may see you in a better light . . . less of a foreigner. This may win you favor among your captors if you can convince them the only reason you want to wear what they are wearing is because it is warmer or cooler or somehow more efficient given your particular physical conditions. As a hostage, you will have to weigh this against the loss of your original identity. If you are planning an escape, traditional clothes will certainly be an asset.

Nowhere have I said that negotiation is easy, but you must look for ways to counter your captor's efforts to dehumanize you. Negotiation while in confinement is certainly difficult, but the situation calls for a strength of wills and a battle of wits, often without any feedback indicating whether or not your efforts are having an impact.

Generally speaking, the longer a hostage is held, the more valuable they become to their captors. This is due mainly to the investment of time, money, and risk by the captors. As the hostage's value increases, the less likely they will be killed. This not a hard-and-fast rule, as humanizing is always a contributing factor.

SEXUAL MISTREATMENT

Sexual torture is defined and categorized "as 1) violence against the sexual organs; 2) physical sexual assault, i.e., sexual acts involving direct physical sexual contact between the victim and torturers, between victims, between victims and an animal, or all three; 3) mental sexual assault, i.e. forced nakedness, sexual humiliation, sexual threats and witnessing others being sexually tortured; 4) a combination of the three . . . Furthermore, sexual torture is often carried out in conjunction with other torture, both physical and psychological" (Bosoglu 1992, p. 312).

Hostages stand a fair chance of being sexually abused. Sexual assault lowers a person's sense of self-esteem and aggressive tendencies. The person feels powerless and no longer in charge of his or her own body. Sexual assault is more likely to happen to a female than a male because most, if not all, your captors will be male, and again, so much depends on the psyche of your captors. Initially, sexual assault on a female may be strictly for sexual gratification, but it can also be used as punishment. Males may be sexually assaulted more often as a personal insult, to cause embarrassment, or for pure entertainment. It is also a demonstration of the power and control your captors have over you. They can do with you as they wish whenever they wish. This is demoralizing and dehumanizing.

Psychological warfare must be met with psychological defense strategies.

> He still comes for me when she's [her daughter] asleep. It's not exactly like it used to be, since I have learned to accept it. I still consider it rape, because what else do you call sex with a prisoner on a chain? . . . Even after four months, it's still three or four times a day. (Berry and DeJesus 2015, 167)[8]

---

[8] Michelle Knight, Gina DeJesus, and Amanda Berry, all young girls, were separately lured into the home of Ariel Castro, a local school bus driver in

Again, the use of sexual assault can vary from group to group, depending upon their interpretation of their religion or how it might be justified as punishment for perceived social or political injustices. Some Islamist groups will give a female the respect she is entitled to by the Koran, such as those who held Melissa Fung (CBC journalist), who told her that one of her male captors must always accompany her even while she was held in the underground hole. This was entirely different from those who held Canadian humanitarian and journalist Amanda Lindhout and abused her in every possible way.

> The book (the Quran) was explicit about what such possession meant: You were basically owned by your captors. There were verses instructing that captives be treated with kindness and granted freedom if they were well behaved. There were others that made clear that a female captive was fair game sexually. (Lindhout and Corbett 2013, 170)

You can forget about attempts to reason with your captors against raping female captives. You may be told that you fall under the Koran's description of "those whom your right hand possesses." This means that if you are a legitimate enemy of Islam, which they will justify that you are, then you are a bona fide and legal prisoner and your captors may do with you as they wish. Your Western marriage traditions, criminal laws, and sexual ethics do not apply here.

The Koran permits Nikah al-mut'ah. *Muta'a,* as it is commonly referred to, is the temporary marriage for sex with or without a woman's consent. It requires that the woman be unmarried, a Muslim, or a "person of the book." The marriage duration can be a few days or a few months. Obviously, this is a one-sided, chauvinistic excuse for having sex with almost any female, anywhere, anytime. If the perpetrator can also justify his actions under *taqiyya* (do anything

---

Cleveland, Ohio. He kept them for over ten years. They were often chained, starved, frequently raped, psychologically abused, and threatened with death if they attempted to escape.

to any infidel in order to achieve the goals of jihad), all the better. As we have seen time and time again, justification is never a problem.

Following is an excerpt from an article illustrating this point. The full article can be found in appendix 3.

> American hostage Kayla Mueller was repeatedly forced to have sex with Abu Bakr Baghdadi, the leader of the Islamic State group, U.S. intelligence officials told her family in June.
>
> "They told us that he married her, and we all understand what that means," Carl Mueller, Kayla's father, told The Associated Press on Friday, which would have been his daughter's 27th birthday. Her death was reported in February.
>
> Her mother, Marsha Mueller, added, "Kayla did not marry this man. He took her to his room and he abused her and she came back crying."
>
> Mueller was held with three other women, all Yazidis, the Muellers were told. All were sexually abused. When al-Baghdadi visited, he would take Mueller to his room, the witness told American officials. She would tell her fellow captives—sometimes tearfully— what had happened.
>
> "Kayla tried to protect these young girls," her mother said. "She was like a mother figure to them." (Dilanian 2015)

According to an annual UN report released on April 13, 2015, by Secretary-General Ban Ki-moon, extremist groups like Islamic State and Boko Haram are increasingly resorting to rape and sexual violence as a tactic of war.

The year 2014 "was marked by harrowing accounts of rape, sexual slavery and forced marriage being used by extremist groups, including as a tactic of terror," Secretary-General Ban Ki-moon said in the report.

The review found that sexual attacks in Iraq, Syria, and Nigeria were not incidental but "integrally linked to strategic objectives, ideology, and funding of extremist groups."

Sexual assault and physical assault are a frequent punishment for attempted hostage escapes. Sexual assaults for this purpose are much more violent and injurious than when they are committed for sexual gratification or to cause embarrassment. When you think of it, how else can your captors punish you any further? They have already kidnapped you and taken away your freedom; they have locked you in a room, accused you of being a spy and their sworn enemy, and caused you to be undernourished. What else can they do to punish you? There is only the physical and sexual. During these times, applying your survival strategies is all the more important. You must recognize that sexual and physical assaults affect only your body; you must mentally separate your physical pain from your mental determination to survive and return home safely.

In 1991, Rhonda Cornum, an American flight surgeon, was captured and made a prisoner of war. During her confinement, she was sexually assaulted by one of her Iraqi captors. In addition, she and other prisoners were subjected to mock executions. Nevertheless, as she was the senior-ranking prisoner, she took responsibility for other POWs. She later co-wrote a book about her experiences, *She Went to War: The Rhonda Cornum Story*, in 1992 (Cornum 1992).

> In an interview . . . she said, the sexual assault in Iraq in that winter of 1991 "ranks as unpleasant; that's all it ranks. Everyone's made such a big deal about this indecent assault . . . . But the only thing that makes it indecent is that it was nonconsensual. I asked myself, 'Is it going to prevent me from getting out of here? Is there a risk of death attached to it? Is it permanently disabling? Is it permanently disfiguring? Lastly, is

it excruciating?' If it doesn't fit one of those five categories, then it isn't important." (Sciolino 1992)

She continued, "There's a phenomenal amount of focus on this for the women but not for the men," citing the "mistreatment of fellow POW Major Jeffrey S. Tice of the Air Force, who had a tooth explode from its socket when he was tortured with jolts of electricity."

"When torturers torture a man in his anus, they proclaim him to be gay or 'no longer a man.' Coupled with physical violence against sexual organs, regardless if the victim is male or female, the torturers say that now it will no longer be possible to have children or should offspring be produced, then the child will be deformed" (Bosoglu, p. 312).

Of course, this is simply paring physical torture with mental or psychological torture. However, this fear may be accepted by the victim and persist as a nagging doubt.

SEXUAL SURVIVAL STRATEGY

I have interviewed people who were sexually abused as a child and as an adolescent, people who had recently been sexually abused, and a female corrections officer who was taken hostage for weeks and sexually assaulted. Most of them developed the same coping or survival strategy, one that helped them during the actual time of the assault and for years afterward. One female victim described to me how as a youngster she had learned to mentally disassociate herself from the body of the person being sexually assaulted. She had learned to imagine herself leaving her physical body, gently floating up into the corner of the ceiling, and looking down dispassionately at what was happening. She described how, while in this state of psychological separation from the actual victim, the physical pain and mental anguish associated with the act itself were significantly reduced. After the assault was finished, she would gently float back down again, taking over the victim's body and carrying on with whatever she had been doing before the assault. This strategy also helped her reduce the symptoms of posttraumatic stress, as she was able to lessen the long-term psychological impact the assault had on her.

Amanda Lindhout bravely recalls her experience.

> Bracing myself, I pushed my hands harder against Abdullah's chest, and something happened. A searing blast of heat hit my palms, a delivery of some sort, a quick shock followed by a strange, spreading calm. I wasn't in my body anymore. I was somewhere else, my mind dissipated into a vast canopy, a thing hung over this place, stretched like a collection of tiny lights.
>
> Maybe I had died. I wasn't sure. I was high up in one corner, looking down at what was below.
>
> From above I could see two men and a woman on the ground. The woman was tied up like an animal, and the men were hurting her, landing blows on her body. I knew all of them, but I also didn't. I recognized myself down there, but I felt no more connected to the woman than to the men in the room. I'd slipped across some threshold I would never understand. The feeling was both deeply peaceful and deeply sad. (Lindhout and Corbett 2013, p. 306)

For some victims, regrettably, it took a period of time before this strategy was learned; for others it was a coping strategy that came to them surprisingly quickly.

> Every time he climbed on top of me, I just tried to disconnect. From the abuse. From my life. From myself. I got to the point where I could make myself not even notice that he was on me. I would make my brain go someplace far away, like to a lush island or to a peach-colored sunset.

175

> This scene went down at least three times a week for the
> next three years. (Knight 2014, 57)[9]

The positive use of this disassociation strategy has been recognized for many years by psychiatrists and psychologists. This disassociation is a valuable skill to learn, and many might find it relaxing—a form of meditation. Some chronic pain sufferers regularly use meditation to reduce the severity of their pain and to relax tense muscles.

In order to effectively use this dissociative strategy, it must be practiced. Anyone can practice it, anywhere, at any time. People who regularly practice meditation, by itself or during a physical exercise such as yoga or tai chi, may have a head start. Many runners experience a wave of euphoria during a run that emanates from physical and mental wellness.

I recall one victim of frequent sexual assault who realized that if she went limp and lifeless during the assault, the assaulters soon lost interest and the assaults eventually stopped.

> To battle for survival among so many hostile males, I instinctively took to behavior I suppose shared with female captives as far back in time as you'd care to go. I did everything I could to avoid provoking what might be called an "enthusiastic male response." The precautions included letting my appearance completely go except for the basic cleanliness, such as it was. I also guessed right in advertising my status as a "mother." As far as I could tell this was keeping the men at bay. (Jessica Buchanan and Erik Landemalm, *Impossible Odds* 2013, 176)

These survival strategies for sexual assault are similar to many other strategies presented in later chapters of this book—they all involve

---

[9] A twenty-one-year old single mother, lured into the home of a local bus driver in Cleveland Ohio, Michelle Knight was held for over eleven years. She was often half-starved, chained, and repeatedly raped, and she suffered numerous abortions at the hands of her abductor.

a strong mental component. Considering that most hostages endure weeks or months chained to a wall, handcuffed, tied, and bound in any number of ways and locked in a small room or even imprisoned by the environment of a desert or jungle, it's critical for them to remember that their mind is still their own—it may be the only tool they have.

Your mind—your imagination—can free you from the depths of reality. It can be your refuge. Your days and weeks of captivity will be boredom beyond compare, so you will have plenty of time to practice and exercise your mental strategies. As you learn and apply these strategies, your mental capacities will be called upon in ways they have never been called upon before. As stated earlier, these strategies have been used, and used successfully, by hostages who were held for months and sometimes years under the very worst of conditions and treatment.

Resolve to not let sexual assault break your spirit and interfere with applying your strategies and plans to return home safely because "all responsibility and guilt must rightly be placed on the torturers" (Jorgen Ortmann, *Sexual Torture and the Treatment of Its Consequences*, Bosaglu 1992, p. 317)

LATER INTERROGATIONS—CONFESSIONS

Interrogations can occur at pretty much any time during your confinement. It is common among terrorist groups to demand that you sign a confession admitting to the activities that you, your company, or your government have committed. These confessions may be handwritten or video-recorded.

Of course, your first inclination is to refuse, and you are the best one to judge if you should refuse now or refuse later. Again, you are in a position of strength because your captors need your compliance. My advice, strictly from a negotiation point of view, is to refuse. Of course, your interrogator will not be pleased if you do, and you are likely to suffer some form of punishment. But if you give in to this demand too early or too easily, you will not be in any position to negotiate. As I mentioned earlier, negotiation occurs only when each party has something the other party wants. If you have nothing of value, you have nothing to trade. If whatever you do have is seen as worthless or not worth having, you have nothing to bring to the table. Just as a poker player needs money to be invited to the game, you must barter your compliance. Barter compliance for something of value for you. Is it more food, better treatment, or better conditions?

It has long been recognized in Western countries that any written confession or verbal statement that was obtained under such circumstances was obtained through intimidation or physical force. Therefore, do not be overly concerned—your statements are worthless to the outside world.

We only have to recall the admissions of the CIA's "enhanced interrogation techniques," a.k.a. torture, as testament that any confession is worthless unless corroborated by other reliable information. No government is going to believe anything you say under these circumstances as the truth and will never hold you responsible for its content. Your family will not believe any statement, as they too understand that it was given under duress and threat of physical punishment. The general public will not judge you poorly after hearing of the atrocities committed against Vietnam POWs and, more recently, from testimony from released hostages from the Middle East, in which confessions were obtained solely by force. However, as unimportant as a confession might be to people back home, it appears to be something of value to your captors, so hold out as long as you can—and then negotiate. The longer you hold out, the more valuable your confession will become. The more valuable your confession, the more you will benefit in return. This is basic supply and demand. They want it; you've got it.

Again, recognize that your interrogator has bosses too. He was ordered to have you write a confession or give a videotaped confession or statement as to how well you are being treated. He needs to look good in front of his subordinates, and he has to follow instructions from his boss. He is under pressure to perform. If it is a videotaped confession he is asking for, he can't have you looking beaten; that discredits the whole purpose.

If he gives you a mattress to sleep on or a blanket to keep you warm, so what? His boss won't mind as long as he gets results. If he gives you reading glasses and provides you with some books to read, another victory for you. It's likely no big deal to him personally to give you books, as long as he has your "confession." If you sense you might be able to negotiate for more significant concessions, you may even ask your interrogator to get rid of a particular guard that abuses you too often or is the worst of the bunch because he is resisting your humanizing efforts and influencing the other guards against you. Again, you will be in the best position to understand your needs and priorities.

Just because you're a prisoner doesn't mean you have nothing to trade.

During the Vietnam War, departing American soldiers were taught that if captured and forced to give a tape-recorded or videotaped message, they were to speak more slowly than usual as a sign that the statement was given under duress. Some POWs would deliberately beat their own faces as a tactic of revolt against their treatment so that a promised POW press interview could not go ahead because it would be obvious they had been beaten. Some POWs were compliant backstage, and when told to go onstage, they stood like automatons with dumb robotic stares. Yes, they were punished later for appearing as though they had been brainwashed, and of course they made their captors look stupid, but it was their way of demonstrating to themselves and to others that they still had power. Knowing that in some small way you have altered or disrupted your captor's plans can give you a sense of power when you thought you had none. This can be psychologically rejuvenating to a hostage.

RELEASE PROMISES

One often-successful tactic that terrorist groups use to get hostages to write out a confession or perform a video interview is to promise to release the hostage if he complies. Here's how it works. You're sitting in your cell and you are informed that one of your family members has been involved in a terrible traffic collision; the family member is in intensive care and has only a few days to live. If you sign a confession now, you will be freed, and you are likely to make it home in time to visit the person. If you ask who the family member is, the guard says he doesn't know exactly, but that adds more suspense, doesn't it?

Your captors are playing to your weak side—your sense of loyalty to your family—and capitalizing on how very much you want to be released. If you fall for this ruse, you will, of course, say anything you're told to say and write anything you are told to write. Your interrogator will leave, and you will be left wondering who was involved in the accident and what repercussions this will cause to your family. As the days pass, your questions about when you will be released will be met with vague promises such as "maybe tomorrow" or "maybe the day after tomorrow." After a week or so, even these replies will fade and disappear. You will be left in your cell with nothing, and they will have a free confession. So don't believe everything you are told by your captors. Treat everything they say or promise with distrust and suspicion. Remember, taqiyya and halal.

Another tactic often used among Islamic terrorists is the promise that "if you were a Muslim, we would have to set you free." They may quote lines of scripture supporting their statement, but this is a lie. Remember, they are allowed to lie to infidels. The Koran promises significant rewards to any Muslim who converts someone to Islam; the more evil the convert, the greater the extra credit. There are many released hostages whose conversion to Islam made absolutely no difference in negotiations or their eventual release. Considering the amount of time, money, and risk put into your abduction and confinement, to release you at that point just because you converted to their religion is unrealistic. If you do convert, there is the chance you will be confronted and asked if you are a real convert or just a pretender. This is a catch-22. You will likely be asked, "Are you a real convert?" If you say yes, they will say, "If you are a true convert, you will realize your place is to stay and fight with your brothers and sisters, and you would not wish to go home. Now, are you a true believer or just a pretender?"

Included with religious conversion is a name change. Your captors will give you a new name which you will always be known by. This detail was not explained to you prior and it may sound insignificant, but it is not. This dehumanizes you. It immediately changes your view of who you are and everyone else's view of who you are. You will be treated differently and you will be expected to act differently. This is a whole new road.

There are hostages who have converted to Islam and still sit as captives waiting for their release. That said—and to their credit—these hostages may have seen this as an opportunity to engage with their captors in an activity that would humanize them. Some converted and were released; some converted and were not.

FAKE EXECUTIONS

Hostages are sometimes told a few days or a few hours ahead of time that they have been slated for execution; maybe today, maybe tomorrow. Captors will often advise the hostage that their demands have not been met, that the hostage's country and his family have done nothing to help his situation, and that he has been abandoned. Giving the hostage prior notification is designed to cause as much mental anguish as possible. The hostage now perceives every sound and every footstep as activity in the planning for his execution. He begins to wonder about every detail of his execution. Will he be shot in the back of the head like he's seen on TV? Will he be beheaded? He wonders if there will be a video. Will he be buried in an unmarked grave in the desert, never to be found, never to be returned home? How will this affect his family? Of course he's always wondered about how it will end, but now that it's finally here, it's a reality.

> I discovered a special form of living hell in that combination of helplessness and terror to be endured while waiting for execution. No doubt the horror of this moment is known to all condemned people. They would surely recognize that sensation of sharp

nausea, the loss of fine motor control, the difficulty
with balance when smaller support muscles spasm
and misfire. (Jessica Buchanan, 83)

These are the times when predeployment planning shows its
real worth. A hostage faced with death—real or imagined—can
find solace in knowing that he prepared his family well for such an
outcome.

The exact scenario will differ from group to group. Some groups
might tell the hostage he will be executed along with other hostages.
His hands are tied behind his back; he is blindfolded and taken
outside. There is a short walk, and he is told to kneel down with his
head bowed. Sometimes he is made to dig his own grave. There is a
speech justifying why these executions are necessary—more realism,
more fear in the hostage's mind. Just for more drama, the hostage
might be told "You are number three." Of course, as the hostage hears
the first shot, he believes one hostage is dead and this is for real. As
he hears the second shot, another hostage is dead, and this is for
real. As he prepares for the third shot, his life passes before him—so
this is how it will end. Then after what seems an eternity, the gun
goes *click*, his blindfold is removed, and everyone points at him and
laughs. Now someone who was once strong and defiant is blubbering
and emotionally crushed. Now his captors put him on the phone to
plead with his family to pay the ransom or ask the government to
comply with the terrorists' demands. You can imagine the emotion
expressed by the hostage and the effect it has on the family on the
other end. Back in his cell once again, the hostage will go through
bouts of crying and depression.

FAKE RELEASES

Again, in a practice that varies from group to group, hostages may
be subjected to fake releases. A fake release might only be a promise:
"today or tomorrow." These are meant to keep the hostage on edge or

just to tease him, strictly for entertainment. Again, you have to take into consideration that your guards and captors are also hostages in a sense. They can't leave either, and they too get bored. Sometimes fake releases are designed to keep the hostage on good behavior, as hostages are not likely to want to jeopardize their own release.

A fake release or a fake execution is used to demoralize a hostage—to break the hostage down or punish him. A roller coaster of faked releases and faked executions will take its toll mentally, as they will cause intense feelings of hopelessness and despair. Mental strength is everything during times like these. Fake executions are commonly carried out just before a phone call for ransom. Having just gone through what the hostage believed were his last minutes on earth, a hostage will most certainly sound desperate and plead for whatever demands or ransom the hostage takers want. A fake release or the promise of an impending release may be a psychological ploy to ridicule, punish, or humble the hostage.

Common demoralizing lines are "Nobody is willing to pay for you," "Your government doesn't care about you," or "Your family doesn't want you back." These statements are intended to make you more submissive and controllable or for your captor's own entertainment. The hostage takers might use a fake release to demonstrate their power and control over the hostage. They might use a fake release or a fake execution to cause the hostage a complete breakdown and present a better plea during a phone call for ransom. They may use a false release to keep the hostage quiet during transportation to another location. Or they may use the promise of an impending release as a way of keeping the hostage on good behavior. "One or two more days, and you will go home."

I fully understand that it's easy for one person to sit back and tell another to be strong, to get his head around the problem, basically "to get over it." However, when you as a hostage hear these words, try to see them as cues to recognize exactly what they are trying to do and then counter it.

When you understand what they are doing and why, you can plan your mental defense. Get back on the horse and stick to your plan.

GENDER-SPECIFIC HUMANIZING STRATEGIES

Do not underestimate the behavioral and situational humanizing strategies identified in the last two chapters and the long-term strategies to come. There are many examples of male captors developing a strong social, paternalistic, or even romantic attraction to their female captives.

One day while Judith Tebbutt (2013) was visited by a number of her captors, she noticed one staring at her.

"What is it?" Judith asked.

Her translator Ali replied, "My friend here"—Ali jerked a thumb at Scary Man—"his grandmother was English, and he wants English wife."

"Oh, does he? Where's he going to get one of them from?"

"He looking for wife, he look at you." (Tebbutt, p. 260)

Later that same day, as Ali was escorting her across the yard, Ali asked for Judith's book and pen, and she watched as he carefully inscribed a phone number and e-mail address on the page.

"When you go home," he said, "please, ring me, text me: 'Blue room hotel.' Then I know you're home." (p. 261)

"When you see Ollie [Judith's son]," he said, smiling, "you say hello from Ali."

"I like to see London. If I come to London, you take me out?"

"I don't think so" was the reply.

A few minutes later, Ali returned with a fellow captor named Gerwaine, who looked a little sheepish.

"This man," said Ali, "he ask, do you think he is a bad person?"

Again, Judith had to ponder if she should be honest here.

"I don't know him as a person. But what he's done is very bad. It's ruined my life, ruined my son's life [the death of her husband]."

"If Gerwaine come to London, would you say hello?"

"No," she said, feeling her patience stretched. "I would ignore him. You understand *ignore*?"

"So you no say hello?" (pp. 261, 262)

Jessica Buchanan (2013) had similar "proposals." "He fancied himself an artful molester. He made weak excuses to justify sitting next to me, maybe placing a reassuring hand on my shoulder, my arm, my thigh."

"Jesses, I come to America [stroke, stroke, pat, pat]. Stay with you."

"No, Jabreel. No, I'm married."

"I am your good friend [stroke, rub, pat]. You're my good friend."

"I am your married friend, Jabreel."

"Erik?"

"Yes, Erik. I love Erik."

"I come live with you and Erik! We are happy [pat, pat, pat]. I will sleep on floor. By your bed."

"By my . . . God."

"What you say?"

"I said I'm married, Jabreel. So are you."

"You are beautiful [stroke, stroke, pat, pat, pat]." (pp. 176, 177)

However, Jabreel doesn't get the message. Later on he repeats it. 'Jesses, I come America, live with you."

"No, Jabreel. I keep telling you I'm married."

"I live with you and Erik . . . You hear me, Jesses? You hear me?"

"Yes, I hear you, Jabreel. I'm still married. I love my husband."

"But I love Jesses. When Colonel talk to me about you, we call you *lei*, you know that? In Somali is 'golden.' I marry to you, all these men wish to be me." (p. 201)

No doubt about it, there are strong sexual overtones in both Judith's and Jessica's situations, but let's also look at it from a cultural perspective. Ali's, Gerwaine's, and Jabreel's culture is very much male-dominated, paternalistic, and of course, sexist . . . all of that.

Having cared for their female hostage/guest for months, bringing her food every day, bringing her a (smelly) blanket to sleep on, allowing her to visit the washroom (after asking permission), and protecting her from rogue terrorist groups, these men begin to see themselves not as captors but as caregivers and protectors. They begin to believe that these women must recognize this treatment and the women must certainly appreciate all they've done for them, maybe even love them for it. If a captor has had sex with or has raped their hostage/guest, he might even see this as a consummation of their *mutual* affection. Ah, the male ego.

If hostage/prisoner rape results in a child being born, this strengthens the paternal instincts of the male captor, who will begin to see the "union" as a "family." This was strongly demonstrated in the case of the three young girls kidnapped in Cleveland, Ohio, Amanda Berry, Gina DeJesus (Berry, DeJesus 2015), and Michelle Knight (Knight 2014), during which Berry gave birth. Their kidnapper, Ariel Castro, repeatedly explained to the police that they were "a family."

As a negotiated resolution comes closer and there are real plans to transport and release the hostage, at great risk to themselves, the captors begin to believe they are doing the hostage another great favor.

As pointed out in earlier chapters, a hostage must walk the tightrope of passive compliance. A hostage must endear themselves to their captors, humanize themselves. Judith Tebbutt and Jessica Buchanan certainly accomplished all of that and, obviously, more than they had wanted, but in their case, the physical line was not crossed. Humanizing served its purpose. It kept them alive. Frightened, nervous, and afraid, yes, but alive. After all, the object is to stay alive . . . no matter what.

On June 12, 2015, the RCMP announced the arrest of Ali Omar Ader in Ottawa, Canada, a few days after he arrived from Africa. The RCMP describes him as the "main negotiator" in the fifteen-month hostage taking of Amanda Lindhout. His arrival in Canada almost seven years after the hostage taking has many people speculating as to the real reasons Ali Omar Ader would risk coming to Canada.

Ali Omar Ader is actually the man Lindhout refers to as Adam in her book. After his arrest in Canada, Amanda Lindhout said that during her confinement, Adam had often mused about marrying her.

These feelings of affection by the captor and the expectation that these feelings are mutually held by the captive are a zookeeper's syndrome.

The zookeeper feeds and waters the animal every day, ensures they have comfortable and clean sleeping quarters, oversees the animal's physical health, and protects them from harm. The zookeeper expects that the animal recognizes these activities as a demonstration of their genuine affection and assumes a strong mutual bond between them.

What the zookeeper fails to recognize is perspective. To the caged animal, the zookeeper is the one responsible for their captivity. The zookeeper keeps the animal locked inside its enclosure. The zookeeper decides what and when the animal gets fed. The zookeeper decides when the animal goes to bed and when the animal wakes up only to repeat its boring, depressing, and unnatural life day after day. The animal hates the zookeeper.

One day when the zookeeper gets attacked by the animal, the zookeeper is astonished, dismayed, and emotionally hurt. However, the zookeeper strongly defends the animal and attests that the attack must have been an accident. The zookeeper will always believe the animal loves him; the animal will always look for another chance.

CHAPTER 10
LONG-TERM STRATEGIES

The long-term strategies outlined in the next few chapters are designed to assist the hostage with maintaining good mental health throughout the term of his captivity. A hostage needs a resilient mental strength to go the distance. A strong will to live comes from continued good mental health; however, good mental health requires constant nurturing and support.

> As soon as Omar had finished explaining the rules of our imprisonment we were joined by Jack and what we came to think of as his senior staff. This time the interrogation was a little more formal and aggressive, but not markedly so. He explained that we were his prisoners, that he led one of the AQIM *mujahideen* and, speaking through Omar, outlined the organization's objectives. He also asserted that he and his *frères* were strict and devout Muslims who unreservedly followed God's word as revealed to the Prophet in the Qur'an without deviation or interpretation and to the letter.
>
> He then, in quiet and measured tones, launched into a tirade against the hypocrisy of the Western-toady, "apostate governments" . . . and the debauchery of the Jew-crusader, American-led Western governments . . . that send vast armies to rage and occupy "Muslim lands." (Fowler, 60, 61)

LOSING HOPE

So now you've met your hosts, your kidnappers, your interrogators, and some of your guards; you've been given the reason for your kidnapping. You've been informed whose fault it is that you've been kidnapped, and your life has been threatened. Has the depth of the reality of your situation set in yet? When it does, you will go through mental calculations about what will happen next, how long you will be held, how you will be treated, the likelihood that you will be killed, and how that will happen. But you are trying to make calculations without any information; you're trying to do complicated math without an equation and without any numbers. You are trying to predict your future or at least get some kind of handle on what is going to happen to you, but you have no information with which to solve that puzzle. You can't predict your own future; you have no control over your next minute or your next day. It's the first time in your life that you can't see past right here and right now. It scares the hell out of you; it might be time to cry again. You are wrought with self-pity and regret. You might end up crying on and off for hours or for days. You are a hostage—this is your new reality. You have decisions to make.

RESOLVE

As your brain tries to make sense of what this means for you in the coming days, weeks, and months, it's time to think. It's time to recognize just how serious your situation is; it's time to get off your butt and start doing something constructive. You can't afford to leave your situation to your family and friends back home to sort out. You can't leave your situation for politicians to sort out. You can't expect a hostage rescue mission at any moment, and divine intervention hasn't really happened for thousands of years.

It's time to stop chastising yourself, blaming others for how you got here, and feeling sorry for yourself. Realize that you have to play an active role in your release. Your captors have given you information about themselves, about your role as a hostage, and about the rules of your captivity. During your predeployment training and through reading this book, you have learned about survival strategies; you have learned how to interact with your guards and humanize yourself to them. You have learned how to discuss religion and politics in a manner that endears you to your captors; you have demonstrated to them that you are a God-fearing, religious person with a family and real human feelings. It's time for resolve. It's time to recognize that you do in fact have the necessary information that will help you develop and carry out an action plan. Be proactive; resolve to play a part in your own release. Resolve to be a factor in your own mental and physical health; resolve to maintain focus and that you will return home safely. This is the will to live.

When Amanda Lindhout was recaptured after her escape attempt, locked in a small windowless room, alone for months with her legs chained and padlocked she lamented, "I lost the sky." (April, 2016)

> *When you have shut your doors, and darkened your*
> *room, remember never to say that you are alone, for*
> *you are not alone; but God is within, and your genius*
> *is within—and what need have they of light to see*
> *what you are doing?*
> —Epictetus, *Discourses,* chapter xiv

Aron Ralston, aged 28, was hiking alone in the mountains of Utah, United States, in 2003, when he dislodged an eight-hundred-pound boulder that fell and wedged his hand against a rock wall. After spending five days in this situation, he thought of his family and friends and the many things he still wanted to accomplish with his life. He found the courage and made the decision to save himself by amputating his own right forearm with a dull pocketknife. But before he could do so, he had to break his arm so that the knife would cut all the way through without being hampered by his bones. He first applied a tourniquet, broke the bone, and then cut off his own arm.

After he freed himself, he rappelled down a twenty-meter (sixty-five-foot) cliff face and then faced a hike of eight miles to his vehicle (Ralston 2004).

Aron Ralston came to realize that what's done is done; there is no going back. From here on in, if he wanted to survive, he would have to find the courage and the means to do it himself and do it alone. He found the courage to do what it took to survive. As a hostage, so must you.

Ralston's story is like so many other stories of survival that highlight the tenacity of the human spirit to survive in extreme circumstances and against incredible odds. Every year, we hear stories of lost or stranded hikers who survived against the odds or shipwrecked sailors and fishermen lost at sea . . . and then found alive. One such sailor was Steven Callahan who, in 2002, drifted in a life raft for 76 days and traveled over 1,800 miles at sea (Callahan 2002). Movie director Ang Lee used Callahan's story as inspiration for the award-winning movie *The Life of Pi*.

We have all heard the stories of people stranded in cars for days in snowstorms . . . and they survived. We have heard of people stranded for days in the desert . . . and they survived, lost hikers who survived on squirrels and snakes and found their way out, little girls who survived a plane crash in the woods and walked miles to get help. Be one of those who survived.

PERSEVERANCE

Perseverance is sticking to the plan. No doubt there will be days when you feel that regardless of what you have been doing, regardless of your best efforts, nothing is changing—you don't see any results. That's when perseverance comes in; perseverance is seeing this through. Let's face it—do you really have any other choice? As the popular engineering saying goes, "Plan the work and work the plan."

Hostage rescue teams say, "Fail to plan, plan to fail." A hostage must have a plan. A plan provides the hostage with direction and goals; a plan provides focus.

Your life now depends upon your ability to focus and recognize your situation as a challenge—a challenge of your will to survive and return home versus your captor's will to use you as he wishes—his identity as a fighter versus your dignity as a human being, his power versus your freedom.

Difficulty shows what men are. (Epictetus)

BARBED-WIRE PSYCHOSIS

A hostage must recognize his own symptoms of "barbed-wire psychosis," also referred to as barbed-wire fever. This is a mental state of shutting down and becoming passive and numb due to the continuous mental and physical pressures of being a captive.

Psychosis is a loss of contact with reality, often brought on by helplessness and hopelessness. Helplessness is believing that no matter what you do, you are unable to change your present situation and you feel frozen by your circumstances; hopelessness is believing you cannot influence the eventual outcome. Unchecked, hopelessness and helplessness can lead to depression and suicide as they are symptomatic of a cycle of surrender. A hostage may recognize the first signs of barbed-wire psychosis when they have fallen into accepting the routine of their captivity as normal or mechanical . . . and they don't much care. They have lost faith; they have lost hope. They lie around, do nothing, they are lethargic and sometimes don't even bother to eat. They are content to just waste away and leave their life to fate. It is crucial to a hostage's survival that they recognize this as a serious threat . . . they are losing their will to live. Essentially they have fallen into a deep well, a well of despair and apathy.

You can acknowledge feeling fear and loneliness.
You can get mad, bored, resentful, anything at all.

But despair is the one big no-no. Despair isn't just a
mood or a state of mind, it's a disease and it can kill
you by making you give up. Despair is a killer as
sure as the Black Plague. (Jessica Buchanan and Erik
Landemalm, *Impossible Odds* 2013, 107)

If a hostage is being held alone, he must recognize for himself
that he is in great danger. He must become self-reliant. Just as
an alcoholic or drug addict will glimpse their reality through the
fog of addiction and recognize their poor physical health, the fact
they are living on the streets and committing crimes to support
their addiction, as true indicators of just how far they have fallen,
so too must the hostage recognize their symptoms of barbed-wire
psychosis. Addicts often need to hit rock bottom before they come
to this epiphany, this realization that if they don't do something right
now, they will die.

If he is being held with others, his fellow hostages must recognize
this for what it is and take action.

We agreed not to allow hopelessness into our
conversation, and neither would we permit it in our
thinking. (Jessica Buchanan and Erik Landemalm,
Impossible Odds 2013, 107)

At this stage, a hostage must remember all that he is fighting for,
who he is fighting for, and all the reasons why he wants to return
home. The hostage must dig deep within himself. Hostages must
call upon their survival strategies: faith and prayer, exercise, mental
visualization, positive thinking, physical games, song, personal
grooming, smiling, and their anchors.

Hostages can accept their circumstances for what they are, but
they must never accept their circumstances as being static, inflexible,
and permanent.

YOUR ANCHORS

To help with your resolve to return home, you need to identify anchors to rally around. An anchor can be social, mental, or spiritual.

Anyone in crisis, not just a hostage, will benefit from some sort of focal point that helps him remember what he's fighting for. For an alcoholic or drug addict, it might be getting sober or getting clean so he can return to his job or be able to visit his children once again. It's that "keep your eye on the prize" sort of thing.

Many hostages will use the sound of their children's laughter or their children's voices and play these sounds over in their heads when things get tough. In these situations, just saying the names of those children out loud is a reminder of why you will keep on fighting until you are released and back home.

For those who are devoutly religious, it is their faith. They will find solace in prayer. They may recite their favorite prayers or even say prayers with family members in their heads. They might imagine they are in their church. They may speak with their God or a favorite saint or engage in a favorite ceremony that brings them spiritual comfort.

A hostage can use his anchors during his morning and evening rituals as he greets his family "hello" or says "Good night and see you tomorrow." This anchor will provide strength against the loneliness of confinement.

The benefit of an anchor is that it can be called upon at any time for comfort and support. It is one of the strategies that can be called upon for short-term, mid-term, or long-term benefit.

It will assist the hostage in providing a sense of calm in the face of danger. It will become his companion of strength.

Many hostages have written the names of their children on the walls of their cell as a permanent visual aid. You can also write your survival mantras on the wall: "I am strong," "One more day," "I will go home."

You can make up your own "strong song" or "life song"; you can combine it with your "strong dance" and "life dance." Christmas carols can be very uplifting, although they are the wrong religion and might be viewed as anti-Muslim.

These suggestions might sound silly, but to a hostage who is looking for something to hold on to every day, to be able to reach out and grab a memory, a voice, a prayer, or a mantra which represents all that he wants to live for and which will strengthen his will to live, he needs to build anchors.

CHAPTER 11
STRATEGIES AGAINST TORTURE

The reader is reminded that the situational or event strategies discussed in earlier chapters can be applied to any of the situations identified in this chapter, to be used as and when required.

A precise definition of *torture* is surprisingly difficult because of the more recent inclusion of psychological pain or mental suffering. Is forbidding someone to speak for days or weeks a

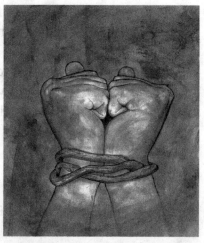

torture? Maybe, maybe not. Is having a light turned on twenty-four hours a day torture? Maybe, maybe not. What about a strobe light going on and off? What about loud noise? The following was the 1984 UN definition, which came into force on June 26, 1987.

> "Torture" means any act by which severe pain or suffering, whether physical or mental, is intentionally inflicted on a person for such purposes as obtaining from him or a third person information or a confession, punishing him for an act he or a third person has committed or is suspected of having committed, or intimidating or coercing him or a third person, or for any reason based on discrimination of any kind, when such pain or suffering is inflicted by or at the instigation of or with the consent or acquiescence of a public official or other person acting in an

197

official capacity. It does not include pain or suffering arising only from, inherent in or incidental to lawful sanctions. (United Nations 1984)

Torture is the "deliberate, systematic or wanton infliction of physical or mental suffering by one or more persons acting alone or on the orders of any authority, to force another person to yield information, to make a confession, or for any other reason." (World Medical Association in its Tokyo declaration 1975)

Hostages will be exposed to both physical and mental torture. Torture has evolved over the years, its methods learned through experimentation and limited only by human imagination.

TORTURE

Torture is hostage taking's evil twin.

"By torturing the body, the torturer's aim is to destroy his victim's mind. The physical injuries, sometimes present for life, have the effect of continuing the torture long after the detention. Pain, scars, and deformities will be a continuous reminder of the torture. Torture is always aimed at the victim's vulnerable points, both physical and psychological." (Grethe Skylv, "The Physical Sequelae of Torture," Bosaglu 1992, p. 38).

Torture has been around for hundreds of years, and there are almost a hundred different kinds. It has been practiced by different cultures, armies, religions, and governments. Torture was—and still is—used to obtain confessions. Confessions under torture used to be accepted as truth, and many went to their deaths because of them; today (hopefully) they are not.

Torture has been used both as a punishment and as a deterrent. Watching a person being whipped, burned at the stake, or buried up to his neck and fed upon by animals was an excellent deterrent, and recidivism was very low to nil. Historically, torture focused mainly on physical pain. There are the famous machines of pain such as the rack, the thumb screw, the boot, burning pokers; disfigurement by pulling out fingernails; shredding the tongue; being boiled to death; or just being left to die and rot in a cage. Some torture instruments and practices were specific to the crime, such as breaking the jaw or cutting out the tongue for crimes of blasphemy. Many torture methods were learned through trial and error. Some punishments were specific only to the instruments of the crimes committed, such as cutting off the hands for crimes of theft, and some types of torture were just the method of choice by the torturers themselves.

Although written initially to protect captured soldiers, the Geneva Convention has been expanded by its many treaties to protect civilians and noncombatants from cruel and unusual punishment such as torture. The Nuremberg Trials and the World Court have heard many cases where the Convention and its treaties were violated; however, the definitions of *war* and who is a *noncombatant* or a *civilian* in each particular conflict have often come into question. As with religious interpretations, there are always legal interpretations of what constitutes freedom fighting, fighting against repression, fighting for human rights, self-defense, legitimate rebellion against repression, and fighting against foreign occupation. Your captors will have their own justifications as to why none of the rules within the Convention applies to them. They have likely never heard of the Geneva Convention, so there's not much sense bringing it up unless your interrogator brings it up first. If you bring it up before they do, they will suspect you are more learned about war than you have admitted, and you will be considered a spy or a soldier posing as a civilian; both situations are bad for you.

A study of torture finds that instruments of physical pain slowly began to be applied in conjunction with instruments of torture of the mind. These mental techniques began to show themselves in the late

1940s but became well known in the early 1950s during the Korean War. From 1973 to 1985, Uruguayan and Honduran authorities used psychological torture on a large scale (Conroy 2000). Mental torture began to show promise and became popular, as results could be achieved without the victim showing physical scars. Methods of mental torture became the preferred treatment, especially if victims had to appear in court to answer to a charge that was supported by their "confession." Practices such as Chinese water torture, isolation, social and sensory deprivation, plus sleep deprivation soon became popular and were applied with a mix of new physical tortures such as electric shocks and chemical injections, again depending on the desired results and whether or not the victim would ever be seen in public again. Since 9/11, new psychological tortures have focused upon activities that embarrass a victim or are an affront to their religious or cultural beliefs. The United States' treatment of Iraqi prisoners at the Abu Ghraib prison in 2003 was a collage of both physical and mental torture. The mental torture in this case was the religious and personal tortures of shame or embarrassment and personal nudity witnessed by females. Even more recently, the daily practices in modern Western prisons of segregation, isolation, and social deprivation have come under increasing scrutiny by human rights groups, who see them as inhumane and argue that they meet a definition of torture.

As a hostage in my scenario, a nonmilitary Westerner held in a Middle East or African conflict zone, taken by religious fanatics, where hostages are held for political leverage, ransom or as human shields, there is not likely to be much "traditional" physical torture outside of the usual beatings and sexual assaults. The most likely forms of torture are described in the following sections.

For many hostages, the physical conditions of their daily confinement alone are a form of torture.

PHYSICAL BEATINGS

Physical beatings are carried out initially as an expression of anger against the West, your company's activities, or your political and religious beliefs. These beatings are just the release of the many frustrations this particular terrorist group has experienced in achieving its goals. Their frustrations may be from the number of years they have struggled, the many fighters and supporters that have died along the way, the day-to-day pressures of being hunted by the police and intelligence agencies, and the setbacks they have experienced. As stated earlier, they feel the frustration of all the planning, expense, and physical risk that went into your capture. The type and extent of physical abuse will depend upon the psychological makeup of your captors, their experience of handling other hostages, the sex of the hostage, and the religious or political justifications or restrictions of the group.

During initial beatings, a hostage will be handcuffed or tied and may also be hooded, which by itself induces isolation and dread. Hooding increases a person's anxiety, as he doesn't know when or where a blow will land. Later on in his cell, a hostage may just be kicked or punched without warning and for no apparent reason other than those previously mentioned.

I cannot provide any strategies on how to lessen the injuries you receive during a beating, and I doubt a medical doctor could either. Tensing your muscles may lessen the impact and the damage a blow might cause in the short-term, but if your captors want to inflict pain upon you, they will continue to beat you until they see you are in pain. Don't be alarmed if you see yourself bleed from the lips or mouth or over the eyes. When your captors see blood, they will realize they have inflicted damage, and the beating may soon be over. This is just like during a boxing match, where it is not uncommon to see a boxer suffer a cut over his eye or bleed from his nose. These are not major injuries, and they are not life-threatening. If your captors want to beat you, they will beat you regardless of how you act; regardless of what you say, it's going to happen. There is some solace in knowing that a severe beating is likely to happen and that it will be over when they're done. A severe beating is likely to happen earlier rather than later, and you can look forward to knowing that any future beatings will be less severe.

If you've played a contact sport such as hockey, football, or rugby, you have, no doubt, left the playing field with a bloody nose or a bleeding cut somewhere. Even playing baseball or soccer, you can get a bleeding nose or need a couple of stitches now and then. The point is, don't let minor injuries bother you. As anyone who has suffered a severe beating or been involved in a serious car crash or other serious accident can attest, the human body is capable of withstanding a lot of punishment, and is surprisingly good at healing and repairing itself. Also, your captors are aware that if they inflict serious damage requiring examination by a qualified physician, this may expose them unnecessarily.

I am not qualified to give medical advice. The following advice is taken from my years as a first-aid instructor, related first-responder training, and a layperson's understanding of human physiology and should be taken only as suggestions. I have, however, discussed them with a medical doctor.

If you suffer a beating, do not just sit or lie curled up in a corner for hours afterward. You must take proactive steps to help your body heal and prevent any future complications.

The human body is made up of many miles of arteries and veins that carry red blood cells (the body's nutrition) and white blood cells (the body's infection fighters) to every living cell in your body. Human muscles compose much of the body's soft tissue and are built in bundles much like handfuls of drinking straws. Blunt force trauma can cause muscle fibrosis, which is essentially a buildup of torn connecting tissue between the rows of muscles. After receiving a physical beating, it is important to assist your body in its healing processes. This is done by standing upright and slowly stretching and flexing the body's arteries and veins to allow blood flow to return to its normal function. Sitting or curling up on a hard floor may only serve to flatten or compress arteries and veins, which will restrict blood flow and may contribute to the formation of blood clots. Increased blood flow is beneficial as it will carry swelling away from the injury sites; this also helps speed up healing and recovery.

Gently stretching the body's blood vessels and muscles in a fashion similar to that of a tai chi exercise will help heal your injuries and stimulate or realign muscle groups. Any stretching exercises or massaging after a beating should be done slowly and with caution, as swelling may have shortened a muscle or put extra pressure on blood vessels. If you believe you have a broken arm or such, immobilize the suspected area to allow the break or stress fracture to mend itself. That said, it is uncommon for a hostage in my scenarios to be beaten to the point of broken bones. One exception to this is broken ribs, which are common. Broken ribs are painful but rarely fatal. I recall interviewing with one hostage who said he had been beaten so badly during his confinement that he wanted to die, but he didn't suffer any broken bones. Although it may not feel like it at the time, these beatings are survivable. Painful, yes, but survivable.

After receiving punches to the stomach and abdomen, monitor your urine for signs of blood. If your urine shows a reddish tinge, it may indicate the presence of internal bleeding, possibly some broken minor blood vessels in the stomach or intestines. If the injury is minor, it should heal in a few days. The bright red color will fade in a day or turn a dark ruby color in another day or so and, later, black. Also check your stools for a dark-red or black tinge, which may indicate blood in the intestinal tract. This too should disappear in a few days. When your urine and stools return to their usual color, it is likely the associated bleeding has stopped.

If you do believe you have suffered a serious injury as the result of a beating, or you believe you may have a related infection or an illness such as malaria, ask for medical attention. You can expect to have better medical knowledge than your captors, so if you can present them with a credible self-diagnosis, they may be more inclined to have a doctor attend to you. If a doctor attends and confirms an injury, your captors should take this as a warning against future beatings. As mentioned earlier, you are a commodity that must be guarded from serious harm. As a further matter of interest, I spoke with a hostage who, having complained of illness, to his surprise, was visited by a Western-trained medical doctor who examined him and, within a few days, provided prescription drugs delivered by his captors.

FAKING INJURIES

Hostages may be tempted to fake an injury in the hope that it will deter further beatings. As tempting as it might seem, however, faking injuries can have serious consequences. Faking might help in the short term, but you must be well versed in human physiology and a good actor to get away with it for long.

You can never be certain when your guards are watching; if they suspect you're faking it, you'll be severely punished. Also, injured hostages may get a visit from a qualified medical doctor, and if you don't pass the medical examination, you will certainly be punished and lose all credibility. Don't get caught crying wolf. A hostage who is trying to humanize himself and improve his treatment cannot afford to lose credibility.

MALNUTRITION

Malnutrition is recognized as a form of torture as it causes a person to lapse into a state of mental confusion; it can also cause hallucinations brought on by the lack of glucose (sugar) to the brain. While in this state of diminished mental capacity and confusion, the person is susceptible to suggestion and influence. Malnourishment will also reduce a person's physical capacities, as he is also less likely to show aggression or attempt to escape. Mental confusion can also be a symptom of dehydration, so drink more water.

There was some evidence in the 1980s of terrorist groups in the Middle East adding arsenic to hostage food as a mild sedative. This drug reduced their aggressive behaviors and made hostages more manageable. There are suspicions that ISIS may be drugging hostages to make them more docile and, therefore, less troublesome during beheadings; however, this is purely speculation at this time.

You will likely receive the same meal and in the same amount as your captors unless you are being punished, then of course you will receive less. As you can expect, you will lose weight, which translates into a loss of muscle mass. You will feel lethargic and inclined to sleep more often. However, it has been scientifically proven that given every opportunity to sleep as much as a person wishes, unaided by any sense of day or night, a person will sleep an average of only eight to nine hours in a twenty-four-hour period. You can't sleep through your captivity.

You are not likely to enjoy your daily meal. Firstly, it will not be what you're used to, and you will be eating it in a place you'd rather not be. People in the hospital dislike the food, but much of their dislike may be caused by not wanting to be in the hospital in the first place; in that situation, it is common to hate most everything in your immediate environment.

You must eat every chance you get and drink every chance you get. If you're not hungry because you're upset, take the food and save it for later. If your captors are Islamists, during the month of Ramadan you will not be fed during daylight hours; you will eat when they eat.

Given the tentative surroundings and your situation, you might be relocated at any time and have to suffer long hours in the trunk of a car or on foot, or your guards may be called to other more urgent activities and you may not be fed on time or at all for a day or two. For these same reasons, I recommend you do not go on a hunger strike as a protest. Your captors will not have the necessary medical knowledge to force-feed you in a noninvasive manner, and if they have to force-feed you, it will cause physical injuries. Also, after any prolonged hunger strike and based on your previous nutritional intake, it may take weeks to regain the muscle mass you will have lost, if you ever do. I cannot imagine any hostage situation where refusing to eat is a beneficial strategy.

Malnutrition can cause your teeth to loosen and, in extreme cases, to fall out. If you are hungry, ask for more food. Your captors realize they must keep you properly fed, watered, and warm for you to survive. If they feel your health may be at risk, they may feed you more. Your captors might be feeding you less just as a punishment for who you are or might be having a game with you about how long it will take you to ask for more food. Just because you are a hostage doesn't mean you can't ask for more food, more water, or warmer clothing.

If you are so hungry that you cannot sleep, make a fist with your hand, push it into your abdominal area, and fold your body around it as best you can. If you have an extra item of clothing, you can roll this into a ball and press it into your abdomen. This will push your stomach walls closer together and provide a false sense of fullness, thereby reducing your feelings of hunger.

SLEEP AND SLEEP DEPRIVATION

Sleep deprivation was not always considered torture because, as the definition implies, it seems somewhat mundane and not life-threatening. But it can have the same disorienting, confusing, and hallucinating mental effects as solitary confinement or social deprivation; it can also cause many physical effects such as tremors, aching muscles, and increased heart rate variability.

Menachem Begin, prime minister of Israel from 1977 to 1983, was tortured as a young man in the Soviet Union, and in his book *White Nights: The Story of a Prisoner in Russia*, he tells of fellow prisoners who had endured extreme tortures under other regimes and had not cracked, but who lost their will to resist when subjected to sleep deprivation. "In the head of the interrogated prisoner, a haze begins to form. His spirit is wearied to death, his legs are unsteady, and he has one sole desire: to sleep. To sleep just a little, not to get up, to lie, to rest, to forget . . . Anyone who has experienced this desire knows that not even hunger or thirst are comparable with it. . . . He promised them—if they signed—uninterrupted sleep! And they signed . . ." (Conroy 2000)

Captors can use a variety of methods to keep hostages from sleeping. Hostages have been hung from the walls or ceiling with only their toes touching the ground. This causes severe pain in the shoulders and joints; the hostage attempts to relieve this pain by trying to support himself by his toes, which then causes pain in the toes and feet. A hostage may be subjected to very loud and disturbing music and then doused with very cold water to keep him from dozing off. Hostages have also been subjected to continuous pain, such as being whipped, or have had weights suspended from their genitals or other sensitive body parts in an effort to keep them awake.

Suspension is closely related to binding as the side effects are muscle cramps, joint, and hip pain. There are many types of torture related to binding and/or suspension with ropes or sticks and each may cause general or specific damage to the body. It doesn't serve the purpose of this book to go into specific detail.

If a hostage is subjected to a number of less intrusive tortures— let's call them sedentary tortures—such as solitary confinement, tight binding, and malnutrition all at the same time, it is easy to see where he might begin to hallucinate and experience extreme anxiety and panic to the point of going mad. It is easy to sympathize with institutionalized patients who suffer with these disorders, real or imagined, and who resort to repetitive rocking, head banging, or self-inflicted pain as a diversion from these conditions.

If you feel too cold to sleep or you have been shivering while trying to sleep, of course, ask for more blankets. They will smell bad, but they will keep you warmer; you will soon begin to smell the same anyway. If you lie down or sleep on a hard floor such as hard-packed dirt or cement and you feel cold, don't lie in the fetal position. The fetal position exposes too much of your body to the hard floor and your body's valuable heat will be absorbed by the floor. The body loses more heat to the ground than it loses to the open air. Try sleeping on your knees with your head bowed onto your forearms. You can also try sleeping on your haunches with your head resting on your knees or in your folded arms.

If you have a blanket, try sleeping with it underneath you as opposed to over you. By reducing the amount of contact by soft body tissue against the floor, you will lessen the amount of heat lost from your body. It won't be comfortable, but it may be warmer. Of course, if you are cold and are being held with other hostages, sleep together and spoon—that is, sleep front-to-back. This is not time to be sensitive about gender—I'm talking about survival. You would do this if you were lost in the woods on a cold night, so do it here. You can laugh about it later.

BEING CHAINED OR TIED FOR LONG PERIODS OF TIME—BINDING

In my civilian scenarios, at the outset of confinement, it is common for hostages to be tied up, handcuffed, or chained for long periods of time. Initially, this is done because the captors are concerned that the hostage may attempt to escape. This practice also protects the captors against a possible physical attack from the hostage. Although many Middle Eastern terrorists have become more familiar with the physical and mental abilities of Westerners, they are still apprehensive of Westerners' fighting skills and their escape potential. Being chained or tied for a long period of time restricts your movements and may cause parts of your body to cramp up. You will have to stretch or exercise one part of your body at a time at the expense of other parts. Again, a type of slow extension and retraction of the muscles and joints will allow the blood vessels and muscle groups to realign themselves and prevent blood clots.

Some hostages spent months or years chained to a wall. (Terry Waite spent four years chained to a wall.) Some hostages spend weeks chained to one another. I spoke with one hostage who had been handcuffed together with a number of other hostages every night. He said it was very embarrassing if someone had to pee during the night, as you had to wake up the other hostages and have everyone stand in a circle as you peed into a two-liter Pepsi bottle. They later fashioned a handcuff key from a nail and unlocked themselves at night and rehandcuffed themselves in the morning before the first guard entered for an inspection. This was a major accomplishment, as it significantly improved their ability to sleep independently of one another and, of course, urinate whenever they wished. They also attained a sense of power and control over their situation and their environment—a small victory.

If you are tied too tightly and believe this is causing or is likely to cause circulatory problems, ask—even demand—that your bindings be eased. One of the first signs of bindings being too tight is a swelling in the extremities beyond the actual binding. If this swelling is not relieved, you may notice the swelled area turning a shade of blue. Many Vietnam POWs were tied with wire and suffered from swollen extremities for many days in a row. When they were untied, it took a few days, or sometimes a week or more, of gentle massaging and flexing to regain full feeling and control of the muscles in the affected areas. Binding can cause damage to underlying tissue and ligaments.

It is beyond the intent of this book to outline techniques for escaping from or breaking handcuffs, tie wraps, ropes, or padlocks. There are a number of Internet sites detailing how handcuffs work and how they can be picked, shimmed, or broken, plus how tie wraps can be cut without a blade or even broken using the proper leverage.

SOCIAL AND SENSORY
DEPRIVATION—BRAINWASHING

Two relatively new tortures that may be used in long-term hostage situations are social deprivation and sensory deprivation. These are carried out in a number of ways, but the deprivations are more likely to be situational and accidental than deliberate.

Sensory deprivation is the removal or absence of all sensory information or stimulation. This would be the complete absence of light, sound, and touch. Although at first this might seem like a relaxing place to be, sensory deprivation causes a person to hallucinate, panic, and fear the worst of everything. A sense of dread and confusion takes over a person's mind. In this state he is easily confused and easily influenced. This used to be referred to as *brainwashing*, where a person's thoughts and his very sense of identity and realism could be erased or at least significantly diminished, and then a new sense of identity, purpose, and realism could be introduced.

During the Korean War, a number of American POWs vehemently denounced the activities of the United States. This caused considerable concern within the US military, as they believed the communists had discovered how to effectively brainwash American soldiers. The United States immediately began a number of scientific experiments, code-named MK Ultra, to discover how this could be done. The CIA secretly commissioned experiments on American and Canadian human subjects during the 1950s. It was officially sanctioned in 1953 and halted in 1973. They used combinations of social deprivation, which could last for many months; hallucinogenic drugs such as lysergic acid diethylamide (LSD), psilocybin (magic mushroom), electroconvulsive therapy (ECT), hypnosis, as well as verbal and sexual abuse. The belief was that the human brain would undergo such stresses that its internal wiring could be broken down, hence the terms *mental breakdown* or *brainwashed*, after which it could then be "rewired" with new behaviors and new beliefs. All they ended up proving was these experiments altered the subject's memory, often forever. When the POWs who had earlier denounced their country's actions returned home to their normal environment, their beliefs quickly returned to their original predeployment sentiments—support for the United States.

What the result of these experiments and the use of torture to elicit a confession from a hostage have in common is that the effects are short-lived and ephemeral. That is, if you are a hostage and you are tortured to the point where you have to falsely admit to some act or transgression in order to stop the pain, this will not impair your real beliefs. You do what you have to do under the circumstances. Your religious beliefs, your political beliefs, and your ethics will remain intact.

There have been many scientific military studies undertaken to either prove or disprove this brainwashing theory, as well as the hypnosis theory that a person can be psychologically convinced to carry out various acts of violence. All of these studies have proven that it cannot be done. However, that never stops Hollywood. We see extreme fictional examples of this in Hollywood films such as *The Bourne Identity* (Liman, Crowley, and Gladstein 2002), where an individual forgets his own past and is turned into a totally new person. As this new person, he can be made to carry out all sorts of violence, including multiple murders and complicated espionage. The Hollywood version often includes in the plot the use of unpredictable experimental drugs to erase one set of memories and identity and replace it with another set of memories and personal identity. Right—let's leave Hollywood out of this.

As human animals, we rely on our senses to keep us informed about where we are in relation to everything and everyone in our environment. We need to know if it is daytime or nighttime; whether we are sitting, walking, or talking alone or with others; whether we are hungry or feel warm or cold. Our sensory inputs collect details that inform us if we are comfortable and safe or in danger. Without sufficient sensory input, we initially become uneasy; if this situation is not rectified, we begin to be anxious and then afraid, and then we feel panic and begin to hallucinate. We hallucinate because our senses strain to find light and sound and touch, and then, in a state of confusion, our minds provide hallucinations as a substitute for reality. If you have no experience using meditation for either physical or mental relief, lack of sensory information is more likely to have an earlier effect on you than if you do.

In my scenarios, sensory deprivation is likely to be by accident than by design. If a hostage is tied tightly to a chair, wall, or table in such a manner that he cannot move, is hooded so he cannot see any light whatsoever and either has earplugs inserted or is kept in a hole in the ground or in a cave that eliminates all sounds, he will be sensory deprived. Interestingly enough, even partial sensory deprivation can render a person meek and subdued. If a hostage is bound with just a hood over his head, he becomes almost instantly submissive because he has no clues about his immediate environment and, as such, cannot respond appropriately and safely. Just from the fear of harm alone, a hostage will become passive.

We have all seen nature shows where hawks or eagles are suddenly made quiet and almost tame when a hood is placed over their head and eyes; we have seen how a hostile and aggressive poisonous snake or a ferocious animal is calmed simply by putting it inside a cloth bag—they can't fight what they can't see.

Loneliness can also be used as a tactic. Social deprivation is designed to make you come to them seeking social interaction. Loneliness can make you more submissive and, therefore, more likely to follow every command immediately and without question, just for the reward of human companionship.

> "Can I have a hug?" I say. "I just really need a hug."
> I can't believe I said that. I know it's not right. It's strange. But just now I do need a hug. It's hard to be so filled with anger and hate all the time. He puts his arms around me and holds me. "Don't worry," he says, "everything is going to be okay. I'm going to take you home one day, and you'll be back with your family." "I'm so confused." "Why did I ask for a hug from this monster? Is this what prison does to you?"
> (Berry and DeJesus 2015, 107)

Both sensory deprivation and social deprivation can be overcome by mental imagery, which will be covered extensively in upcoming chapters.

HOODING

If a hostage has been hooded continually since his abduction and transport and is threatened to not remove his hood under any circumstances or is allowed to remove the hood only in the privacy of his cell, this may be a good sign. Hostage takers who keep their hostage continually hooded likely do so because they fully intend to ransom and release him and don't want him to be able to identify any of his captors. Again, knowing the real purpose of your abduction and interpreting your treatment for signs as indications of intent or purpose can aid in your ability to survive.

Hooding for longer periods of time is likely to cause the hostage to hallucinate, as the hostage's level of anxiety increases with the threat of death. This hallucination often takes the form of mental imagery.

A hostage held in absolute darkness such as a cave or an underground cell will often experience the same symptoms of visual hallucinations. In order to counter these hallucinations, the hostage must first relax and then substitute their own images through visualization (see chapter 13).

FALANGA

Falanga, sometimes called *bastinado*, is the beating of the bare soles of the feet with a stick or a cane. The soles of the feet are very tender, and beating them causes severe pain and swelling. This swelling makes it difficult to walk. In some cases, the victim's shoes are left on so that the feet swelling within the confinement of their shoes produce more pain. In many cases, the victim is forced to walk over stones or gravel to increase the pain. Falanga is routinely being used today against Somali refugees in areas of East Africa.

The victim is sometimes tied to a chair, and then having the chair tipped over onto its back exposes the victim's feet in the air. A much easier method is to seat the victim down into an empty vehicle tire, which serves to hold the victim from squirming and holds the victim's feet in the air, again for easy access to beating. Even the poorest torturer can find an old tire and a stick.

First aid for most swellings caused by injury is slightly elevating the legs and feet, which aids in draining the swelling fluid from the affected area.

BURNING

Burning a victim alive is not a torture per se, unless it is done to demonstrate to other hostages what might happen to them. Burning someone alive is also for spectacle, intended to warn off other attackers, be they competing gangs or government soldiers. Often, the most painful execution methods are used against government soldiers or police officers as a way to punish the hostage, demoralize their colleagues, and reduce their willingness to fight. The threat of incurring such treatment is a psychological variation of a human shield.

In some areas of South and Central America, the "flaming necklace" was used as entertainment and to scare off government soldiers. The victim was seated and bound with an empty automotive tire placed around his neck. The inside of the tire was filled with gasoline and set alight. A variation of this was the "hot dog." A victim was placed inside three or four empty tires; sometimes the victim was left standing, sometimes lying horizontally inside the tires. The tires were doused with gasoline and set alight. This often did a much better job of getting rid of the dead body than the burning necklace. The names and variations of these tortures or executions vary from locale to locale.

In many hostage situations or even corrupt prison situations, prisoners are burned with lit cigarettes. The most sensitive areas are often targeted: the chest and nipples, the face, the genitals, or the inner thigh. This is a relatively inexpensive torture and, although painful, leaves only small circular scars on the victims.

In East Africa today, hostages are being tortured by having flaming plastic dripped onto them from a burning plastic bag or plastic jug. As with many other tortures, this is often done in conjunction with or during a phone call for ransom. Live torture phone calls serve to transfer distress from the hostage to the family.

ELECTRIC SHOCK

Torture by electric shock has been available since the invention of the static generator used in the operation of the earliest telephone. The generator—a coil of wire turned inside a magnetic field—is turned by the crank handle of the telephone, which sends a brief but powerful electrical current down the wire and rings a buzzer at the telephone operator's switchboard.

In the correct proportions, water will conduct electricity; the human body has those correct proportions. All human beings— all mammals, actually—control their muscles by sending minute amounts of electricity to particular muscle groups, which causes the muscles to contract in direct relation to the amount of electrical current applied. Small amounts of electrical current cause the muscles to react minimally; when larger amounts of electricity are sent through muscle tissue, the lengths of muscle tissue contract fully and rapidly.

Our bodies are designed with both flexor and extensor muscles. As the term suggests, the flexors are responsible for flexing, or contracting a muscle, and the opposing extensor muscles are responsible for extending, or straightening the muscle. We all remember the high school science experiment where a small current is sent through a detached frog's leg—it makes the muscles in the leg contract. When large amounts of electricity are sent through a human body, it causes both the flexor and extensor muscles to contract completely, violently, and simultaneously in opposition to each other; sometimes, the contractions are sufficiently violent to break human bones. These muscle contractions are intense, painful, and exhausting and can cause lesions between muscle fibers. Violent contractions can also cause irregular heartbeats, fluctuations in blood pressure, and organ shutdown.

In electric shock torture, two cables are connected to a small electric generator or a car battery; the other ends of each cable are clamped onto the victim's skin, and the current is sent through the end of one cable, through the victim's body and out the other cable. This causes all of the muscles between the two cables, as well as many other muscle groups in the vicinity, to contract violently. The cables can be placed on different parts of the body in order to target certain muscle groups. Besides causing pinch bruising and burns at the site of the cables, sometimes a victim's teeth are fractured as the victim involuntarily clenches his teeth when the shock is applied. There have been many reports of electric shocks causing teeth to fracture when jaw muscles violently clench the upper and lower rows of teeth together.

Experienced torturers may adjust the intensity of the current in order to surprise the victim about what may come next or even pretend to flip the switch and cause the victim to falsely anticipate the shock.

I cannot provide the reader with a reliable strategy to reduce the pain or the effects of electric shock torture except to say that it is possible that dehydration may reduce the conductivity of electricity, though this is unlikely. Also, biting on something between your teeth may lessen tooth fractures, though it is unlikely you will be provided with such a luxury. On the plus side, some survivors have reported that the first few shocks seemed to numb their bodies and therefore the following shocks were less painful.

WATERBOARDING

Waterboarding is not a new torture, but it has seen a revival since 2000, and it is extremely effective. It has a history of use as early as the 1500s and was used by the Khmer Rouge regime during the

1970s. More recently it was on the CIA's list of enhanced interrogation techniques, released in 2014.

Initially, waterboarding involved tying the victim onto a narrow board and then tilting his head into a large cauldron of water until he almost drowned. Just before that point, the board and the victim would be lifted up out of the water long enough for a quick breath and then tilted back down into the water to experience drowning all over again.

Waterboarding, as it is currently used, involves strapping a person to an inclined board or a table, usually with his feet raised and his head lowered. In most cases, the person's entire face is covered—his eyes, nose, and mouth—with one or more layers of towels. The victim's eyes are covered so he can't see and, therefore, predict what is coming or when. This, of course, adds an element of terror to the exercise. The interrogator then repeatedly pours water onto the towels. As the person attempts to breathe air in through the towels, he inhales water through the nose and mouth and proceeds to drown. The person believes he is drowning because, physically, he is. His gag reflex kicks in as if he were choking. The more he gags and chokes, the more water he inhales.

At this point, the victim experiences the psychological terror of death by drowning and he is helpless to do anything about it. If a victim tries to hold his breath as a way to defend himself against what is coming, the interrogator will often punch him in the stomach, thereby forcing him to exhale and inhale just as suddenly. The victim frequently gags and vomits and sometimes goes into full-body spasms.

The board is inclined so as to encourage water to run up the nasal passages and into the sinuses. A variation on the theme is to use human excrement as a substitute for the water.

The attractiveness of waterboarding as a method of torture is the high probability of a confession without the physical evidence of torture.

By all accounts, the CIA's own admissions plus the reports of actual waterboarding victims, no one can hold out for very long under waterboarding. Then again, no one expects you to hold out forever, regardless of the type of torture to which you are exposed.

SUFFOCATING

Suffocating and waterboarding elicit similar panic and fear responses. A low-tech and much cheaper form of suffocating can be achieved by tying a plastic bag over the hostage's head, which causes the person to hyperventilate, panic, and believe he is dying by suffocation, which he is. The victim loses consciousness due to a lack of oxygen to the brain. As a torture, the bag is removed just prior to the victim losing consciousness so he can experience near-death over and over again.

EXERCISE AS A DEFENSE STRATEGY

Although many hostages may feel the desire to maintain their pre-abduction fitness level, excessive exercise is not advised. Your caloric intake will be significantly reduced and, with it, the amounts of vitamins and minerals required by the various organs in your body. Prior to your capture, you may not have had any medical issues related to vitamin or mineral deficiencies, but a sudden decrease in these levels might trigger a medical event that would not have otherwise occurred. With the possible combination of dehydration, a sudden decrease in caloric intake, and a vitamin and mineral deficiency, the potential for medical complications will increase. These complications may be aggravated by increased physical exercise and exertion. Therefore, I suggest you don't take that chance.

Hostages Robert Fowler and Louis Guay (2011) and Judith Tebbutt (2013) all used walking routines as a means to maintain mental and physical health. Fowler and Guay used walking in the open desert, and Tebbutt paced barefoot around her cell on a linoleum floor.

> We decided that we needed a business plan. We would strive at all costs to maintain healthy bodies in the extremely hostile environment in which we found ourselves, with the hope and expectation that physical health would help preserve mental health and maintain morale, which we took to be our greatest challenge.

So we designed a track, or *piste*, in the immediate vicinity . . . one sufficiently modest in its dimensions, we hoped, to avoid arousing the suspicions of our kidnappers that we might be up to something. We paced out a richly contorted route, nine-teen circuits to the kilometer and decided to walk it twice a day— at dawn and dusk—with a view to putting in a total of between four and six kilometers each day . . . Although four was our minimum, we often managed five to six kilometers each day.

Our cost-benefit analysis of the physical and psychological advantages to be derived from exercise versus the calories we had to expend, which we knew were not being adequately replaced, capped our ambitions at six, although on occasions of extreme stress I would exceed this.

For each of us our exercise regime was very therapeutic. It never failed to reduce anxiety and help us to sleep in the evenings. (Fowler 2011, 110, 111)

However, Fowler and Guay recognized their daily walking demanded its toll.

Initially, this regime was quite a challenge: first because this was exercise that neither of us managed for decades in Canada; and second because we had not anticipated any of the psychological, climatic, or nutritional challenges we would face in maintaining such an exercise regime.

Deteriorating shoes presented the most serious challenge to our health.

With a lot of painstaking work Louis kept the soles of our shoes more or less attached to the uppers. But the holes were inevitably getting larger, a few tearing through, and the leather of the upper parts was becoming ever less able to withstand being worked. (Fowler, 110, 111, 83)

That being said, Fowler's description of a "richly contorted route" gives me mind to suspect their activity may have served another purpose. See chapter 14.

For Judith Tebbutt,

Walking was rhythmic, meditative: it put me in touch with myself and was remarkably effective at driving any thoughts of the pirates from my mind. In my head, I was walking home. And at the end of each day I was exhausted, so aiding restful sleep.

Still, I wondered too if I could try some slightly more vigorous exercise, without having to get down on the floor with the insect life. (Tebbutt 2013, 102)

However, for Tebbutt, her walking regime dangerously overextended her physical limits and put her health at serious risk.

My days felt changeless, interminably long and monotonous, hot, sticky and unventilated. I walked on and on, barefoot, for half an hour on the hour from 7 a.m. to 8 p.m.—unless faintness came over me or the painful twinges of my blisters became unmanageable. Even then, I would try to walk on the edges of my feet, just in order to keep with the programme. (Tebbutt, 145,146)

Weeks later,

> There was, though, no masking the terrible physical condition I was in. My feet were blistered and bloodied from walking, and by the end of each day they had swollen, freakishly so, as if pumped full of water, the skin smooth but strangely "cushioned." My scarred ankles and toes ached. The swelling would recede somewhat overnight, but in the morning my feet had the look of Gorgonzola cheese, veins awfully prominent, so that I could trace them, dark blue and risen just as they were on my hands and arms—a frightening sight. As my hair began to come out in handfuls, my fears heightened and rattled me. (pp. 219, 220)

Tebbutt had taken up physical exercise as a solution to keep her from thinking about the death of her husband (killed during their abduction) and the hopelessness of her situation. She had earlier chastised herself for imagining she was back at home enjoying her friends. She took such thoughts as somehow self-indulgent and saw them only as a weakness which would worsen her mental state. Undaunted by her failing health, walking was her mental anchor.

> I was still walking home, though. Home was still there and I had to walk to it, had to carry on. Part of me knew I wasn't being too clever—indeed, bloody silly, on some level . . . But walking was so essential to my state of mind that I was going to have to make mind triumph over matter. (p. 220)

Even at this point of revelation and admission that she was doing herself serious physical harm, Tebbutt continued her walking regime to the point where the blisters on her feet broke and she knew she risked serious infection. Even a relatively simple infection living under her squalid living conditions of captivity, remoteness, and lack of medical assistance could have proven fatal.

It is a widely recognized symptom within psychology that often people will seek out physical abuse and physical pain as a distraction or a diversion from mental pain.

As mentioned earlier, malnutrition can cause a person to lapse into a state of mental confusion; it can also cause hallucinations brought on by the lack of glucose to the brain. While in this state of diminished mental capacity and confusion, and without the luxury of an objective opinion or intervention, a hostage can easily travel down a path of self-destruction.

The only benefit—and I repeat—the only benefit to a hostage being in serious physical health is your kidnappers are likely to recognize they are in danger of losing their money if you die. All their physical risk, their time and expense guarding, feeding, and caring for you would be for naught. They will be forced to turn over a sick and dying hostage and settle for whatever the present negotiations can offer . . . if they haven't left it too late.

A hostage cannot allow a physical fitness strategy intended to combat boredom take priority over their mental and physical well-being.

"We ate badly, and worried about scurvy and other ravages of vitamin deficiency and nutritional insufficiency" (Fowler, 90).

The benefits of any exercise program while in captivity must always be weighed against the cost of valuable calories, the likelihood of dehydration, and physical exhaustion. In Fowler and Guay's case, as in many similar cases, their water source was often tainted with diesel fuel or other contaminants and was likely a significant factor in the intestinal problems they encountered. An exercise regime that dehydrates the body and thereby causes the hostage to ingest greater quantities of contaminated water is counterproductive. A nutritionally deprived and physically weakened body cannot defend itself against the endemic diseases of foreign environments, human and otherwise.

If you are driving a car that's low on fuel on an unfamiliar highway, is it a better strategy to slow down and improve your gas mileage or drive as fast as you can to get to a gas station more quickly? As I will identify later, there are a number of mental strategies that do a much better job of battling boredom without costing you valuable calories and water.

Fowler, Guay, and Tebbutt used physical exercise to keep them "in the moment," as it were, and help keep them mentally grounded. Although Tebbutt enjoyed her "real" dreams about family and friends, she did not allow herself to daydream or visualize about those same people. She felt that if she did mentally visualize, it would be a sign she was losing some level of mental control, and she would inevitably go downhill from there. She believed her walking routine provided her with a necessary mental and cognitive stability as well as provide a predictable daily schedule. Fowler and Guay did not, or at least did not publicly admit, to spending hours visualizing (see chapter 13) as a means to combat boredom or to sustain a positive mental attitude.

I believe that the walking regime used by Fowler, Guay, and Tebbutt provided them with a sense of control and purpose which they had lost; they felt that doing something was, at least, doing something.

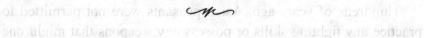

I believe the comparison between the needs for the physical exercise routines of Robert Fowler, Louis Guay, and Judith Tebbutt versus the mental visualization exercises of many other hostages such as

Amanda Lindhout, Michelle Knight, Jessica Buchanan, Jim Loney, and others to be worthy of further study. Their examples demonstrate that a hostage must continually weigh the mental benefits of exercise against the physical cost of exercise.

ISOMETRICS

Isometrics is a form of exercise based on alternating between tensing and relaxing your muscles while remaining stationary. It is one muscle group being used against another and then alternating which group is pushing and which group is pulling. Isometrics can be used standing or sitting. You can use isometric exercises to maintain some degree of muscle tone while also increasing blood flow and providing the vascular pumping action that is so beneficial to maintaining healthy, flexible blood vessels. Many athletes will stand against a wall and push the wall with their hands and arms without moving themselves. This maneuver provides the muscles and blood vessels with the flexing and stretching exercise they need without having to move and exert energy.

You can exercise your upper body by placing both palms together, either out in front of you or even behind your back and alternately pressing one against the resistance of the other. Lower arms can be exercised by placing one fist inside the other palm and slowly pushing the palm away from the body, or side to side, and then resisting the fist as it is being pulled back into the body, a tug-of-war between muscle groups. Chest and leg muscles can also be tensed and relaxed, providing muscle exercise and increased blood flow. Systematically exercise every muscle group from your head to your toes, multiple times a day. This can be an isometric exercise or a tai chi–type exercise, or you can mimic swimming or even dance.

Hundreds of years ago, Asian peasants were not permitted to practice any fighting skills or possess any weapons that might one day be used against those in power. In order to circumvent this law, they invented karate and kung fu katas, which were passed off as dances but were actually a series of martial arts punches, blocks, and kicks. Celebrated as dances, these fighting skills could be passed on covertly within families and between neighboring towns and villages. They also incorporated actual farm implements into weapons, and these weapons are still used today in martial arts training, katas, and competitions. A person may be surprised at just how much healthy exercise isometrics, tai chi, and katas can provide.

Isometric exercise can reduce both physical and mental tensions, which will allow you to manage stress, regain focus on your thinking skills, and help you relax before sleep.

Light to moderate exercise will assist the hostage in maintaining a sense of well-being, which in turn will assist in physical and mental relaxation, improve cognitive ability, and enhance psychological fitness.

CRYING AS A STRATEGY

As a final note on physical torture and prior to examining the psychological aspects of torture and behavioral strategies, it is of the utmost importance that hostages understand crying as a strategy.

Again, the hostage is the best judge of when to cry and when not to cry. If you have been told you are to blame for the suffering and deaths of many of your captors' countrymen, if you are told you are to blame for the social, environmental, or economic hardships your captors and their families now face, it is likely that a physical beating will be handed out as punishment, retribution, or sheer venting of frustrations. If this is the situation you are now facing, you can expect to be beaten until your captors have satisfied their anger or until they see that they have indeed hurt you both physically and emotionally. They will know this only when they see real physical damage as evidenced by blood and a crying, sobbing hostage. If you try to tough it out and show them how much you can take physically and emotionally, they are likely to continue well beyond where they would have stopped, had you cried earlier. If it was their intent to hurt you, you must show them you are hurt; you must bleed. If it was their intention to make you suffer emotionally, then you must show them they have succeeded; you must show them tears—lots of tears.

As in all other strategies, physical and mental, you must be the judge of how and when to use crying. You must not be discovered as a fraud.

> I knew these men despised female emotion. It's a common trait in the culture. A woman's emotional plea is regarded as an unfair and dishonest attempt to manipulate circumstances in the female's favour. It is looked at as being done without regard to consequences for the male. (Jessica Buchanan, 84)

> These kidnappers made it plain how they hated the tears. Crying caused them to poke at me with the barrels of their loaded guns. (Jessica Buchanan, 199)

Crying as a strategy has its place. When a hostage is being beaten or tortured as punishment for acts or crimes, crying by either a man or a woman can be effective. In this circumstance, crying conveys to the torturer that his actions have achieved his goal of physical pain and suffering. In other circumstances, crying is seen as an expression of emotion meant to induce some sense of shame or guilt upon the hostage taker. In this sense, it is seen as unwelcome. Recognize the difference.

As I wrote earlier, no one will believe any statement you make while in confinement. Just as importantly, it is worth repeating here that "innocent" civilians taken hostage for ransom, for political leverage, or as human shields are not likely to be carrying state secrets or knowledge of military movements or military tactics; therefore, they are unlikely to experience waterboarding or other forms of extreme torture designed to extract information or confessions.

These are only a few examples of the most common types of torture. Certain types of torture go in and out of fashion, and torture has its variations, which, unfortunately, are only limited by human imagination. Sexual mistreatment is likely the most frequent and widespread of tortures because it is degrading and humiliating and leaves virtually no physical scars—only psychological ones. And it's readily available.

UN peacekeeping personnel, UNDP employees, as well as NATO and any other international peacekeepers and soldiers must be provided with torture awareness training so they can more easily identify torture implements or torture rooms within prisons, police stations, government buildings, or in training facilities that may have held and tortured prisoners. These UN and UNDP employees, as well as supporting police and military personnel, should have training in recognizing people, alive or dead, who may have been victims of physical or mental tortures.

Investigators must also be aware that torture survivors have often indicated there was a symptom-free period lasting months and even years between the time of the torture and the onset of physical symptoms (Grethe Skylv, "The Physical Sequelae of Torture," Bosaglu 1992, p. 43).

CHAPTER 12
PSYCHOLOGICAL ASPECTS OF TORTURE

I have gained an extensive background in the study of torture through a variety of methods. Studying the history of torture from medieval times through to the present, reading firsthand accounts of political prisoners tortured during oppressive dictatorships in Central and South America, reading the personal accounts of POWs in both German and Japanese prison camps, POWs from the Vietnam War, personally interviewing survivors of both physical and mental tortures incurred during captivity, and then actually visiting the sites of their torture. Based on this information and testimony, I have concluded that there are three psychological aspects to torture:

1. Imagined torture is likely worse than the actual torture.
2. Waiting for torture is likely worse than the actual torture.
3. Hearing another's torture, or having caused another's torture, may be worse than being tortured yourself.

IMAGINED TORTURE

As alluded to earlier when outlining how you might be treated during your initial interrogation, your fear of how you might be interrogated by physical beatings or of being exposed to your own phobias may be worse than your actual beatings. As the saying goes, "You have nothing to fear but fear itself."

I have studied numerous accounts of how prisoners sat in a cell and began to wonder about what would happen next. Would they be dragged from their cell like on TV or in the movies, taken to a room and tied to a chair with a single lightbulb dangling from the ceiling? They wondered about just how many times they would be punched in the face. Would they suffer broken teeth, a broken jaw, or a broken nose perhaps? Would they be hung from the ceiling by their wrists and whipped, like they've seen in the movies? Would their interrogators know about their phobias and lock them in a trunk or bury them in a hole? Would their interrogators know they are afraid of the dark and put a bag over their head? Would they put them in a pit of snakes like Indiana Jones? How long would all this last—two hours, three hours, all night, perhaps?

The worry goes on and on. With unchecked and rambling thoughts such as these, the hostage is actually submitting himself to mental torture. He is creating a sense of fear, confusion, terror, and anxiety in his own mind; he is doing the interrogator's job for him, and he hasn't been asked a single question yet.

Overwhelmingly, the physical punishment the prisoners actually received was significantly less than what they had imagined. After sitting for hours, imagining and fearing the very worst, when it was all over, many prisoners were surprised. Some even joked, "That's it? That's all?"

I certainly don't mean to downplay the very real pain these prisoners and hostages received, nor the many days or weeks it took to recuperate and heal from the beatings they did receive. What I am saying is that in an overwhelming majority of cases, prisoners/ hostages imagined physical mistreatment or torture that was much worse than what they would actually receive. Therefore, you may be doing yourself more harm by unnecessarily worrying about what is going to happen rather than just accepting that what is going to happen is just going to happen.

A hostage's focus at this time should be on preparation—preparing and rehearsing answers to possible questions as a strategy to reduce the amount or the intensity of physical punishment. What are they going to ask? What might they accuse me of? How will I answer?

This is not much different from sitting on a chair outside the principal's office and wondering how much he or she knows and what your answers should be. Except in the current situation, you have practiced your lines during predeployment, when you and your fellow employees, your media relations personnel, and senior executives discussed plausible replies. "My company/country was invited to help your family and your children." "My company/country has brought building materials for homes and schools." "I have been sent by my company to help." The real difference between here and the principal's office is that this interrogation is life and death; this is for all the marbles.

This is serious business, and you must spend your time thinking. Not sulking, imagining, and worrying. Many of us are familiar with promotional boards or annual performance interviews. We have a good understanding of what questions will be asked during these interviews, and we mentally prepare and verbally rehearse a number of possible answers. We know before going in that our activities over the past months or years will be brought up, often with examples, and we will be asked to explain our actions, both good and bad. This situation is no different. You will be accused of working against whatever this fundamentalist group believes in. Proper predeployment training will have provided you with an understanding of cultural sensitivities as well as some very plausible and logical replies to their accusations about your activities. Remember what these responses were. Your captors will question your movements around the country and ask who you've met. Again, your answers will support your company's or your country's altruistic intentions: "to help farmers produce better crops," "to provide better irrigation," "to set up banking and loan privileges to generate and support small businesses" (the Muslim faith prohibits collecting interest on loaned money), "to help set up schools," "to stop police corruption"—whatever.

You must know your answers inside out. Memorize them because as your beatings continue and your thinking becomes muddled and confused, your answers must remain consistent and automatic. Relax, focus, and practice. This will give you confidence.

Rational and consistent responses are more likely to convince your captors of your innocent activities than repetitive, flat denials to their accusations. Your repetitive denials are more likely to be followed by their repetitive blows. Do not make this interrogation a test of whether you can deny accusations longer than they can continue beating you. Providing short, rational, and believable responses is more likely to reduce the intensity and the amount of physical abuse than outright refusal and resistance.

WAITING FOR TORTURE

Many tortured hostages admit that waiting for their torture to begin was worse than the torture they actually received. These hostages recall the many hours they sat and waited in their own cells while hearing the cell doors of other prisoners being taken out and questioned, not knowing if they were being tortured, released, or killed and never returned. Am I next? They listened and analyzed the sound of every footstep in the hallways, the rattling of keys, the chatter of the guards. Am I next? They analyzed the time of day most prisoners were taken out of their cells and interrogated, the guards' shifts, and even the most likely day of the week they would be tortured.

> A survey of two hundred torture victims conducted by Dr. Ole Vedel Rasmussen ("Medical Aspects of Torture," *Danish Medical Bulletin*, January 1990) found that when survivors were asked to indicate what they thought was the worst part of their detention, they often cited the periods between torture sessions, when they were frightened of what was going to happen. For the torturer, each session may last for only a few minutes. For the victim, there is often no break, the mental anguish filling the void between sessions. (Conroy 2000)

Many hostages/prisoners confess to becoming so frustrated by these thoughts of "anticipatory anxiety" (Sherwood 1986; Faber, Harlow, and West 1957) that they came to the point of "Let's get this over with." Again, as with imagining the torture, the hostage begins to interrogate and torture himself. Don't do this. Relax and plan.

When it finally was their turn to be tortured, many prisoners found it was only a simple interrogation to reexamine their previous responses, reaffirm their identity, or just answer new accusations. If it involved a beating or torture, again many prisoners found it was much less than what they had imagined. They often chastised themselves for their earlier anxious and even foolish thoughts while they sat in their cells, waited, and wondered.

If you look at the situation from your captors' perspective, if they bring a hostage in for simple questioning, they may feel foolish, almost embarrassed, to just ask him a few simple questions and return him to his cell without knocking him around at least a little bit to reaffirm their dominance and control. A hostage must refrain from waiting and wondering when it will be his turn and what might happen. Again, a hostage's time is better spent trying to predict what the next line of questioning might be and prepare his responses.

HEARING ANOTHER'S TORTURE OR CAUSING ANOTHER'S TORTURE

Released hostages, political prisoners, and POWs have all recalled how psychologically difficult it was to sit in their cell and listen to the sounds of torture being inflicted upon others. These sounds of torture might be from the instrument itself, such as a whip or electrical cord hitting bare flesh, or the screams of pain from the tortured person . . . then the screaming stops. As in the other psychological aspects of torture, listening to another's torture being carried out makes prisoners think of, even graphically picture, exactly what is happening to the other person and imagining what it must feel like. When there is little else to listen to in their own cell, prisoners will strain to eavesdrop on all other sounds. Hostages will attempt to identify the sounds and make sense of them in order to establish or maintain some sense of presence as they continually construct a mental picture of their surroundings. However, paying too close attention to these kinds of sounds can make a hostage restless and apprehensive. Of course, he will wonder how that tortured person must feel—that's only natural. Plus, it is almost impossible to cover his ears and totally eliminate these sounds from registering in his brain. Some prisoners and hostages have admitted to covering their ears and singing or humming to try to eliminate the sounds.

"I didn't mind the pain so much. It was the cries next door I couldn't bear" (survivor, Basoglu 1992).

All this anxiety, distress, and apprehension is amplified if, for some reason, the listening hostage believes he is in any way responsible for the other hostage being tortured. This guilt might be obvious, such as blaming another hostage for his own transgressions or something as simple as sitting farthest away from the cell door when guards enter, looking for someone to torture. If there are multiple hostages in one cell, there is always the potential for tension among hostages, even hatred. Similarly, there is also the potential for attraction—even affection—as one hostage might take torture intended for another. If there is any sense of guilt, shame, or remorse, the listening hostage may never forgive himself.

This particular torture is called "contingency abuse". When captives are forced to witness the torture and punishment of other captives and realize that their torture and punishment is contingent upon their compliance in the captor-captive relationship (Sherwood 1986).

Again, in situations where there are multiple hostages in one cell or even hostages who know one another but are kept in separate cells, a stronger hostage may wish he was the one being tortured because he knows the tortured hostage may not have the mental or physical strength to withstand this kind of treatment.

> One night he raped me while I was chained to Gina.
> She sat in the corner of the mattress and tried to look
> the other way. . . . The dude would take either me or
> Gina off to the side of the bed; the other one would
> sit there feeling helpless to stop it. . . . Sometimes we
> would reach out and touch the other's hand . . . It's one
> thing to have someone break your own heart; it can

be even more painful to watch another person's heart get crushed. (Knight 2014, 196)

When there are multiple hostages, either of the same sex or different sexes, each will be keeping mental accounts or calculations of who has been tortured the most often, who has been tortured the worst, and in what manner each has been tortured. Each hostage will have a mental picture of who has been treated best and who has been treated worst. If you are the one who has been treated best, for whatever reason, you are likely to feel guilty that another hostage is being tortured in your place and you may wish you were being tortured instead. In these circumstances, there is always the potential for suspicions—suspicions that one hostage is being given preferential treatment over others and why. In these situations, there is a strong likelihood that jealousy, animosity, or hatred will develop. This complication breaks down the social fiber of the group and puts a strain on relationships. It negatively impacts the survival odds of all hostages.

All this said, a hostage may be taken by a group with no plans to physically abuse him, so the risk of deliberate physical torture may be very low.

PARALLELS WITH DOMESTIC ABUSE

As a short aside, years ago, as I pondered these three psychological aspects of torture and reflected on my years of police service, I came to the sudden realization that these three aspects of torture were strikingly similar to the everyday situations experienced by victims of domestic abuse.

I believe that comparing aspects of torture with examples of domestic abuse will provide the reader with a perspective that may be better understood.

The spouse or the children of an abusive person will remember the kinds of abuse suffered in the past, the kinds of pain it caused, and the physical marks it left on them. Like hostages anticipating torture, the victim's imagined abuse can be worse than the actual abuse. Will it be the same this time? Will there be a weapon involved again? If the abuser comes home and the family is subjected to only verbal and not physical abuse, their thoughts and worries while just waiting and wondering about what they might have had to endure affect them regardless.

Also similar to a hostage waiting for torture, the spouse or the children of an abusive person often sit and wonder just what might happen when the abuser comes through the door. When will the abuser come through the door? Will the abuser be drunk or just angry? Abused family members try to calculate the likelihood of abuse and the type of abuse, based on the day of the week. After the abuse, they compare this time against previous times, this pain compared to that pain, and it is often less. But again, the time spent worrying and wondering has taken its toll regardless.

In another parallel with hostages, an abused spouse or child will feel significant guilt and shame if he or she has in some way, real or imagined, been responsible for another family member being abused. Listening to another family member being abused and knowing it should have been him or her is likely to cause guilt and animosity that may last for many years, or forever.

Often a spouse will gladly suffer the abuse in order to protect the children; sometimes older children will opt to suffer the abuse to protect the parent or younger children. In either of these situations, being abused themselves is preferred over listening to others being abused.

CHAPTER 13
LONG-TERM MENTAL STRATEGIES

What is the difference between behavioral, situational, and psychological long-term strategies? For the purposes of this book, when I refer to your behavioral strategies, I am speaking about your day-to-day outlook, your mood, and how others see you . . . for the duration. Your situational strategies are the ones you apply as you need them. Your long-term mental state is how you feel overall—your continuous feelings of frustration or anger and your feelings of general happiness, sadness, and depression. Your psychological state is your level of determination, your attitude, your resolve, focus, and your preparedness to continue applying your strategies until all this is over—your will to live.

Although this book identifies strategies that focus on each of these components separately, each component strategy will always have a level of influence on the others. Sometimes this influence is significant; sometimes it is minimal. It depends on the magnitude of the outside factor and upon which component it is concentrated.

Our daily at-home routine and lifestyle establishes a personal sense of mental and physical balance or equilibrium—this is our normal. Certainly, there are days when we experience more physical or mental activity, but these usually average out, and the balance of physical and mental activity we are comfortable with returns.

This sense of what is normal is different for everyone, and much of it depends upon our particular stage of life. We might be newly married, just starting out with new jobs, a mortgage, and car payments. These activities and the stressors they bring are our normal. We may be semiretired, with no children at home, and enjoy a more relaxed lifestyle; this has fewer stressors, but it is our normal. What is normal is very subjective, and we become somewhat satisfied or at least familiar and content with our physical and mental lives. Whenever it changes, we notice. Your assessment of a possible impending illness or your desire to exercise is based upon your own assessment of your physical self. Nobody knows you like you know you.

We know we have a physical self and a mental self. Through our daily socialization, we also understand where we fit in with our family and friends, our work colleagues, and our community, so we have a concept of our social self. I don't have to go into Freud or Jung or other famed pioneers in psychology to tell you we all know that our physical and mental selves cannot be physically separated. They have grown up together, they interact with each other, and each depends on the other to survive. When one fails, the other fails. If one dies, the other dies.

When you become a hostage, you can expect a catastrophic shift in this balance between your mental self and your physical self. Some people can handle the shift better than others, and some can't handle it at all. This is because we all have different life experiences that shape our personalities, and as such, some of us have been through significant family problems, medical situations, or work problems and have learned important problem-solving skills along the way. Others have not.

After the first week or so of captivity, hostages realize that their body has begun to weaken; the weeks of reduced nutritional intake and unclean water that often leads to bouts of diarrhea, lack of restful sleep, and lack of physical exercise—even the lack of sunlight—have taken their toll. Hostages begin to feel the difference. Some people who may be more in tune with their bodies perceive this change sooner than others, but all will notice it eventually.

Every hostage I have interviewed that was held in captivity for more than a few weeks emphasized how vitally important it was when they reached this landmark. They came to the realization that their physical body was weakening and that their mental toughness alone would determine their survival from this point onward. It is at this crossroad that a hostage must make the decision to either curl up, feel sorry for himself, and leave his very life in someone else's hands (barbed-wire psychosis) or make the conscious decision to be mentally strong, to not give up, to not give in, and to not die. Arriving at this positive conclusion is critical to a hostage's survival.

These hostages recognize that their physical captivity is a given. They accept that they no longer make the decisions about where they can go or what they can do. Just as a captured wild animal has tested the physical limitations of his cage over and over again, the new hostage must resign himself to the fact that his physical self is captive. This is now his new normal.

A hostage who recognizes this inevitability that his psychological self must now support—even rescue—his physical self, needs a specific set of long-term survival strategies. These strategies depend upon the hostage being able to mentally separate his psychological self from his physical self. Some hostages handle this situation better than others. Just how each handles it depends on a number of factors, which incidentally also determine the incidence or severity of any PTSD later on. These factors include the following:

FACTORS IN THE ABILITY TO SEPARATE THE MENTAL AND THE PHYSICAL SELF

Family Ties

A hostage with strong family ties and strong social ties has better mental strength and a more positive outlook than a hostage who does not. Strong family ties give the hostage the awareness of a broad range of love and support back home. This hostage has a larger repertoire of happy family events such as birthday parties, family outings and vacations, and likely a strong recognition of parental support and the knowledge that his immediate family will have the support of their larger and extended family. This hostage will recognize that there are many loving people back home that are expecting him to do whatever needs to be done to return home safely.

Strong social ties provide a hostage with a broader variety of happy memories and the comfort of knowing he has many friends, which provides him with added confidence and a strong desire to see his friends once again. Brom and Kleber (1989) reported that approximately 80% of all people who were confronted with a trauma, utilize their own resources and social network support to work through the after affects.

Strong family ties give the hostage consolation, strength, and resolve. During her captivity, Kayla Jean Mueller, age 26, from Prescott, Arizona, found strength in her faith and her family's love, which she wrote about in a letter released on Tuesday, February 10, 2015. (See appendix 2. Also refer to appendix 3 for letters from executed hostages Peter Kassig and James Foley.) As a humanitarian aid worker, Mueller had an unquenchable passion to help others and wrote that such service brought her closer to God.

"I have been shown in darkness, light + have learned that even in prison, one can be free" (*The Guardian* 2015). The letter was smuggled out by captives and received by her family in early 2014, who in turn released it to the press after her death.

Age

Generally, middle-aged people are more aware of and experienced with survival strategies than younger people. They have more life experiences that required the use of problem-solving skills. They have met with a greater variety of people and personalities in a variety of social situations. They have dealt with people they didn't like and have developed strategies to live with them or work with them, as each situation dictated.

Education

Higher education often brings an academic awareness of individual psychology, group psychology, and social psychology, as well as an anthropological understanding of religions and cultures. It can bring a learned tolerance for different points of view, exposure to a broader range of cultures, and problem-solving experience. People with higher education often have greater self-confidence. That said however, depending upon their personality, some may exhibit arrogance and attempt to show their captors the errors of their ways.

Religion/Faith

Hostages with a strong sense of religious faith generally have a stronger will and more stable emotions. They have learned to temper their adverse feelings toward other people with kindness and forgiveness. They tend not to hold a grudge. Religious hostages believe there is a savior and therefore they are never alone. Religious people tend to have a more positive outlook and can rationalize their situation in a number of ways. "This is God's test," "I know He is watching over me," or "Whatever happens, I will be with God." Religiously devout people can be referred to as eternal optimists. (Don't forget that as a hostage, you too have become more religious.)

Business Experience

A hostage with business experience has dealt with a variety of economic, personnel, and business challenges and, therefore, has more practice applying a range of problem-solving skills. A hostage with extensive business experience is also more used to the loneliness of command that comes with being a person in charge, as a supervisor or business owner.

Preplanning

A hostage who knows he has left his family with fewer problems, having followed a number of predeployment suggestions, will have fewer mental distractions than one who did not.

Rank

Similar to a hostage with significant business experience, a person with high military rank or senior business position will have the advantage of having handled many difficult personnel and situational problems and will, therefore, have a larger repertoire of problem-solving skills to draw on. That said, senior military and senior businesspeople may be less sympathetic and may not be good listeners.

Personality

People with Type A personalities are more outgoing and gregarious and often have a more positive outlook than those with Type B personalities, who are more likely to be reserved and shy and may tend to be pessimistic.

These factors—the pluses and the minuses—will determine a hostage's overall mental strength and abilities.

SEPARATING THE MENTAL AND THE PHYSICAL SELF

The above factors also influence an individual's ability to separate the mental and physical self. This ability allows the hostage's mental self to take responsibility for the well-being of his physical self when he is otherwise unable to do so.

There are several examples of people with experience in separating the two: someone who has been diagnosed with a physically debilitating disease or undergone a significant medical procedure that severely limited physical movement to the point of being bedridden for a length of time or someone who has suffered major injuries as a result of a car crash or other significant accident. These people have experienced the realization that their physical body is held captive by their medical condition, and their day revolves mainly around their mental activities. They will have gone through their days of depression stemming from their lack of mobility and not being able to do the things they want to do, anger about why this happened to them, self-blame that they should have taken better physical care of themselves or listened to their doctor's advice, and frustration that they are powerless to change their present situation. When patients have finished going through these stages and have come to the decision at the crossroads that they will overcome this obstacle by whatever means, they shift their focus to their mental abilities and rely upon their mental toughness—their resolve to see them through. They call upon their will to live.

This situation is identical, although to a lesser extent, to that of someone whose mobility is restricted only by, say, a broken leg. They recognize the limitations the injury has on their ability to do all the things they want to do and, having likely tried to work through the pain, they eventually resign themselves to more sedentary mental pastimes, such as reading or doing crossword puzzles or cryptograms. The level of frustration, depression, and self-blame is different for a stay-at-home parent, the family income earner, an athlete, or an elderly person.

There is a third situation where certain individuals, by design, separate their mental self from their physical self, almost every day—athletes. The average daily runner who runs by choice for physical health learns that adding music to his daily run can essentially set his physical body on autopilot while distracting his mental self by the input of music. During their early days of running, these people began to realize that their body would continually inform their brain that this activity was causing it physical pain and that it should stop doing it. Of course runners know this "complaining" is normal, but they have decided that to achieve their goal of improved physical health, they have to overcome—essentially ignore—this almost continuous complaint from the physical self. To accomplish this, they find something else for their brain to do—listen to music, a distraction.

Each of the people in these examples has come to the same decision—to separate the physical self from the mental self. Two were by necessity, and the third was by choice. This is no different from hostages who find themselves physically captive, though under different physical conditions.

There are also many people who practice separating from their physical self through mental activities such as meditation. These people practice focusing strictly on their mental state and leave their physical self behind; this helps them experience a different level of consciousness and achieve a sense of mental relaxation. They often describe their experience as "out of body." When they emerge from their meditation exercise, they feel mentally and physically refreshed.

As a hostage, in order to survive months or years of captivity, you must come to the realization that your kidnappers control your body but they cannot control your mind. With your mind, you can go anywhere and do anything; you can escape into your imagination. Being able to accomplish this is one of your major survival strategies. It has been used successfully for many years by many hostages in a variety of situations; it will be your game changer. It can help you survive the unsurvivable.

On a personal note, for the last twenty years or more, I have used this same mental technique for ignoring pain while in the dentist's chair. My dentist provides me with headphones and AC/DC music. I turn up the volume, and the dentist goes to work. I have had numerous fillings replaced, teeth capped, even a root canal with only nitrous oxide, but no higher level of sedation; no freezing. New dental assistants frequently do not believe the dentist when he tells them they are working on a patient without freezing. I recall one assistant who, upon hearing this, pushed away from me in shock, her chair colliding with the wall. My dentist just laughed. He has even copied his best AC/DC music onto my personal disks and keeps them especially for my visits. Such is the power of being able to separate the mental self from the physical self (Dr. A. Camastra, personal information).

MENTAL STRATEGIES

As mentioned earlier, your behavioral self defines your mood, your day-to-day outlook, your mind-set, and your attitude. Your long-term behavioral self will influence your feelings of frustration or anger and your feelings of general happiness or sadness. These feelings culminate as a significant factor in defining your personality. Genetics is also a significant factor in determining personality, but that is beyond of the scope of this book.

Like the balance between our mental self and our physical self, our personality is pretty much fixed, but it too will fluctuate day to day depending on our circumstances. We all have a pretty good idea of our personality because we see and hear ourselves every day and we see how others respond to us every day. This is the psychology behind the Looking Glass Theory. We act, then we judge those actions by how others react to them, and then we adjust accordingly. Just as there are daily fluctuations in the balance between our mental selves and our physical selves, there are also fluctuations in our daily mood of happiness and sadness. Of course we know that regardless of how our day starts out, our mood is greatly influenced by the people and the circumstances we interact with each day. As these circumstances change throughout the day, so does our mood. This is where that sometimes humorous, sometimes antagonistic line comes in: "So how was your day?"

When you're a hostage, it's difficult to maintain a positive outlook and be in a good mood every day, all day long. You're being held captive against your will, you're not properly fed or clothed, and you certainly don't care for any of the people or personalities that you interact with every day. However, in order to effectively carry out your daily humanizing strategies, focusing on being passively compliant and reconciling with your physical treatment, you must learn to adjust your mood or at least learn to live with your mood. Here are some survival strategies to help you accomplish that.

Relaxation Techniques

In order for mental strategies to work, you have to relax. If you are not relaxed, you cannot think straight. If you cannot think straight, you cannot plan, organize, or make informed decisions because your brain—your mental self—is confused and disorderly.

Relaxation is the key to strategic thinking and making informed decisions. We experience this time after time in our everyday lives. We often hear, "Just give me a minute to think" or "I can't think with all this noise." You must relax your brain in order to apply it; you must apply your brain to problem-solving and focusing upon the survival strategies that will get you home safely.

Breathing

The most important technique in achieving relaxation is proper breathing. To regulate your breathing, use the 3-3-3-3 rule. Take in a long, slow, deep breath through your nose for three seconds, hold that breath in your lungs for three seconds, and then slowly exhale through your mouth for three seconds. Wait three seconds, and begin the cycle again. (You can adjust this to 4-4-4-4 or as required.)

Repeat this over and over until you begin to feel a sense of calm. Your goal is to achieve a calming rhythmic breathing sequence. This may take a couple of minutes, but there is no time limit because the longer you do this, the more relaxed you will feel. Breathing in through your nose and out through your mouth also increases the amount of oxygen your lungs will absorb per breath—an added benefit.

Smiling

Another factor in relaxing is changing your mood. We all know that our mood affects our facial expression. What our brain feels, our face shows. If we are angry, we form wrinkles across our brow, we tense our lips, and our face shows a scowl. If we are sad, our lower lip pushes out, and the corners of our mouth turn down. On the contrary, if we are happy, our lips turn up at the corners, and our lips and mouth form a smile. No surprise here. But conversely, you can just as easily change your mood by changing your face, and all you have to do is *smile.*

While you read this, hold a pen or pencil between your teeth—horizontally, sideways, corner to corner in your mouth. This artificially forms a smile, which remains until you remove the pen or pencil.

There have been a number of psychological studies involving smiling and its effects on mood and behavior. It has been scientifically proven that as much as your brain (your mood) affects the appearance of your face, conversely, so too will your facial expression affect your brain (your mood). One study showed that if a person holds a smile for at least forty-five seconds, it will have a positive psychological influence on the person's mood. This is a direct causal relationship. I have used this often, and it works. You can easily prove this to yourself any day when you feel angry or upset for any reason. Hold a nice big smile for forty-five seconds or more, and you will feel your mood change . . . for the better.

Meditation and Progressive Relaxation

Meditation practitioners often use a relaxation technique in which they mentally relax every muscle in their body through a systematic top-to-bottom or bottom-to-top sequence, that is, after they focus on relaxing through controlled breathing.

The person finds a comfortable position, lying down or sitting, and closes his eyes. He concentrates on mentally locating and identifying muscles—let's say in the toes; he focuses on mentally feeling each individual toe and consciously letting every muscle in that toe relax, feeling so relaxed and loose that he can feel it droop.

In the beginning, it may help to physically massage each muscle, digit, or limb to better assist the brain in locating it. The person then moves on to the foot, focusing on relaxing every muscle in the foot, the bottom of the foot, and then the ankle. The larger muscle groups such as the calf and thigh muscles are easier to mentally visualize because when they relax, there is discernible physical feedback. The person continues this technique all the way up the body, across the hips and abdomen, through the chest, shoulder, arms, wrists, and fingers. He finishes off with each muscle of the neck and face, which also provide a higher feedback response and then relaxes even the top of the scalp.

Once this is completed—and it can be done multiple times until the person is relatively confident he has relaxed each major and minor muscle group—the person finishes by visualizing a wave of relaxation flowing up and down his body. If you're not familiar with this technique and haven't used it before, it will take practice until you can achieve a level of relaxation. Many people with insomnia routinely use it.

This relaxation technique is very similar to the mental relaxation that a hypnotist strives for to access a gateway into your mental processes. A hypnotist can do so in only a few minutes. (Of course the volunteers have agreed to let him take over their mental self.) If you have ever been to a live hypnotist performance, you have seen the volunteers lined up on stage as the hypnotist goes down the line, testing and selecting which volunteers are the most relaxed and are most susceptible to suggestion. The ones that are visually not relaxed enough or the ones that are resisting his instructions are asked to take their seats. This level of relaxation is exactly the result you want to achieve. Once you have relaxed physically and mentally, you can begin to apply the visualization strategies that I will cover shortly, strategies that will provide you with the ability to escape the inescapable.

PSYCHOLOGICAL STRATEGIES

All military and police basic training camps share a common goal: to prove to every recruit that he or she is mentally and physically capable of more than they realize. Recruits are put through days and weeks of physical endurance activities that go far beyond anything they have experienced thus far in their lives. They are often sleep-deprived while exposed to physically exhausting activities presented in tandem with mentally challenging tasks, all the while being exposed to verbal ridicule and personal insults. To the casual observer, it might just look and sound mean, but it has a much higher purpose.

A critical component of these boot camps is the staff's constant mocking and teasing that the recruit should quit, that it would be so much easier if they just quit. All the pain and suffering would stop if they just quit. "Just say I quit and you can go home" or "Just say I quit and all this will be over" or "Just walk over and ring the bell."

Psychologically, what the training staff is doing is underscoring and verbalizing what the recruit's own brain is telling him to do—to quit. Of course the recruit's physical self is saying "This hurts, let's quit and go home," but the recruit's mental self is saying "No, I want to do this, I must do this, I will not quit." The valuable lesson the recruit learns is being able to separate the suffering physical self from the determined mental self.

Boot camp staff could preach to recruits all day long that they are physically and mentally capable of much more than they could ever believe, but the recruits must learn this for themselves—their spirit, their psyche must be taught this. When boot camp is over, every recruit will have experienced more physical pain and mental anguish than ever before in their lives. But they have learned the objective of the camp—they have mastered themselves. They can psychologically separate their mental from their physical self. They are now able to go physically and mentally further than they have ever gone before, because they have redefined their own personal limits. They have taken their minds and bodies further than they would ever have believed possible. They have taken their minds and bodies to a higher level; they will never be the same person again. Most parents of these recruits say the same thing—they came back changed. More confident yet more relaxed—some called it *character*. What they experienced was pain and suffering; what they learned was resolve and determination. *They learned to overcome physical adversity through the application of willpower.*

Every person's mental and physical abilities are like the speedometer in a car. The car is engineered and built to go faster and farther than you would normally drive, yet virtually no one ever pushes their car to the limit of its speedometer. These boot camp recruits have pushed their limits—they have a new personal maximum.

This experience teaches the recruits that when carrying out their duties in the field, when they feel physically exhausted and when they want to quit, they will not quit—they know they are capable of so much more. They will continue to fight the good fight. Military mottos and chants are made of such things: "Be All That You Can Be" and "An Army of One," United States Army; "Semper Fi" (Always Faithful), US Marine Corps; "Never, ever, ever give up," attributed to the fighting philosophy of Winston Churchill.

This boot camp lesson demonstrates how a hostage must act if he wants to survive. A hostage must continue to bear up against impossible odds; he must persevere. A hostage must continue to fight the good fight even though his body or his brain wants him to give up and quit. His family and friends do not want him to quit; they want him to keep fighting. The hostage must continue to survive—he must do whatever is necessary to survive. He must hear in his own head the voices of his spouse and children saying, "Don't give up," "Don't give up, Dad," and "Don't give up, sweetheart." The hostage must push his limits of mental and physical endurance; he must set himself a new maximum.

I had to "go deep within myself to see what I had to survive" (Lindhout and Corbett 2013).

Be Positive

Psychological survival is aided by maintaining a positive and constructive mind-set. A hostage can maintain his positive outlook by restating supportive chants such as "I am alive," "I am not sick," "I have my imagination and my memories to keep me company," "I am fed," and "I can get through this." Remember the parallel strategy with outdoor survival. Take personal and material inventory, identify a goal then establish a strategy for reaching that goal. Hostage survival is no different.

The definition of *survival* is existence, endurance, subsistence, and staying alive. A hostage can set up a daily routine of positive chants. He can tell himself every morning, "I can survive *one more day*" and then *do it*! He must also remind himself of his survival strategy plans: "I will work to improve my living conditions," "I will continue with my religious prayers," "I will not let them defeat me," "I am better than they are," "I will go home."

Even hardened combat troops such as SEAL teams, HRTs, joint task forces (JTF2), the SAS, and so on use these same reinforcing mental mantras: "I will not die today" and "I am strong." The commanders and the instructors of these elite troops recognize the strength that such mentally supportive mantras can bring to a soldier deployed in the field while living and fighting in overwhelming and life-threatening conditions.

Mental Imagination and Visualization Strategies

Imagination and visualization techniques can reduce your stress, improve your mood, provide positive reinforcement, and enhance your overall positive outlook. Imagination and visualization can help you escape.

For Jim Loney, the worst part of his months in captivity, "worse than the physical pain, worse than the mental stresses, was the 'excruciating boredom.' The pain of bruises was nothing compared to the psychological pain" (Captivity 2011).[10]

Visualizing is constructing familiar sights, smells, and sounds, visually constructing a safer, happier, and relaxing place where you can meet friends and family and do the things that make you happy.

Amanda Lindhout visualized the planning, designing, and decorating of every room in a large, brand-new house for many hours a day, hence the name of her book depicting her fifteen months of captivity, *A House in the Sky* (2013).

---

[10] In November 2005, James Loney and three other men, all peace activists, were taken hostage at gunpoint in Baghdad. They were held by a previously unknown group called the Swords of Righteousness Brigade, who demanded the release of all persons taken prisoner by the United States during the occupation of Iraq. During their 118 days of captivity, one hostage was killed by his captors and subsequently the other three were rescued by Task Force Black, a joint British SAS and US Special Forces counterkidnap group.

This technique has proven to be so helpful for so many hostages that to me, it is the premier strategy to escape the daily physical pain, the mental anguish, the boredom and the suffering that hostages must endure for months and sometimes years on end. Imagination is your sanctuary. Imagination is your escape. Imagination is your freedom. If you lose your head, your body will be close behind.

VISUALIZATION: GETTING STARTED

> Something happens when you're alone most of the time, when there are no distractions. Your mind grows more powerful—muscular, even. It takes over and starts to carry you. . . . I could feel a new sort of energy making itself known to me. It felt physical and also not physical. (Lindhout and Corbett 2013)

For those readers who are not familiar with the practice of imagination and visualization, imagination is using your mental capacity of daydreaming, but you take it to a whole new level; you take it to its maximum. It is thinking of a place you know so well that you can rebuild it in your own mind. Visualization is the practice of training your brain to recall the colors, the sounds, and the smells; recall and add every little nuance that will reconstruct a place, an event, or an activity in as much detail as possible—so much detail in fact, that it will appear real. Just like when you awake from a dream that was so vivid, so exact in detail, so realistic in sound and smell that it was "real," you can also do the reverse.

Just as smiling for over forty-five seconds changes your facial expression, which in turn directly affects your brain and your mood, so too can visualization affect your brain and your mood. Visualization is essentially constructing your own dreams—dreams that are so realistic, so vivid in visual and acoustic detail, so intense in the smells and the voices that you can convince your brain that you were really there. You can actually build your own dreams. You have the memories, you have the mental capacity, and you most certainly have plenty of time. You have every day, all day long to focus on treating yourself to what you want to do and where you want to go. All you need is an idea and the willingness to try and practice.

It is important to be relaxed when you want to visualize. As I wrote earlier, you cannot think clearly or mentally focus if you are not relaxed. So relax first, visualize second. The more relaxed you are, the easier it will be to visualize.

> Once I got myself into the groove, the force of memory
> was nearly hypnotic. I found I could pass hours that
> way. (Buchanan 2014, 223)

If this is a new technique for you, a little instruction is in order. Close your eyes and imagine seeing the color red. Do it again and see a red so bright it almost hurts your eyes. Now look again and see a deeper red—say, a maroon or a burgundy red, like a red wine perhaps. Close your eyes and picture your favorite apple—did you also see it as red, round, and plump or green with a soft brushed surface?

Close your eyes and picture the color green, like a lush and healthy green lawn. Now picture the many shades of green like you might see when the sun shines through the back side of an ocean wave as it rises up and begins to curl and then seems to stand for a second before it drops and breaks onto the beach. Now see another wave rising up with all those same greens, but add the blues of the ocean behind it. As it too rises and then drops, add the sound of the wave collapsing like thunder. See, listen, and hear the sound of the water and white foam hissing toward you as it climbs the sand upward and onto your sandy beach. Can you hear the clattering and clicking rocks as retreating waves pull them back to the sea?

As you get better at visualizing this particular scene, add the view of a long, white, crescent-shaped beach stretching out in front of you, and then feel yourself walking along this beach, your toes sinking gently into the sand with each step while your sandals hang from the fingers of your hand. You can see and hear wave after wave crashing along the shore ahead; you can smell the saltiness of the ocean and hear the seabirds as they circle and squawk in the blue sky overhead.

Watch as the little sandpipers scurry up and down as they search for morsels of food brought in by the waves.

If you've spent time at a cottage on a lake, you can recall the sound of an aluminum boat gently thumping against the dock. You can see the early morning mist rising off the lake as you sit with your first coffee in this serenity—this peaceful scene.

Of course it's easier to visualize what is most familiar because you know it so well. You have many memories of what is familiar because you have seen it over and over again and under a variety of circumstances. Everyone can visualize every room inside of their house or their apartment and from a variety of angles. When you're sitting as a hostage in a dark room and you want to feel like you're at home, you can.

You have walked into your house or your apartment hundreds—maybe even thousands—of times. Close your eyes, relax, and walk through your front door. What do you see directly ahead of you? What colors are on the walls beside you and ahead of you? What pictures are on each wall? See the light fixtures, the floor coverings, and each piece of furniture. Take your time and do this in the very finest detail.

Then do whatever you habitually do next. Take off your jacket, undoing it button by button, remove your arms from each sleeve, grab your jacket by the collar, open the closet door and select a hanger, slide the hanger into each shoulder of your jacket, lift and hang your jacket onto the closet bar that holds so many other jackets, and close the closet door.

Then do whatever you normally do next. If you take your keys out of your pocket and place them in a bowl on the table right beside you, then do that. If you take off your shoes and place them on a mat on the floor beside you, then do that.

As you walk forward, what next comes into view? Do you see your living room or dining room next, or do you see your kitchen? Visualize each of these rooms down to the finest detail. The exact size, color, and texture of each piece of furniture, the color of each wall, the artwork on each wall, the floor covering, each window and how much light is coming into the room and from what angle.

What can you hear? Can you hear music from the radio, or is the television on? Can you hear what song is playing, or can you tell what show is on the television? The more detail you can bring into this trip home, the more rewarding your experience will be.

> Instead, my days blended away inside my imagination. Since I didn't know if I would ever see my home again, I visited it in my mind and made it a point to visualize every detail I could, to deepen the experience and prolong the amount of time I might have away from my surroundings. . . . I pushed myself to focus. (Buchanan 2014, 223)

For many, visualizing a familiar activity or hobby may be easier and more rewarding. For those so inclined, build a house. Draw the plans, line by line; watch the excavators dig the foundation, pour the concrete. Visualize getting into your car, and while driving to the lumber yard, remember every turn, stop sign, and traffic signal. At the lumber yard, go through ordering and purchasing every kind of framing lumber, nail, and fastener you'll need for the first phase.

As you build the house, visualize measuring for every 2 × 4 and stud, mark each one with your pencil, pick up your saw, and watch yourself cutting it, then put the stud into position and go through hammering every nail. Do this piece by piece for every piece of wood for the framing, the window openings, and the door openings.

> I tried to climb away from the shock of what my life had become. In my mind I built stairways. At the end of the stairways, I imagined rooms. These were high airy places with big windows and a cool breeze moving through. I imagined one room opening brightly onto another room until I'd built a house, a place with hallways and more staircases. I put myself there, and that's where I lived, in the wide-open sky of my mind. I made friends and read books . . . I ate pancakes drizzled in syrup and took baths . . . . This

wasn't longing, and it wasn't insanity. It was relief. It got me through. (Lindhout and Corbett 2013)

My imagination had begun to occupy more of my awareness than physical reality. As happens with anything practiced for hours every day over a period of months, I had developed visualization skills that made living either in memory or in fantasy a convincing experience . . . And I felt how deeply this kidnapping ordeal had amplified my natural desire for human closeness, far beyond anything I'd known before. On most nights, that meant a silent conversation with my mom. (Jessica Buchanan and Erik Landemalm, *Impossible Odds* 2013, 145)

If you get interrupted at any time by one of your guards unlocking your cell door because it's time to empty your toilet bucket, you can easily pick up building your house where you left off or continue your walk along the beach.

Build a life-size boat—again, in detail. Design the boat with all the sails, rigging, floor plans, electronics, anchors, and fenders. Visualize laying the keel, putting in the ribs, putting in the knees—screws or wooden pegs? Put in every screw, one by one. Lay every plank, one by one. Paint the hull, stroke by stroke.

If hobbies aren't your strength, how about commuting or travel? How many times have you driven from your house to the office, from your house to the cottage or to a friend's house? Visualize it. You have commuted to the office maybe hundreds of times. Every house, every traffic sign, every sight and sound is imprinted on your memory; it is there in your mind. Find it. Use it.

Walk out of your front door, look around, and recall every detail—the sights and smells of your yard and the house across the street. Feel the wind on your face, describe your car, unlock your car, sit down into it, and look across the dashboard, remembering every detail, every gauge, and every button. You have sat in this car hundreds of times—now test yourself on how much detail you can recall. After you start and drive out of your driveway, recall every little pothole or nuance in the roadway. Can you see and describe every house on your street as you pass it by? Do this for every street on your drive. You have done this before—remember which stores are along the way, what color they are. Even see and hear the other traffic on the roadway.

Do in your head what you have done many times before or something you have always wanted to do. Build a wooden boat, build a model airplane, sit on the sand by the seashore in every little detail. This stuff works. Using it will help you pass the hours in the days, the days in the weeks, and with them, the months of captivity with their never-ending boredom. Visualizing will help you keep your sanity. *Your imagination is your refuge.*

When Terry Waite was held hostage for over four years, he passed the time by writing his autobiography . . . in his head. When he returned home, he simply published it: *Footfalls in Memory* (Waite 1997).

Then there are always the movies. If hobbies don't work for you, perhaps your favorite movies will. What movie do you like so much that you've watched it five or ten or maybe even fifteen times? Visualize watching that movie from the very beginning. Watch it from the opening scene with all the dialogue and detail until the end, and don't forget to add the music. What a great way to spend the afternoon in your cell, watching your favorite movie! What about visualizing a favorite book, a story you know so well you could actually reread it in your head.

Many hostages visualize talking to people—their spouse and their children. With very little practice, they could hear their children's voices and their laughter. They could hear their words of encouragement: "You can do this, Dad," "You can survive this, Dad," "Don't let this beat you," "You can do one . . . more . . . day." These voices can be your anchor.

Many hostages spoke with people they'd had disagreements or arguments with in the past. They apologized to them and made amends. This act of contrition alone has given many hostages the important peace of mind that comes only with the absence of guilt and regret. They felt good making amends to those they may have offended or hurt, and as a result, a huge psychological weight was lifted off their shoulders.

"I made peace with anyone who might have been an enemy. I asked forgiveness for every vain or selfish thing I'd ever done in my life" (Lindhout and Corbett 2013). If the worst should happen, a hostage can face this tragedy with peace of mind. He can feel he has righted wrongs and made amends. This sense of relief, this peace of mind, this closure and resolution will bring calm where there was once only fear.

Many hostages have spoken about how their confinement and treatment caused them psychological pain as well as physical pain. Psychological pain is brought on by emotional suffering. The origins of this suffering can often be from an unrelenting sense of guilt or remorse. Untreated or unresolved psychological pain can often lead to psychosomatic disorders as the mind attempts to camouflage this sense of psychological guilt by providing a real physical pain as a diversion. Amanda Lindhout's usage of visualization to make peace and ask forgiveness had the added benefit of a significant positive impact on psychological pain.

Amanda goes on to write about the voices of fear in her head that had been replaced by a stronger voice, a voice of calm.

> It said, See? You are okay, Amanda. It's your body that's suffering, and you are not your body. The rest of you is fine. Things became more bearable then—not easier, just more bearable. I was alone and shackled, but the rest of me was okay. The rest of me knew not to panic. It had a place to go. Anywhere, anywhere, I reminded myself, I could go anywhere. (Lindhout and Corbett 2013)

Visualization can also serve as an anchor to the future. Jessica Buchanan visualized a warm, tender moment in which she and her husband shared feeling the gentle breath, soft smooth skin, and clean baby hair of their yet-to-be-conceived baby. "That scene helped me keep going, much farther than I would have been able to do on my own, reminding me I had to survive this ordeal and allow the images to become reality" (Buchanan 2014, 228).

> "And then the strangest thing happened. I felt the gentle pressure of a clasp on my hand, and in my head I heard David's voice, true as life, as clear as my dreams: 'You're going to do this. I know you will. You're much stronger than me'" (Tebbutt, p. 135).

Hostages—or anyone who has used visualization as a mental aid—will tell you that their visions were so real and so lifelike that they actually miss them. They miss the house that they built; they miss that seashore and the quiet cup of coffee watching the sunrise with friends. These visualizations can be that real, that cherished.

Science is strange. Sometimes healing the body also heals the mind, and sometimes, healing the mind also heals the body.

CHAPTER 14
ESCAPE

No circumstances of hostage confinement can be considered without mentioning escape. In my scenarios, escape decisions must not be taken lightly. Escape should be considered only if the attempt is likely to succeed to the point of rescue—to the point of freedom. Escape for the sake of escape must be attempted only if death is imminent. That said, you are the hostage; you have more information than anyone  else, and you are the best one to decide what you should do. But to be successful, you must think it through.

As mentioned earlier about criminals, there is always more planning put into the actual robbery than into the getaway. Considering what may be facing you when you escape, the easiest part may be escaping your confinement. Like the dog chasing a car and then the car stops, so you're out—now what do you do?

An escape plan is more than just getting out of the window. Do you know where you are? Do you know where you're going and how you will get there? If you escape in a large city, there may be police or military patrols that you could flag down; if you're in the country, the only people on the road will likely be from your village or camp, and they will quickly recognize you. If you are held in a rural Middle Eastern country or in North, West, or East Africa, in arid or semi-arid climates, there is sparse vegetation, so hiding will be difficult.

Many hostages have escaped confinement in Somalia only to die of exposure in the desert.

Which way is north, south? Where is the closest village? Will you be better off in that village? Will you be given up and returned by those villagers? If you escape confinement without knowing where you are or where you're going, you may escape only to travel into rebel territory and be taken hostage by another terrorist group, who may treat you even worse than the one you have just escaped. When they find out that you escaped confinement somewhere else, you can bet you will be confined, bound, and treated accordingly.

We know that politics in many of these regions changes rapidly, and territory that was once held by terrorists or organized crime groups may now be in the hands of government forces or vice versa. You may think you're running toward safety when you are actually running toward more trouble.

Do you have the physical strength to make it? Do you have food and water? clothing? a disguise? You are probably estimating your ability to travel based upon your preconfinement health and fitness level. You will have lost weight, and much of that weight loss will be muscle mass and, along with it, physical stamina.

Do you have the proper clothing necessary to make a successful escape? Most hostages are relieved of their shoes for this reason alone. As a fugitive, are you able to be disguised as a local until you get out of danger? Can you take a blanket with you for warmth, sun protection, and as a disguise? Remember, you are a foreigner, and as such, you are easily recognized—you stand out. The more rural the location, the more obvious you will be. Can you speak enough of the language to ask for help?

Is the unknown better than where you are? If you are held captive in a desert or on a ship, the environment is your fence; the environment is your prison. An environment like the famed prisons in barren and frozen Siberia or in the southern swamplands of Florida and Louisiana are still used today for this reason. It also reduces the overhead. Remember the movie *Papillion*? Escape was the easy part; surviving was the real test. Although prisoners in Alcatraz could hear partiers in San Francisco, Alcatraz was successful because of its long cold-water swim, with strong bay currents and sharks. If you escape only to be recaptured, you will likely be seriously punished, and the remainder of your captivity will be made worse—much worse. Amanda Lindhout escaped, only to be quickly recaptured and dragged back to an awaiting vehicle by her ankles and sometimes by her hair. As a direct result, she endured unbelievable physical punishment.

> He bound my arms together just above the elbows and below the biceps. My shoulders and chest pulled up awkwardly . . . my whole torso arched. My hands and feet were roped together, pulling in opposite directions. I was immobilized. My body had been drawn into a taut bow. My muscles immediately began to scream. . . . I was trussed like an animal. My panic was immediate. I couldn't last a minute this way. I couldn't even last a second. I couldn't form a thought beyond the pain of that position, my back straining from neck to tailbone. . . . The twisted sheet cut into my arms and ankles, cutting off circulation. My lungs felt compressed. I struggled to breathe, gagging as if someone were pouring sand down my throat. . . . Pain tore through my shoulders and back, searing the length of my spine. (Lindhout and Corbett 2013)

Later that night a guard entered, and she pleaded to be untied.

> Whoever it was, he was tugging at my sheet, using his bare foot for leverage. I felt a new tension in my shoulders, my thighs lifting higher off the ground. He'd only come to tighten the knots. By morning, I'd peed myself . . . (Lindhout and Corbett 2013)

Many hours later . . .

> Someone had entered the room and wrapped what seemed to be a scarf around my neck, so that any

time my head started to sag, the tension on the scarf
caused me to choke. They've studied this, I thought.
They've consulted some manual on how to make a
person suffer. (Lindhout and Corbett 2013)

*Since her release, Amanda Lindhout has admitted that accounts
of her worst treatment were not included in her book.*

Possibly the most important decision you must make before
you attempt an escape is whether you are prepared to fight. Are
you prepared to injure or kill a guard in order to escape? Can you
overpower your guard and take his keys? How will you do that?
Will you use physical strength? Do you have a weapon? If you are
successful in unchaining yourself and climbing out of the window
only to drop down in front of one of your captors, are you able and
willing to kill him? This is not a situation where you can just say
"Oops, sorry" and climb back into the window. If you injure or kill
someone during an escape attempt, there is no turning back; if you
can escape without causing injury or death, well done.

If you are being held with other hostages, be careful to whom you
tell your escape plans in case one of your fellow hostages informs the
guards, hoping to receive better treatment or even release. You may
be surprised, both positively and negatively, about the behaviors your
fellow hostages may display under stress.

If recaptured, you will lose all hard-won rapport, and you will
never be trusted again. You may also lose your hostage ranking. If
you were initially kidnapped strictly for ransom, the problems and the
embarrassment your escape may have caused your captors, especially
if there were injuries involved, may change their minds. They may
now hold you for execution instead. Your treatment from now on may
also be based upon the kind of problems you caused for your captors,
especially if any of your guards were disciplined or beaten as a direct
result of your attempt.

Again, as I mentioned earlier, you are the hostage; you have more
information than anyone else, and you are the one to decide what
you should do. It is your life that hangs in the balance, not mine or

anyone else's. I have only outlined what must be considered before you attempt an escape.

Hometown Escape—Active Shooter

Just for a moment, if you find yourself outside of my particular scenarios, that is, if you have been abducted from your family in your own hometown, escape if you can. You know where you are; you speak the language—of course, escape. You know very well that if you can escape your initial confinement, just walking down the center of the street will attract attention or elicit a phone call, and soon the police will arrive. Is there a computer in the house that you can use to send an e-mail? Is there a cell phone to call 911? If you can pull a fire alarm, you may well have your freedom. Even if you have to escape your confinement stark naked and walk down the center of the road to attract attention, so what? Do it.

If you are held hostage in a coffee shop or in a school classroom and you see a clear opportunity to escape unharmed, take it. Can you safely jump out of a window or run out through an unlocked door?

Just as abductors in my foreign scenarios are nervous—and yes, even frightened—so too are hostage takers and lone gunmen in your hometown. Lone gunmen are unpredictable, yet in many ways, they are predictable. The first few minutes of the situation are chaos. There are people screaming and running in all directions. The hostage taker or the active shooter has to make countless assessments of people, places, times, and actions and make an immediate decision for each one. His earliest decisions might be more irrational—made in the heat of the moment, as it were. Later decisions, made after some thought, might be more rational. Before the hostage taker or the active shooter can get all the doors locked or all the windows locked, search for and round up everyone—there will be more opportunities for escape. The larger the building he is trying to command, the more avenues for escape. If you can't escape, what can you hide in or hide behind that may be bulletproof? What about behind the vending machines, the photocopier, or the filing cabinets?

Single hostage takers, especially, grow weary from the continued pressure of the countless mental stresses brought on by their own actions. Their mental and physical fatigue will soon cause them to make mistakes in judgment; take advantage of these mistakes. Their fatigue will cause them to doze off and fall asleep; take advantage and escape. These hostage takers have become hostages themselves, by their own actions. They are now victims of their own poor planning; take advantage of their lack of forethought. Look for an escape opportunity and take it.

As I mentioned earlier in my definition of being a hostage versus being a prisoner, it is very difficult for anyone on the outside—or on the inside, for that matter—to be able to make an early accurate assessment of the shooter's intentions. Is this a hostage situation or an active shooter situation? Is he a terrorist, a criminal or mentally deficient? The answer to those questions will determine if you will be held and exchanged for some consideration or if you will be hunted down and murdered. Just as my philosophy throughout this book has been that a hostage must take active steps in his own physical and mental health, so too must a person who finds himself in what might be an active-shooter situation take deliberate action to preserve his own life.

One very important question is, again, are you prepared to kill this gunman? Are you familiar with the weapon? Just as in your escape planning during a long-term hostage scenario, in a lone gunman situation, your escape may depend on your being willing and able to kill or overpower the gunman. This book is not a "how to" in that regard, but in many situations where the hostages or prisoners outnumber the lone gunman, such as on an aircraft or a train, in a café, and as prison staff are trained to do, each hostage/guard takes one arm or one leg and holds on, regardless of what happens. You may have seen this same technique on television, when police arrest someone during a riot. It may look like police brutality, five against one, but it is actually the safest and most effective way to restrain and take somebody into custody without injury to the officers or the prisoner. Each officer is assigned one specific duty: left leg/right leg, left arm/right arm, weapon, handcuffs, and so on. When it happens, it must happen quickly and completely; the gunman must be overwhelmed. After the gunman is subdued, use belts, neck ties, or nylons as ropes to tie him up.

Lone gunmen may have planned *what to do* for a long time, but they don't devote a lot of time planning *how to do* it. After the first few seconds of chaos and pandemonium, the element of surprise is gone, and they don't really know what will happen next. You are likely to be very familiar with the physical layout of the building, so you will have information about nearest escape routes and good hiding places. Plan ahead. During your normal activities in your office building or your school building, look for escape routes and hiding places. Mentally prepare how to lock and barricade doors. Remember to pull the fire alarm before you hide, as this will often be the quickest way to alert first responders. It will also get the attention of everyone else in the building and may also scare the shooter and cause him to leave the building. Think, plan, then act.

Again, you have the most information about your situation, its opportunities, and your abilities. The decision to escape cannot be made by anyone but you.

The December 2014 hostage taking at the coffee shop in Sydney, Australia, is an excellent example of many hostages recognizing an escape opportunity and taking it. In first-world countries, police hostage rescue teams, SWAT teams, and uniformed police officers are aware that civilians are being held hostage, and therefore, they will be watching for hostages to escape. You are not in any danger if you escape and maintain a nonthreatening posture. Be aware that once you are in police custody, they must physically search you and confirm your identity, to determine that you are who you say you are and not the hostage taker trying to escape disguised as a hostage. You can expect to be immediately debriefed by the police, who will be seeking information about the number of hostage takers, the kind of weapons, the number of hostages, where they are, and so on. Do not be in a rush to leave and get home. Take the time to provide as much information as you can to assist other hostages that may still be held.

These "hometown" situations are certainly not the focus of this book, but escaping long-term hostage situations and escaping lone gunmen situations have their similarities.

HELPING YOURSELF, MESSAGING AND SIGNALING FOR HELP

Back to my Middle East scenarios. Part of any survival strategy—and any escape strategy, for that matter—is looking for ways to improve the odds for your own rescue. You're already applying humanizing strategies every chance you get. You're attempting to improve your living conditions by building rapport, you're passively compliant, and you're openly practicing religion. You're using mental relaxation and visualization to combat boredom to relieve any regrets or guilt and improve your overall mental health. But you must never become complacent. You must always consider every activity that even in some small way may lead to your freedom. You must always be thinking, "What else can I do?"

A hostage can sit back and grumble, "What's the use? That's never gonna work" or "What are the chances of that happening?" But consider that every single lottery winner beat the odds.

A hostage has an obligation to himself to do everything in his power—using both mind and body to assist in his own rescue. Look around—what do you see? What can you use? Like the old TV series, what can you "MacGyver"? (MacGyver was a mild-mannered government agent who refused to wear a gun and always found ingenious ways to escape tight predicaments by fashioning escape tools from everyday items, toys, and trash or household chemicals.)

Can you fashion a handcuff key from a nail, from a piece of tin can, from a brass shell casing, from a piece of wire or a bottle cap? Can you spend hours loosening a chain from the bricks in the wall by twisting it? If there is a window with a blind, can you poke tiny holes into it so that at night when the light is on inside the room, the letters *SOS* or *USA* or *CDA* or *HELP* shine through? *SOS* in Morse code is dot-dot-dot, dash-dash-dash, dot-dot-dot. Can you write a note on a piece of trash that might be found? How about a note in a bottle? In many countries, kids still collect bottles for money. Could your note be found and turned in to authorities? If the house where you are being held is being watched for any reason, be it as a terrorist hideout, a drug-smuggling operation, or a weapons stash, authorities may be inspecting the trash for evidence. If they find your note, things could change for the better very soon.

If you are held in the open desert, what can you do? If you are allowed to walk around, can your footprints make a message or a simple arrow? Can you signal an aircraft with the shiny lid of a tin can? Again, SOS is probably your best bet. I am not aware of any country where the government does not have air supremacy, so any aircraft will be "friendly." Also consider that many aircraft—manned and unmanned—may not be visible, so signaling to an apparently empty sky may still yield results. Be careful to signal only into the sky.

If you camped in the open desert, for days or even just for the night, can you leave a note under a rock or buried in the sand where it might be found? Again, this is in case some enforcement agency is following your vehicles and looking for evidence. They may suspect you are in the group, and a note will provide confirmation and proof.

If you are held in a cell, a small room, or even in the open desert, leave some kind of message behind. If out in the open, you can scratch your initials and the date on a rock and leave it face down for someone who may be following you to find. In a cell or in a room, scratch your name and the date on a brick in the wall or in the corner of the room. Remember to keep the date current from time to time.

In order to leave a DNA trail behind, leave a small lock of hair possibly tucked into the corner bricks but showing slightly. You can leave behind small pieces of paper that you have covered in saliva or blood and dried. These can be examined for DNA matches and used to trace the locations, health, movements, and timelines of hostages.

These strategies are tools that can be applied to whatever situation you need to fix. As you assess your situation and as your situation changes for whatever reason, your strategies will change. You are playing a chess game for your life. You are playing an opponent without him knowing it. You cannot divulge a strategy; you must keep a poker face and be prepared should your opponent change the rules.

SUICIDE

Suicide must be discussed, but *it is never an option*. A hostage has so much time to sit and ponder his options, to consider all manner of possible outcomes of his situation, and to weigh the many do's and don'ts that suicide is always considered. Time, if not properly used, can be a detriment to your will to live. "I think about killing myself. But if I do, he wins" (Berry and DeJesus 2015).

> I considered suicide a valid option among the few available to me . . . I'm glad to note that I was never seriously tempted, and despite the extreme depression and confusion in those early horrible days and nights, I knew that such an act would have to be weighed exceedingly carefully against the devastating impact on my family and, most immediately, on Louis [his co-hostage]. I agree with those—like Mary—who hold that suicide is an essentially selfish act in all but the most extreme circumstances. (Fowler 2012, 183)

In a single-hostage situation, there must be a concerted effort toward maintaining positive mental and psychological health. This is not easy. A single hostage has many responsibilities. He must be his own conscience, adviser, physician, confidant, emotional support, and best friend. This is a huge responsibility for one person to endure for weeks and months on end. This is social deprivation and segregation. It can lead to depression caused by sheer loneliness.

> As hard as this is to admit, I want him to talk to me, just not about sex. I need someone to talk to. I haven't had a real conversation with anyone in eighteen months. (Berry and DeJesus 2015)

It is during times like these that hostages are tempted to convert to other religions, give in to their captor's request to make videos, and sign confessions. Months of segregation and social isolation will tempt a hostage to do anything for some human contact—human social interaction of any kind, good or bad. It's during these times that hostages can become dangerously susceptible to suggestion, especially their own flawed logic and pessimism, born of depression and a sense of hopelessness.

<p style="text-align:center">~~~</p>

People who cannot imagine a future tend to dwell in the past. However, short nostalgic visits to the past are beneficial as anchors.

Nostalgia is reminiscing and reliving happy times. It can bring you comfort. It is a coping mechanism to help you feel good about yourself and improve your mental health. However, a hostage cannot become obsessive about nostalgia because it can lead to increased homesickness and depression.

<p style="text-align:center">~~~</p>

Any hostage who finds himself actually considering suicide must recognize this as a sign that he must concentrate even harder on positive imagination and relaxation techniques. Remember these thoughts are symptoms of barbed-wire psychosis. If you could talk to your spouse or one of your kids, they would say, "Hang in there," "You can do this," "Don't let them beat you." A hostage must find strength in his religion, in his family situation. Live to see others. Consider the sorrow that your suicide will cause to your loved ones. A hostage must reaffirm his resolve to make it home safely. He must work to control his emotions—focus on the positives because there are many, count them.

Remember, there are life insurance implications. No life insurance policy I am aware of will pay any benefits if the policyholder's death was by suicide. Of course this will be difficult to prove one way or the other, given the extreme situation and being so far from home. A suggestion by the captors that a hostage committed suicide while in captivity will not be legal proof, but a family doesn't need another complication on top of what they have already endured. Suicide has financial implications on your family's ability to move forward, your children's education, and their future.

Talk yourself out of depression; recognize the symptoms of onset. Be positive, optimistic, and upbeat. Smile—remember that smiling for forty-five seconds will positively influence your mood. This may be the time for more prayer, time to make up another song. Remember, they cannot control your brain. They may have your body, but in your mind, you can go anywhere and do anything. Force yourself to relax and come up with more options. Realize these times are expected; these times and these thoughts are normal. Recognize that many before you have also come to this point. They too had these thoughts and they made their way through them; you will too. This is a test of your will to live. Go to your anchors; go to your happiest places.

Remind yourself of the many survival stories you've heard, such as around-the-world solo sailboat racers. Many a racer has been rolled over and demasted in the middle of the ocean; no mast means no sails, hundreds, even thousands of miles from shore. Do you think they just said, "Oh well, that's it. Guess I'll just jump overboard and drown myself." No, they didn't. They figured out how to survive. I do not know of a single one that saw no other way to survive and committed suicide. They took stock of their situation, where they were, what equipment they had to work with, and what skills they possessed. Then they got on with it. They got on with figuring out how to survive. Many of these sailors took five, six, or more days in the open ocean fighting seas, winds, and fatigue to make it to shore. Most racers got parts and repairs, which often took many days or even weeks, and got back in the race.

We have heard the stories of fishermen who, for one reason or another, spent days, weeks, or even months floating around in the open ocean before rescue. They took stock of what they had, what they knew, and what they needed to do to survive for as long as it might take. They had no option but to survive. Hostages too must convince themselves they have no option but to survive.

You are capable of much more than you know. You can survive much more mental and physical punishment than you realize. A single hostage must be their own coach, their own cheerleader and their own support group. Consider this as just a long boot camp where your body wants to give up but your mind won't let it.

CHAPTER 15
MULTIPLE-HOSTAGE SITUATIONS

As with single-hostage situations, treatment of multiple hostages is dependent upon the personalities, the temperament, and the experience of their captors, and how well multiple hostages are housed and maintained depends on the resources of their captors. Holding multiple hostages requires larger facilities, which are difficult to conceal in more populated areas. The comings and goings of the numbers of guards, the changing of shifts, the size of the facilities required for the guards, food storage and preparation, plus the amounts of garbage produced by a relatively large number of people are difficult to conceal and, therefore, difficult to keep secret. The logistics alone for keeping multiple hostages necessitate a holding facility in a more rural location or in a much more secure operating environment. This fact alone restricts smaller terrorist groups from holding any more than a few hostages at a time in any one location.

These logistical requirements, however, do not restrict a terrorist group from holding multiple hostages if, in fact, the group is operating with the knowledge and consent of whoever controls the area or the group holds the territory themselves. This is certainly the case for Boko Haram, a terrorist group in Africa that controls a large amount of territory in countries with a weak and ineffective government. Boko Haram routinely raids villages within the country and captures sometimes hundreds of girls at a time. Because they control the territory, they can openly hold multiple hostages in relative safety for months or even years.

This is the same situation for Al-Shabaab, a terrorist group operating out of Somalia. They attacked the West Mall in Nairobi, Kenya, targeting non-Muslim civilians and they routinely take civilian and government hostages inside Kenya and Somalia. Their cousins, the Somali pirates, kidnap vacationing couples in small sailboats anywhere near the Horn of Africa or attack and swarm monstrous international container and cargo ships a hundred miles offshore. At any given time, they hold up to a dozen supertankers for years. They can hold these supertankers and their hostage crews at anchor in the bays off their villages in relative safety, because they control the region. It is instructive to recognize that Al-Shabaab's religious views, which condone the killing of innocent people, scorn the Somali pirates for their acts of theft.

ISIS, Daesh, the Islamic State, presently controls much of Iraq and Syria and is moving toward Libya and beyond, an area of thousands of square kilometers. As such, it has the military and financial capacity to hold single or multiple hostages in any number of facilities across this vast area of the Middle East. It can also capture and move a large number of hostages and use them as human shields at multiple facilities across the region, as required. Due to ISIS's significant military capacity, it is also able to defend its hostages against even the most daring and coordinated rescue attempts. The sheer size of its territory combined with the military ability of this terrorist group is such that a successful escape from any of its strongholds may be next to impossible.

In the Sinai Desert, there are rebel groups who capture Somali refugees attempting to cross into Israel. These hostages, mostly women, who are sexually assaulted on an almost daily basis, are tortured and held for ransom. The rebels are just criminals who are not operating under any political or religious banner and survive solely because of government indifference. This is a relatively small group of less than fifty rebels who hold approximately thirty to forty hostages at any time. As hostages are ransomed and their number dwindles, the rebels can easily abduct more refugees as they try to cross the rows of barbed wire in the open and undefended areas of the desert.

Obviously, the security requirement for either single or multiple hostages depends entirely upon the identity of the captor group and the captivity location. Single or only a few hostages being held in a location that is not under the group's control will require different security from what is needed when hostages are held in a relatively secure and controlled region. Single or only a few hostages held together are more likely to be chained, tied, or handcuffed for all or most of the time. This tighter control over hostages serves to better control their movement and reduce the likelihood of escape, which in turn requires less security and fewer guards.

BENEFITS OF MULTIPLE-HOSTAGE SITUATIONS

For a hostage, multiple-hostage situations are easier to survive than single-hostage situations, but they each have their drawbacks. In a multiple-hostage situation, being held in the same room or cell with other hostages has a definite survival advantage, both physically and psychologically. Multiple hostages benefit from "combat bonding." Like soldiers, hostages who share similar hardships will feel a kinship to one another.

Physically, you will have others to help tend to your wounds, especially those you cannot reach. As a group, you will have a better pool of medical training and survival knowledge, which will benefit the entire group. You can share scarce resources such as food and water, spare clothing and blankets, even reading glasses. You can huddle or spoon together for warmth and assist each other in personal grooming. If hostages are forced to do menial labor or daily chores, the healthy hostages can assist those less able. If the toilet facilities are outside of the cell, a stronger hostage can assist a weaker hostage in getting to and from those facilities. As a group, hostages can oversee the health of weaker hostages and be their voice in demanding better treatment or medicine for those in need.

As a group, they are better able to defend a fellow hostage from physical abuse by guards. This can be done either by voicing loud verbal objection or by forming a physical barrier around the intended victim. This kind of physical protection will often convince abusive guards to forego their behavior, as they do not want to agitate the hostages unnecessarily. They also may not want other guards to be aware of their transgressions, which may offend their collective religious beliefs or political ideals. This kind of rallying to support one another can provide a valuable sense of power and control to the group.

Psychologically, multiple hostages will have much in common. Firstly, many will have the common denominator of why they were in the country or why they were targets for abduction. They may be journalists or writers for large or small media outlets or just independent writers or researchers. Many will have come to the country to find answers to political, legal, or social questions. They will likely all be foreigners and will have an altruistic ideal, which again is why they were in that part of the world in the first place. Although they will have come from a variety of backgrounds, they will discover they have much in common.

As a group, they can morally support one another through group prayer. They will find ways to pass the time, such as telling stories, reciting poetry, singing (albeit quietly), making up games, or playing trivia. Some hostages have made up card games using paper or cardboard; some have used small pebbles to toss against the wall or to juggle. Some will take the opportunity to learn a new language.

As a group, they will console those among them who are going through tough times. In these situations, only a hostage can best understand the needs of another hostage. They try not to be judgmental. A hug and words of encouragement from another human being can make a big difference in being able to make it through another day or another long night.

Robert Fowler and Louis Guay developed an outstanding set of hostage behavior guidelines, which served them as a means to watch out for themselves and for each other.

> First rule—*no what ifs or if onlys*. We agreed, first tacitly and subsequently explicitly, that it would be perilous, counterproductive, and downright self-indulgent to wallow in any musings about what had brought us to this pretty pass.

Second rule—*no discussing bad stuff after midday.* Very soon we realized that if we shared our worst worries and fears late into the night, we would not be able to sleep with such thoughts . . .

Third rule—*no discussing anything sensitive after dark.* We could not tell where our kidnappers were and they might be close enough to hear.

Fourth rule—*absolute avoidance of rabbit holes.* This was the most important and had to be strictly enforced. As soon as one of us started into some spiral of desperate worry, the other was to use every wile or insult to pull him back out . . . We both understood that we had to be particularity vigilant about diving down separate holes, or the same rabbit hole, simultaneously. (Fowler 2011, pp. 111,112,113)

DIFFICULTIES WITH MULTIPLE-HOSTAGE SITUATIONS

When hostages are held together, group social dynamics, with their hierarchies and competitions, conflicting or complementing personalities, individual biases, and competing needs can sometimes be a negative factor.

Franco-Colombian presidential candidate Ingrid Betancourt was abducted in 2002 and released six and a half years later, in 2008. She was held in the jungle with three American military contractors and ten others.

In their book titled *Out of Captivity,* three American Northrop Grumman contractors, Marc Gonsalves, Keith Stansell, and Thomas Howes, all of whom spent time as captives of FARC with Ingrid Betancourt, described her behavior as selfish, displaying that she felt she deserved better treatment than the other captives due to her political and social standing. The Americans, held captive by the FARC from 2003 to 2008, stated that throughout their captivity,

Betancourt claimed and took more than her fair share of scarce food, clothing, and personal space. Stansell said, "I can get over just about anything, but I don't know about Ingrid. Forgive? Yes. Move on? Yes. Respect? No" (Pilkington 2009).

Not everyone will be in a good mood every day. As we all know, there are those among us who are in a good mood much of the time and others who are almost never in a good mood. There are some who can tolerate another person's bad mood and others who cannot. The more hostages there are in one room, the more mood and personality will play a part in the day's activities and the group's overall physical and psychological well-being.

Let's face it, any time humans compete for scarce resources, there will be difficulties. When there are two or more hostages in the same room, under life-threatening circumstances, each fighting for his own survival, there will be tension. This is the same scenario that reality-television programs like *Survivor* strive to duplicate. The producers deliberately bring together a variety of male and female personalities into a situation where they must all compete for scarce resources in unfamiliar surroundings, yet they must all focus on the same goal. They must identify allies, form allegiances, and plot against one another. When difficulties arise, loyalty and allies are quickly forgotten, and allegiances are broken and then reformed as suits their purpose. All that matters is their goal, their individual survival, even at the cost of another's. It's every man for himself. Participants are thrown into a social pressure cooker, strictly for our entertainment—a return to a time when gladiators entertained the Romans.

For real hostages, living in physically and socially cramped quarters with no privacy, in competition for scarce resources, loyalties are formed, jealousies arise, and even love and hate can play their part in fracturing and fragmenting the group. This struggle for survival is real. These hostages all come to realize, either in their own time or through honest and frank discussions with the group, that each of them wants to be the first to be released, the next to be released—to go home. No one wants to be the very last hostage, the last one sitting alone in the cell, where once there were many. Tensions and frustrations eventually give way to tempers, arguments, and eventually hard feelings. Many will cry, apologize, and make up. For some, forgiveness and healing will take a little longer. During these times, the best of the group will rise to the top: the most empathetic, the most generous, and the most compassionate. The physically and mentally strongest may give up their "turn" for the weaker among them, the person who needs it more than they do. Those who stay behind so that others may go free—go home—they are true heroes.

Even months or years after being released, after being debriefed by law enforcement, counseled by psychologists and in prayer and confessions with religious leaders—even when safely among their family and closest friends—for those hostages who survived months and years with other hostages, promises were made and secrets are kept.

That being said, promises made to your captors do not need to be kept. Like a confession made under threat, by trickery, under duress, or by deceit, promises made to captors in the hope of gaining the freedom they stole from you in the first place are not binding. They are not binding morally or ethically and should be dismissed and forgotten.

CHAPTER 16
HOSTAGE RESCUE

Hostage rescues, like hostage releases, can come at any time. To a hostage who has spent many months secluded in a small room, in a cave, or in a hole in the ground with very little human contact, a hostage rescue is a frightening and traumatic experience.

Hostage rescues are, by their nature, stealthy and secret; they can also be violent and deadly. A hostage may be awakened by explosions, gunfire, and yelling or by a gloved hand over his mouth. Most hostage rescues are during darkness, as it benefits the stealth and surprise factor. Plus, there are fewer guards and civilians nearby. Hostage rescue teams prefer stealth ingress (entry) and egress (exit) with minimal gunfire, as this is considerably safer for both them and the hostage.

When a hostage hears gunfire and yelling, especially at night, he should act as if it were a hostage rescue. A hostage should immediately be able to tell the difference between rescue gunfire and yelling and the celebratory gunfire and cheering he may have heard previously near his surroundings.

As for how the hostage should react, first of all, he should try not to be in a direct line with the door or windows in case a stray bullet comes through either or a stun grenade is thrown into the room.

Note: In December 2014, AQAP militants shot dead two hostages—American journalist Luke Somers and South African teacher Pierre Korkie—during a failed attempt by American commandos to rescue them in southeastern Yemen. During the rescue attempt, one of the terrorists ran into the hostage's cell and executed both of them before they could be successfully rescued.

During a hostage rescue attempt, you should sit in a corner, facing out of the corner, knees in front of you with your hands and arms protecting your ears, head, and face. This position will protect your vital organs from the overpressure in case a stun grenade lands nearby or explosives are used to enter the room. This position will also assist anyone who comes into your cell to recognize that you are likely unarmed and not a threat. As the shooting and yelling comes closer to your cell door, you can expect to hear a rescue team member call out your name. Of course, you must reply to this call. If a stun grenade does go off in your room, you will be temporarily blinded and deafened. You may not hear your rescuers call your name, and they may not hear your reply. A hostage should simply yell, "Hostage, hostage!" You have to understand that the rescue team is moving about your building, not knowing what they might find around the next corner or in the next room. They may have an idea which room you are being held in, but they may not be certain.

When they hear you respond and call out, this will assist them in locating your room more quickly, and they will also not expect to find hostile persons in the room. However, they will enter prepared to shoot and kill anyone who appears to be a threat. If the door is locked, they will tell you to stand back from the door, as they will use specialized gunfire or explosives to destroy the lock or the door hinges. Immediately upon entering the room, they will look for anyone who appears to be a threat, and they will act accordingly.

You can expect to hear your name called again, in your language. Do not immediately stand up and do not attempt to help. Remain sitting, respond to your name, and at most, just lift your hands and wiggle your fingers. Listen to their commands and do exactly as they say. You might not be able to see them, but they will be able to see you. If they are looking for other hostages and expect they may be in the same room, you will hear their names called as well. At this point, they will identify themselves so that you know they are friendly and that this is, in fact, a rescue.

Initially, you can expect to be treated roughly. Because of the proliferation of explosive vests and booby traps, they will need to confirm you are not a threat, not a sleeper. They will then proceed through a number of steps; the order differs only slightly among national rescue teams, but the content and purpose is the same. They will confirm your identity by referring to a photograph and asking you to state your full name and date of birth. If you are chained, bound, or handcuffed, they will have bolt cutters handy and will quickly cut any chain, padlock or handcuff. They will ask if you are injured and if you are able to walk unassisted. If you are injured, they will quickly assess your injuries and apply emergency and temporary first aid. If you cannot walk, they are prepared to carry you.

They will ask if you are aware of any other hostages being held in the same building and, if so, where they are located. Before you leave your cell, time permitting, they will put a bulletproof vest on you, which you will find very heavy and cumbersome. You may also have a helmet put on your head. Of course, these are for your own personal protection. If you have any letters, a journal, or notes you wish to take with you, this is the time to say so, because things will move very quickly. They will tell you to keep your head down and do as you're told.

As you depart the building, you can expect to be held up by at least one arm, probably both arms, as most hostages will stumble as they are led quickly outside surrounded by team members. You can expect to hear more gunfire and yelling as you depart the building and head for your waiting departure vehicle or aircraft. You can expect to be handled roughly at this point but only because the team is trained to move as quickly and effectively as possible. The longer it takes to get you out and loaded, the longer you and the team members are exposed and therefore at risk. You can expect to be quickly loaded, according to your health and mobility, still surrounded by rescue team members, and you will begin to move. Your rescue will likely be as traumatic and as stressful as your abduction. Again, if you know beforehand what to expect, you are less likely to panic. The trauma and stress will be short-lived and therefore less likely to have any long-term negative impact.

During your transportation to a safe area, your rescuers will again ask you about any health issues you might have. This is to ensure that they did not overlook anything and to ensure you were not injured during the rescue. This is also an effort to engage you in a friendly conversation that informs you that you are now safe and surrounded by people who care about you. Depending on how long the transport takes, rescue teams do not usually give you the "welcome back" speech, as this role is often reserved for some government representative. The rescue teams are meant for business, but if your thinking is beginning to clear up at this point, this would be an excellent opportunity to personally thank your rescue team members, as you are not likely to ever see them again.

As you begin to realize that it's over—finally over—you're likely to cry. This is normal. This flood of emotion is the release of the many stressors you have been subjected to over the period of your captivity. The anxiety of not knowing what will happen to you today, tonight or tomorrow is over. The fear of torture, of dying, of your family never knowing what really happened and when or where your body might be found is over. You are simultaneously experiencing fear and relief.

Hostages, their families, and the general public are often not aware of the considerable time, effort, and assets their government puts into finding them and bringing them home safely. As one who has witnessed these efforts firsthand, I can assure you that there are considerable police, military, and political efforts involved at many levels. In most foreign hostage situations, federal police officers and military personnel are dispatched to either a safe neighboring country or into the hostage country itself. For months at a time, they leave the safety of their own country and their own families to investigate, coordinate, and rescue a hostage. Governments never divulge what goes on in the background and are resigned to sit and listen to all manner of criticism from released hostages, their families, or the general public. Only a very few know everything that happened.

As mentioned earlier, regardless of what a government does to secure the freedom of its citizens, regardless of how much time and money is spent, without proper support and consideration of the family along the way, it is unlikely to receive any recognition or sincere thanks. For a grieving family whose son or daughter did not survive the abduction and captivity, there will always be unanswered questions. Even rescued hostages will have questions about the what-ifs and why-nots.

There have been many occasions when hostages have been rescued by armed military personnel. These military personnel may be from the hostage's own country, from an allied country, or from the country in which the hostage is being held. All rescues require the most accurate and up-to-date information possible because hostage rescues place more than just the hostage's life in danger; they place the lives of the rescue personnel and the futures of their own families back home in jeopardy as well. The information comes from political sources, police investigations, informants, concerned citizens, and allied and military sources. Most of this information is accurate and reliable. However, some of it is hearsay, some is conjecture and assumption, and some are just lies.

As mentioned earlier, a number of hostage negotiations are plagued by competing information sources. As every hostage has employers, associates, friends, and family, they all want to help and pass along any morsel of information they can find. In today's social media environment, this information base expands dramatically with the well-meaning, well-intentioned people of the world passing along their information, knowledge, and of course, their advice. Then there is the Internet, with its worldwide media coverage and editorialized reporting, its sensationalism, and its many expert opinions and pseudoscience. With the families being bombarded almost daily with this information and advice, it is no wonder they become confused, skeptical, and demoralized. The task is left to their governments and their negotiators to sift through it all, separate the good from the bad, roll the dice, and commit lives to a rescue.

(See appendix 4, a report released by the Pentagon, outlining a number of American hostage rescue attempts and responding to the Kayla Mueller letters and the concerns expressed by her parents about the government's lack of involvement.)

CHAPTER 17
STAGES OF A HOSTAGE
TAKING—RELEASE

Kidnappers are just as nervous and apprehensive about hostage releases as they are about hostage abductions. While you may sit for months or years wondering if, how, or when you might die or if, how, and when you might be released, your kidnappers are sitting for these months and years wondering if they will be attacked in the middle of the night by a rival gang or killed during a hostage rescue. Your captors are always afraid that ransom agreements and release plans are just a trick to lure them out of hiding and kill them.

ACTUAL RELEASE

A hostage's release by his captors can be as sudden and dramatic as the abduction—so sudden, in fact, that he may not believe it's really happening. Hostages often experience confusion almost to the point of panic; they experience disbelief and suspicion that it's some sort of trick. After all, the hostage by now has plenty of reasons and supporting evidence not to trust their kidnappers. Hostages who for months or years imagined what their release might look like are surprised and in shock for the first few minutes as they try to make some sense of what's really going on. For hostages who have previously been put through the agony of fake executions, there is the return of that mind-numbing fear.

Sometimes, hostages may be told they are being released. Considering all they've been through and the many times they were told "Maybe tomorrow" or "Maybe in two or three days," you can appreciate their skepticism. They might be hooded and bound, driving along a road or in the middle of a desert or some farmer's field; the car stops and they are told to get out. When they get out, again fearing the worst, the car speeds away, and they are left virtually in the middle of nowhere. Soon, another vehicle drives up to them and tells them to get in—they are free.

Often kidnappers tell hostages they are just being transported to another location. Then somewhere along the way, their vehicle stops, and the hostage is put into a vehicle with a government representative who informs him he is free. This can be one of those "pinch me—I think I'm dreaming" moments.

Your first few minutes will be confusing as you begin to reestablish yourself mentally. There are new faces and voices. You may smell cologne, there is a man wearing a suit jacket, the conversation is friendly and nonthreatening, and someone is smoking a cigarette. Surprisingly, freedom may actually take a while to sink in. If your rescue flight with the military or your government drive takes a little while, it will provide you with the opportunity to let all this sink in.

If you are in a car, the first outgoing phone calls will be made by the representative in the car to the appropriate authorities to advise that the pickup has gone well—you are onboard and, for the most part, unharmed. After that, you will be given the phone so that you may call your family. Expect this to be another emotional time for you as you hear the voices you have imagined so many times and have longed to hear once again. If you're in a military vehicle or aircraft, you won't smell any cologne, but take the time to feel the moment, look around, feel the wind on your face, and realize your captivity is over. Take this time to breathe deeply and enjoy the moment because when you arrive at your destination, things will become overwhelming again. As explained earlier in this book, knowing what is coming next and why will inoculate you psychologically, making everything less confusing and less stressful. You will need to be prepared.

POSTRELEASE EXAMINATIONS AND DEBRIEFINGS

The location of your release will dictate where you are taken first. If you are rescued or released near a friendly military base, you will most likely be taken directly to that base; if you were rescued by a military rescue team, you can expect to be taken to their operating base. If this base is offshore, such as a military ship, and depending on your nationality, you may be taken to this ship. If you were handed over to a government official, your first stop may be an embassy or consulate or possibly a secure hotel. All of this will have been organized prior to your rescue or release, but these plans may change depending on whether or not you require medical attention and what sort of attention or treatment that might be. Regardless, your first stop will only be temporary as you will be moved to a location that is secure and more family-accessible.

You can expect to be surrounded by a number of people, which you'll find overwhelming. All of them have a purpose for being there. Everyone there knows who you are and where you've been. Many have worked long and hard to secure your freedom, so expect their jubilation—they have earned it. Although as yet, you don't know exactly how.

You can expect to be taken aback by the amount of light in the many rooms through which you will be processed. Don't be surprised if you find yourself squinting. It might appear as though you're under the spotlights in a television studio or on a performing stage. During your captivity you were likely kept in a smaller and dimly lit space for some time. Your eyes and your brain will be overwhelmed by all the light, but somehow you know this is normal because you remember having previously lived in such an environment. It is both normal and strange at the same time. It is foreign yet familiar—it feels like something you must have experienced in a previous life, maybe? You may feel overwhelmed by the variety of smells—again, foreign yet familiar. You will take a second and wonder if it always smelled like this.

People will be busying themselves around you. To some released or rescued hostages, it feels like walking into a room with a dozen televisions all around them, each on a different channel and all talking at the same time. You will be handed off to a person who will introduce himself, welcome you back, and explain what they are going to do for you here. You may also be introduced to people you will have difficulty remembering, and you'll have trouble recalling what they say to you. Simply smile and nod your head a lot; if you can manage a "thank you," all the better.

The following are some of the things you can expect to happen when you arrive at the safe facility—first things first.

COMMUNICATIONS

You will, of course, be given the opportunity to phone your spouse/ partner and other immediate family members. As much as you may want to stay on the phone for hours, your first few phone calls should be short and sweet. You will be surprised how exhausting these first calls will be. After all, the news is short: "I'm out, I'm fine, I love you, we'll be together soon." I recommend that you take advice from your spouse/partner on who you should phone next. She/he may want to recommend who best to call and in what order. Things may have changed at home.

MEDICAL

Patience. As much as you might want to take a nice long shower and brush your teeth, it is important to you and to the medical personnel that they perform at least a cursory examination of your health before they leave you unattended in a hot shower.

Your first walk past a mirror after many months of captivity will be a sobering experience. Take a moment; the person you see will look foreign yet again familiar.

The medical staff will need to take photographs of injuries that have healed and of recent bruising for evidence of maltreatment. They will need to take X-rays to determine the extent of any injuries and assess the extent of any healing. What might seem unimportant to you is very important to them. They may wish to take samples of the dirt on your skin or under your fingernails for later examination as well as take a lock of your hair.

They will need to take a number of blood samples and a urine sample. These will provide them with considerable information in regard to your present health and certainly to any preexisting medical conditions. The samples will assist them in deciding whether you require any prescription medications immediately or just a vitamin booster. Considering where you have been and for how long, you may have contracted some common regional illnesses such as malaria or dengue fever, or you may have suffered mild bouts of cholera, and so on.

As much as it may seem like another sexual intrusion, the medical staff may request a vaginal or anal swab for DNA. Hopefully, the medical staff will take their time and fully explain the forensic needs of this procedure prior to taking samples.

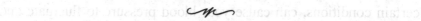

Note: I interviewed a female hostage who was held for weeks, during which she was sexually and physically abused. After her release and during her initial medical examination, male investigators wandered in and out of her hospital examination room at will, without regard for her privacy or her dignity. For this newly released hostage, this was reminiscent of exactly the treatment she had undergone during her captivity—the loss of her privacy and her dignity and the loss of control over her life. Law-enforcement officials had just unknowingly retraumatized her. In these kinds of situations, law-enforcement officials often act as though they are entitled to open any door and walk into any room because they have important questions to ask. They have waited weeks or months to ask these questions—they can wait a few more minutes. Released hostages must feel their rights, their privileges, and their privacy are back under their own control.

The medical staff will be aware of any preexisting medical conditions you may have had from information provided by the FLO. They will be prepared to assess the state or progress of these conditions, if any. They will have on hand any relevant prescription medications you might require. They will question you with respect to any skin rashes or infections you might have had; they will ask about your diet.

The medical staff will inquire if you were given any drugs while you were "away" and why. Were you ever seen by a medical doctor or treated for any ailments? What were the symptoms? They will want to check you for head lice and for any intestinal worms or parasites; they will also give you a quick hearing and visual assessment.

Also very importantly, the medical staff will be judging your mental state—are you medically confused or psychologically confused? There is a very important difference.

These questions about your present condition are important. You might think you are capable of standing in a hot shower for the next half hour or so, but maybe you're not. Exposure to hot water, under certain conditions, can cause your blood pressure to fluctuate and cause you to faint. No sense having you survive a hostage ordeal for months under extreme physical and psychological conditions only to lose you to a fall in the shower within minutes of your release—talk about bad press.

DENTAL

A dental exam may include X-rays for broken, missing, or fractured teeth and abscesses. An assessment for gum disease will form part of the medical examination. Dental health is very much a factor of diet, and you would not have eaten your normal diet for some time. A lack of vitamin C can cause scurvy-like conditions, which might cause your gums to recede and, as a result, your teeth may be slightly loose and therefore susceptible to accidental damage. This will have a direct impact on your choice of a first meal.

PSYCHOLOGICAL

Again, patience. You are likely to feel overwhelmed and crowded. Going from days of extreme boredom and social deprivation to being the center of attention is likely to cause anxiety, mild confusion, or even panic. Relax. This is normal. It is only a symptom of having lived in captivity for so long, having adjusted to the constant fear of not knowing what's going to happen next and learning to survive under the constant threat of death.

You have been afraid for so long, and it will take time to learn to become unafraid. Let's face it—your kidnappers were once strangers. They treated you badly, and you came to fear and mistrust them. Now you are experiencing another kind of abduction, an abduction from your captivity, from what you came to accept as "normal," and you are again surrounded by strangers.

Readjusting to being with "regular" people and being in the kinds of places that were once familiar and nonthreatening to you is far easier than the adjustment you had to make earlier as a hostage, when you were surrounded by the types of people and in the kinds of places that you had never previously experienced.

YOUR FEDERAL POLICE

As mentioned earlier, your own federal police agency would have been sent to your location, a safe location nearby or a safe country nearby, and would have been involved every day in every aspect of securing your release. Their activities involved discussions with an assortment of in-country political, home-country political, local and international law-enforcement agencies, local and international military personnel, a variety of intelligence agencies, and possibly direct negotiation with your kidnappers or their agents. They will ask to speak with you in private.

Because they are trained negotiators and experienced criminal investigators, they have been involved with your situation almost from the start. You may not realize this yet, but you owe them more than you will know. They will be interested in your assessment of your captivity, your treatment, and the behavior patterns of your captors. They will be very interested in timelines. They need your feedback; you owe them your feedback. As negotiations progressed while you were captive, your treatment may have changed accordingly, for better or worse. Any relevant comments made by your captors or any changes in their behaviors during these negotiations will provide valuable insight to your negotiation team.

As probably only a hostage held under these circumstances can appreciate, it is extremely difficult to negotiate with religious fanatics who cannot see beyond the pages of their own scripture and to whom logic and common sense are almost nonexistent. It is important for you to help your negotiation team learn as much as they can from your abduction and from your release. What did your captors call themselves? What were they fighting for or against? Can you provide names and descriptions of your captors? How often were you moved? They need to know what worked and what didn't work. They may ask you what ifs—what if we had done this, what if we had done that? The next hostage will benefit greatly from your insight, your opinions, and your experience. You may also have messages from fellow hostages to pass on.

You may be debriefed by law-enforcement personnel from other countries that represent other hostages whom you may have met or may have been held with during your confinement. They will be interested in how those hostages are holding up mentally and physically.

The negotiation strategies for the release of other hostages may depend heavily on what you can tell their negotiators. Comments made to a hostage by their captors during confinement are likely to be more accurate and psychologically telling than the captor's public propaganda or their conversations with negotiators.

Your federal authorities will take your clothes for inspection and laboratory analysis. Sometimes, a hostage has a bag of clothes waiting for him, provided by the hostage's family and sent by the FLO. Expect to need smaller sizes than what you used to wear. Don't put these clothes on yet, as you have not had the opportunity for a shower.

LOCAL LEGAL—LAW ENFORCEMENT

Local authorities will want you to provide details of where you were held, whether you can identify your hostage takers, what their names were, how many times you were moved, whether there were other hostages, what their names were, and where they are now. They may show you mug shots and ask if you can identify any of them as your captors. This is important information to help them take actions to reduce further incidents of hostage taking. Authorities may also take photographs of you before you are cleaned up and shaven.

Hopefully, at some point during all of this prodding, poking and questioning, your new "captors" will ask you want you would like to do. Maybe you just want to stand outside and feel the wind in your hair or the sun on your face or maybe you just want to sit and watch the clouds go by; maybe a glass of water with ice cubes.

GOVERNMENT SUPPORT

Depending on exactly where your first arrival and examination point is, you will be transported, most likely by government aircraft, to a major medical facility. This facility may be in Europe (considering our scenarios), as this is also a convenient travel destination for your spouse or family members. Depending on your medical condition, you will be kept in this facility for a few days under observation and await laboratory results. Again, you will be provided with communications with family back home. Your incoming calls will be screened. This is not the time to contact any press outlets back home; instruct your family to also avoid doing so. Before you speak with any press outlets, you must discuss any media responses with your FLO.

Early during your stay at this medical facility, you may receive a phone call from your prime minister, governor general, president, king, queen, or ambassador. The polite thing to do is to thank your country and your government for all they have done to secure your release. The dignitary will engage in a short chat with you, chat about your family visiting you, and wish you a speedy recovery and speedy return back home. Regardless of your immediate thoughts about what, when, or how your government should have acted, you don't have sufficient information to pass judgment at this time. Be polite and do the right thing. Back home, a representative of your government will be quick to inform everyone that he has spoken with you and you are in good health and looking forward to returning home.

Your government will arrange for any passport or travel authorizations you or your family may require. If you are transported directly home (or when you and your family are transported back home), you will be accompanied by a federal police officer. This officer will have coordinated your travel plans with local immigration officials and your external affairs department. This officer will ensure that you and your family do not have to deal with any travel, security, or immigration complications on your way back home. Your FLO will coordinate your arrival with any security and press matters, as required.

CHAPTER 18

THE PSYCHOLOGICAL AFTERMATH

RETURN—DISCOVERY—RECOVERY

The psychological aftermath of being released involves a host of issues. Returning home involves more than just the physical reunification with family and friends; it involves the social reengagement with family, friends, work associates, and the general public. While you were a hostage, it may have seemed as though your world had stopped, but for your family, friends, work associates, and community, it never did. Things happened; things changed. The released hostage has to catch up on family situational events, good and bad; family finances, good and bad; plus community and world events. This will require patience, understanding, tolerance, and often, forgiveness. All of this will take time, so don't rush into it—pace yourself. An essential feature for recovery from psychological or social trauma is reestablishing and normalizing attachments to others.

FAMILY MEETINGS

Your very first family meetings will likely be at the medical facility or at the airport when you arrive home. It is important for both you and your family members to stick to the positives. It is vitally important to maintain a positive outlook and receive only positive feedback during the first days of your return; this will be a significant factor in determining your short-term and long-term mental health. Very importantly, this goes for your family members as well.

As I stated earlier, accept that both you and your family are not the same people as when you left. This is paramount. You have all been under tremendous pressures; you have all suffered your own nightmares, and you have made life-and-death decisions without sufficient information. They did their best with the information they had, just as you did your best with the information you had. You may not agree with everything that took place during your absence, and you may not be aware of any social fallout that may have transpired. This is not the time to discuss why things were done or were not done. You may have missed significant family and/or social events; this happens to lots of people whose jobs take them away from home for periods of time. Catch up, but be patient and accepting. Use this time and your early days at home to decompress and ease back into social life.

The first time you drive down your street, you will notice what changes have been made to some neighbor's yard or house, but they are of little consequence. As you pull into your driveway, you will notice every little change in flowers, plants, or trees around your own house. You will find it mildly amusing. When you comment on these minor changes, you'll be told about the storm that broke off a tree limb or the gift of a new shrub or tree. Your family will delight in telling you all about it.

When you step into your residence for the first time since your departure, subsequent abduction and confinement, you will be very surprised. You'll immediately notice every minor change. Your memories of where you lived are strong, and your visualizations of your residence and all that it contains are indelible. For just a moment, you will be almost shocked at how well your memory preserved those details. I speak from experience on this. After spending almost a year on a UN mission in the deserts of North, West, and Central Africa and then over a year in the jungles of Southeast Asia, it was just as much an experience returning home to Canada as it was leaving. If a picture has been changed on a wall or moved on a mantle, you will notice; if a chair has been replaced or even moved, you will notice. Notice it all, but take the changes in stride. Yup, things change. Anyone who has been away at school for a semester or even longer would notice many of the same types of changes. If you were away working for months or years, you would also notice these changes.

The difference between memories held while in captivity and those held while away at school or work is that there was other business to attend to at school or at work—distractions. Memories of your yard and your home and its contents would not have been held in such esteem and reverence by your family as they would by you. After all, you stayed alive just to see them once again; you kept yourself going by your longing to see them, touch them, and smell them again.

For returned hostages, their memories were their lifeboat. Those memories kept them sane, kept them alive, and sustained their will to live. When a returning hostage notices the changes in such minor things as a picture or a chair that has moved, he must immediately realize that there are more changes yet to be noticed. Not just physical changes but possibly social changes as well. This is a crucial time for the returned hostage and his family—a crossroad. For the released hostage, someone has messed with his cherished memories. For the family, this is a time for tolerance and understanding, as it is for the released hostage.

As much as your memories sustained you for so long, it's time to recognize that this is not a new book—it is just a new chapter.

During your first days back, do not attempt to attend any large family reunions or business parties to congratulate you and welcome you home. A family party with your spouse, children, mother and father, and brothers and sisters who live nearby is welcome. Take this early time to reengage with your family and with your life, step by step and at your own pace.

You may have missed your own birthday and maybe Christmas and other important family or cultural holidays. Your first days should include sitting with the usual family members you would celebrate those special days with and opening up the presents you weren't there to open. Enjoy yourself and have a good laugh about the pants or the belt that might not fit just right. If one of your family members says something like "I wanted to get you out earlier but no one agreed with me," just pass it off and say, "There will be plenty of time to talk about that later." As tempting as it may be to talk about your ordeal, let it pass for now.

Family members will, of course, be curious about everything. Most of what they know about your abduction, who your kidnappers were, and how you were treated was learned from media coverage and discussions with on-camera experts. They had so many questions while you were gone, and they are understandably eager to having them answered. As tempting as it may be to enthrall everyone with your stories, take it slow. Some family members may not be ready for your answers. After months of not being in control of very much, you are now in a position of control, but exercise it lightly. Decompression takes time. Relax, think, and plan.

Let's deal with a few housekeeping items. Of course, by this point, you have spoken with your extended family members, but you should also call your employer. Your manager, just like the prime minister or the president, will be glad to have the opportunity to welcome you back, to welcome you home. This is also your opportunity to thank your employer and your coworkers for all the support they showed your family during your absence. If your spouse has mentioned any one employee's support that stands out, mention that person's name when speaking with your manager. Now your manager can announce your thanks and best wishes to the entire company; he's happy. Of course, he'll tell you to take some time off with your family. Everyone at work will be very understanding when you tell them you would love to meet them soon but you need more time. They will always understand.

ANGER AND HEALING

At this juncture, it is important to discuss your anger issues and their impact on your ability to heal. Psychological healing takes time and professional help is the best way to begin so, I will touch briefly on only a few points.

During these early times, it is very easy to fall into the anger trap. You are angry at your kidnappers for taking away your freedom and for all of the physical and mental atrocities committed upon you; you are angry at your government for not paying a ransom, angry at your police or military for not rescuing you earlier; angry at all the time you have lost and angry at yourself. Your spouse and your children, your parents, your brothers and sisters, all of your extended family; your friends and your work colleagues all have the right to be angry. Everyone will have something to be angry about. But, in the spirit of healing, you must not allow this anger to become the topic of conversation because it will only go round and round feeding upon itself until an ugly situation develops or somebody makes the rational decision to stop. Anger begets anger and soon it will begin to eat away at you from the inside.

I'm not saying that as soon as you hit home soil you can't express any anger. Of course there are things that need to be discussed with your immediate family. You will tell your immediate family most, if not everything that happened; you will tell your extended family a little less and your friends and colleagues will get the generic and condensed version. Very few can be trusted with the most personal details.

A little venting is good but beware of family or friends who feel they have to go on about how it could have been worse; the what ifs and the maybes. They are just trying to help and make you feel better, in their own way. But, you have all had enough anger and hardship to last a lifetime. Giving up anger will give you back your life. It's time to get past the anger and begin the healing. The time frame for every released hostage is different. It depends upon the size of the family and its shared religious beliefs; it depends upon the hierarchy, the composition and the overall personality of the family.

I believe it was best said by the mother of Elizabeth Smart (Smart, Elizabeth, *My Story*, 2013)[11] the morning after her rescue when advising Elizabeth how to get on with her future, her life: "If you go and feel sorry for yourself or if you dwell on what just happened, if

---

[11] In June 2002, fourteen-year-old Elizabeth Smart, the daughter of a Mormon family in Utah, was taken from her bed at knifepoint by a religious fanatic. She was kept chained, dressed in disguise, repeatedly raped, often nearly starved, and threatened that if she tried to escape her family would be murdered. She was rescued in March 2003.

you hold on to your pain, that is allowing him to steal more of your life away. So don't do that! Don't let him! There is no way he deserves that. Not one second of your life. You keep every second for yourself. You keep them and be happy. God will take care of the rest." (Smart, Elizabeth, *My Story*, 2013, p. 286)

CRIMINAL PROSECUTION

In the spirit of healing, psychologically, you can forgive your kidnappers. But, that doesn't mean you must also forgive them criminally in order to heal. Forgiveness and prosecution can be coincident. A released hostage can feel comfortable with forgiving their kidnappers and torturers in order to heal while still proceeding with a criminal prosecution.

As I have said earlier, a released hostage is the best witness in a criminal prosecution and a hostage can find important solace in bringing their kidnappers to justice. Testifying should not be viewed as revenge. Testifying can provide a released hostage with a renewed sense of control. There are few acts that can provide the satisfaction and healing that comes with standing in the witness box and, pointing at your kidnapper, saying, "That's him." The hostage often feels as though they have just walked through a door. This act demonstrates the hostage's psychological freedom from the kidnapper. There is the added satisfaction of knowing you have reduced the likelihood of future kidnappings and the world has become a safer place.

MEDIA PRESSURE ON ARRIVAL

The actions of the media during the early stages of a repatriated hostage's arrival home have a tremendous and profound impact on his mental well-being in both the short term and long term. I believe that if better media relations assistance were provided to repatriated hostages and their families during the first few weeks of their return, the symptoms of PTSD would be significantly reduced. Therefore, my first hostage survival home strategy is the FLO or a media relations officer should accompany a repatriated hostage and his family for a short time to coordinate all media requests and provide them with both media and social guidelines on how the released hostage should best reenter his former life.

First of all, let's look at the media from their point of view. Reporters are always under pressure to get the story and are always under a deadline. Newspaper and television news editors are always pressuring their reporters to get a picture, get a live interview, get it first and get it before the next TV news broadcast or the next newspaper deadline. You can expect them to want a picture and an interview, so understand what they need from you and, more importantly, what you need from them.

I recall going to the airport to greet a released hostage upon his arrival back in the country. As I and my fellow FLO entered the Arrivals area, I noticed about twenty or so media people wandering about, carrying cameras and talking on their cell phones—the usual suspects. I recognized the impending swarm. Accordingly, I proceeded to make arrangements with the airport terminal security personnel to have the hostage and his family, with whom he would have already been reunited behind the scenes, arrive though a particular set of doors—done. I returned to the Arrivals area and announced to the waiting media who I was and where the returning hostage and his family would appear. They could take all the pictures they wanted and, of course, ask questions. Later, when those doors opened and the released hostage and his family stepped out, they were met with a wall of lights, microphones, and cameras—at least three times the number of media we had seen earlier. Of course, we had made the family aware of these arrangements beforehand. The newly released hostage stood, read his prepared speech, thanked everyone for their help in securing his release, and told them he was glad to be back home. The media people got all the pictures and videos they needed and had most of their questions answered. The family walked to waiting police vehicles without the usual horde of television and print media tripping over each other, all yelling questions at once and retraumatizing the released hostage.

The object here is to exercise control and manage the newly released hostage's environment until he is capable of doing so himself, just like he used to before he was abducted. During the months or years of captivity, the hostage had absolutely no control over his environment. Now, the objective of the FLO, the family, the employer, and the government is to teach the released hostage how to slowly reenter his society and allow him to exercise control over his own environment—just like it was before. So let's hold his hand and walk him through this.

STRATEGIES AT HOME—THE MEDIA

Dealing with the media has surprising similarities to dealing with your interrogators. You have something the media wants—your story—and they will do anything to get it. Your task, your negotiation strategy, is to get the media to tell your story on your terms.

As a released hostage, your return to society, to your family, and to the life you once led began the moment you realized you were free. This is also the moment when things could begin to go very wrong. Your actions and your engagements in your first few days of freedom, how people treat you, how people interact with you, and how you choose to reenter your new world will have a significant bearing on your mental health for the rest of your life. Just as when, as a hostage, you decided you were not going to let your captors decide what was going to happen to you, you must relax, think, and plan.

First of all, it is important to realize that you have successfully come through a very difficult test of your mental and physical capacities. You have been tested in ways that few have ever been tested. Take the time to congratulate yourself on all that you did to achieve such a feat. It is important that in your early days of freedom, you establish and maintain a positive outlook. Smile and remain upbeat and optimistic.

HOMETOWN MEDIA COVERAGE

One more example. One day, my fellow FLO and I were visiting a newly released hostage at his parents' home in a small town. As we drove up to the house, we saw maybe a half-dozen local and national media people wandering around the street with their media trucks parked nearby. At the former hostage's house, the blinds were pulled and the drapes were drawn, but we had called ahead and were expected. After a few minutes of handshakes, congratulations, and light discussion with the family, I asked about the media outside. We were informed that the family was being pestered by the local media. They had repeatedly come to the door with microphones and cameras rolling, wanting pictures and interviews; they were denied. Local media had been calling the house asking for interviews; they were denied. The media was left to take long shots from the street.

It was time for a Media 101 talk. I told the newly released hostage how, during our visits with the family in this small town, we had seen local fast-food establishments put up well-wishing signs; churches had held special prayer vigils, and we had seen yellow ribbons on trees and telephone poles in support of the hostage. His extended family and his parents were always treated with respect, best wishes, and support whenever they were seen around town or at the local arena watching a hockey game. I informed everyone that this was an opportunity—actually, I remember wording it that it was more of an obligation—for the released hostage and his entire family to thank everyone in town for the wonderful support they had shown throughout this ordeal. They all understood and agreed that a photo op was necessary.

I walked out to the end of the driveway and announced that Mr. X and his family would like to meet the press at the end of the driveway in one hour. Well, of course, immediately the media cell phones went up and calls were made. We spent the next hour having coffee and cake inside the house, while the press gathered at the end of the driveway. When it was time, I staged everyone in the backyard: Mr. X in the middle; Mom and Dad beside him, etc. There were about eight people in all, as I remember. Luckily, the driveway was wide and long. As the family walked from the backyard onto and then down the driveway toward the cameras, the print media got the pictures they needed, and the TV cameras got the family stroll down the driveway for the opening shot of their news piece. The released hostage thanked everyone in town for the support they had shown his family during his ordeal and expressed that he was glad to be back home— done.

What was accomplished here was to free the newly released hostage from the "celebrity" confinement of his parents' home. He could now open the drapes and blinds and look out at the view he had been visualizing during his confinement and had been looking forward to seeing once again. The family didn't have to worry about the local media paparazzi sneaking around their property and trying to steal a picture, and they were able to thank the whole town all at once. There were no more media requests at the door and only a very few by phone.

Certainly, the freed hostage is a celebrity. Of course, everyone wants to see him: his entire and extended family, his manager and everyone at work, the neighbors, and the media. What the released hostage and his family must recognize and learn is how to reenter the life he once knew—and on his own terms.

PERSPECTIVE AND PTSD

What the police, the FLOs, the repatriated hostage's family, his manager and coworkers, or anyone else working with released hostages have to learn is perspective. To the freed hostage, his environment is everything. What everyone else must calculate— what everyone else must assess—is what their plans, with the best of intentions, look like or feel like from the perspective of the released hostage. Here are a few examples:

1. When the police rescue a person from a suburban hostage situation, they should not put the released hostage in the backseat of a marked police car and drive him off to the police station. Everyone knows you can't escape from the backseat

of a police car; it's reserved for prisoners. The hostage has just been taken from one form of captivity to another. What happens if the hostage, while sitting in the back of the police car, looks over and sees his hostage taker in the backseat of another police car? Both are still prisoners; the hostage might just as well be back inside.

2. When the police or medical personnel interview the released hostage, they should not do so in facilities that resemble the one in which the hostage was held. If a hostage just spent two days in a 10' × 12' room painted off-white, they shouldn't interview him in a 10' × 12' room painted off-white. This room would remind him of his confinement, and he would feel like he was still a hostage.

3. If the hostage taker was a man in his fifties and slightly balding, they shouldn't have the released hostage interviewed by a police officer who is in his fifties and slightly balding. This would remind him too much of his hostage taker.

Although this advice sounds simplistic, it has a significant impact on the released hostage. Police activities focus so much attention on resolving the crisis situation they tend not to focus well on the hostage release stage. Okay, the hostage is out—now what? The police must be more familiar with the post-trauma honeymoon factor found in chapter 19.

While we're on the subject of debriefing hostages, it is vitally important for law enforcement personnel to have a better-than-average understanding of how a hostage interview must be carried out. This is *not* a criminal interrogation. Refer to the post-trauma honeymoon period outlined in chapter 19 and remember that hostages do not spontaneously report sexual mistreatment or torture. Hostages often fear religious or social shame and experience self-blame, survivor's guilt, and the fear of social exclusion . . . and it's not their fault. I cannot stress this enough, and it is beyond the purpose of this book to extensively cover the subject except to emphasize that the information a released hostage can provide is analogous to what the black box and cockpit voice recorder are to the civilian aviation investigator. The information cannot be extracted without specialized handling. A released hostage can be the police officer's best evidence and can offer a rare insight into negotiation strategies.

The released hostage from a domestic event where the hostage taker is killed by the police holds the evidence of what happened, what he did to whom, why and how often, and importantly, what he was intending to do next. This evidence would support the police decision to shoot the hostage taker, important evidence in liability suits. Also of extreme importance is whether the hostage taker's intent was to deliberately confront the police and have the police kill him—suicide by cop.

Hostage memories are the most fragile of all forensic evidence.

A released hostage who has undergone the anguish of a number of false executions, where he ended up standing in the middle of a bunch of cheering terrorists, cannot be expected to attend any sort of homecoming celebration where he must stand in the middle of a bunch of cheering people. If a ceremony must take place, possibly it should be done on a stage where everyone is below and in front of him and he knows subconsciously he has an escape route. He feels safer.

4. Do not assume a released hostage wants to be hugged. After months of social isolation and no physical contact, close physical contact can sometimes seem smothering and cause anxiety. What released hostages need is time and space. Allow him to initiate physical contact on his terms until his family and friends can recognize that he has adjusted and

accepts the frequency and intimacy of their contact. He must decompress.

Although a released hostage might not immediately recognize these situations as reconfinement or reenactments of what he went through, he might recognize them subconsciously—psychologically. These situations may directly resemble the event or only symbolize the event. And therein lies the danger. He very much wants to feel free, but something inside him keeps telling him he is not yet free. These are the types of feelings, the nagging voices which foster PTSD and help to maintain it.

To a released hostage, seemingly innocent personal or environmental situations, such as a visual scene or physical location, a particular noise, footsteps, or a creaking door, even a particular kind of laugh, can be a cue. Anything might startle him and evoke fear or panic responses. These little cues remind him of past painful events, and he may react to them today in the same way he did while in confinement. To a released hostage, he is reliving the trauma of the event.

In many survivor cases, new research prefers the term *ongoing traumatic stress* because to the sufferer, many of his symptoms are related to ongoing issues.

Startle responses to similar stimulus in the original event are referred to in psychology as *generalization*. A torture victim tied and assaulted may react when presented with a rope or generalized to a length of wire or even shoe laces. A person sexually assaulted at the rear of a bus will be wary of sitting at the rear of any bus—it reminds them of the sexual assault. But to this assault victim, many things can look like a bus—an airplane, for example, is a long metal tube with windows and seats along both sides and an aisle down the middle, the same as the bus. To the victim, a streetcar or train is a long metal tube with windows and seats along both sides and an aisle down the middle, the same as a bus. A victim may generalize the same feelings of anxiety, the same fear of the assault that took place on a bus, to an airplane or a train. Even the rows of pews in a church could induce generalized fear.

Probably the easiest way for a family to understand how seemingly insignificant events can trigger such extreme reactions is to consider that the newly released hostage developed unknown phobias while he was away. And just to further complicate the matter, the released hostage isn't aware of them. Just as people might develop a medical illness while away and now require sufficient time and the proper circumstances to heal, people who were once hostages and survived a life no one but another hostage can imagine also need time and the proper environment to heal.

People without phobias have difficulty understanding why people with a phobia could ever react with such extreme behavior to such a minor and trivial stimulus. You can argue and rationalize all day long with someone about how silly his phobia appears to the rest of us, but that won't make it go away. Many of the released hostage's senses are hyperactive and they need time to readjust, time to heal.

These are the types of events that might happen relatively early upon the released hostage's return, those that must be handled with the person's perspective in mind. If we can handle the early days for the person, this will provide him with more time to figure things out for himself, begin to solve his own problems, make his own decisions, and regain a sense of control over his own life. Again, he must be allowed to decompress.

LONG-TERM MEDIA DEMANDS

Sometimes, press and media people figure they have the right to know everything about everybody. If there was any government involvement—and hostage situations always have some degree of government involvement—the media consider it their right to know everything. They're wrong—it was your experience and you own it. You choose what, when, and with whom you will discuss any or all of your experience. We have all met veterans of wars who have never discussed any of their experiences with anyone, and that's the way they like it. But the media will press you to give up your story because they are in the business of selling stories. Like a good movie or a novel that relies on drama, desire, and danger to make it worth telling and worth watching, a hostage story has it all. If you decide to release some parts of your experience, keep in mind issues of privacy and sensitivity. If other hostages were involved, their story is their story; their secrets are their secrets. And remember your promises.

If you were held with other hostages who are still in captivity, be extremely careful about any comments that might anger your pervious captors, as they may negatively impact on those hostages who still sit and wait.

During your first days at home, of course, the media will try to find you and get an on-the-spot interview. Stick to your script, wave, be pleasant, and have the courage to walk away. Your FLO or media relations officer may be with you during these early outings, and they can handle the press for you. Don't be taken in by the media's provocative questions, which are meant to elicit an emotional response and get you talking. Stick to the plan; stick to the script.

I should mention at this point that I don't want to scare you into not going out in public during your early days. I think it is important for you and your family to get out there, to get out of the house and feel free—to recognize that you're home. This is why you worked so hard to survive.

During your absence, your family likely gave interviews to the media. During those interviews—especially television interviews—family emotions, tears, and pleas sold the story. The media would like to get your emotions, your tears, and your pleas as well. Recognize that you are still at a vulnerable stage of return, discovery, and recovery. As you did during your confinement, relax, think, and plan; take your time.

The media are insatiable. They will try to manipulate you with patriotism or with sympathies. "Do you think your government should have done more to get you out?" or "What advice do you have for other hostages?" If you feel compelled to release something to the press, your FLO or media relations officer will assist you in writing a statement you can read that will provide the press with the information you wish to give and nothing more. Many of us have seen returned hostages sitting at a long table with their close family members, reading a detailed press release to the television cameras and print media. This is a compelling scene, and it serves both the released hostage's desire to say something to the general public and get the media off their backs, as well as their family's need to get it out of the way and get on with their lives. The freed hostage stands, hugs his family members, waves, and departs.

I strongly recommend this type of media event because the freed hostage has reaffirmed that he is glad to be home among loved ones and thanks everyone for their support. But the most important part is that the freed hostage does not answer questions from the press. The media are insatiable and relentless. If during a press conference, a freed hostage begins to answer unscripted questions, the media will do everything they can to bring his emotions to the surface. This is what their viewers want to see; this is what sells. The media questions will become more and more intrusive as they drag the freed hostage back into the dark nightmares of his captivity for the entire world to see. If the freed hostage even suggests any kind of physical abuse, the media questions will quickly turn to questions of sexual abuse and "What was that like?", "How often did it happen?", and "Did you see it happen to other hostages?" Unstructured media events can lead to media overexposure and will often turn into bizarre theater.

During the first days and weeks of freedom, it is imperative that the freed hostage avoid any situations that might trigger an anxiety response—PTSD. The longer a freed hostage can avoid triggering events, the more quickly he can adjust and ease back into a normal life.

The family should take the opportunity to meet more often during these early days, sometimes at the freed hostage's residence and at other times, a little further afield, at other family residences. Again, let the freed hostage make those decisions.

CHAPTER 19
PTSD AND SUICIDE

This book is not the place for a comprehensive list or an examination of clinical PTSD symptoms and treatments, nor are my comments on suicide meant to be a voice of authority. PTSD and suicide are topics that deserve the volumes of psychology journals and the bookshelves they now occupy. For returning soldiers, civilians, and NGOs of all sorts, these PTSD studies are extremely important and relevant in today's society. The reader can find those lists and authorities in any number of places. My comments are only intended as an overview or a sketch of what sorts of difficulties hostages may experience when they return home and some options for managing those difficulties.

It is important at this point to briefly speak to the differences in the causality of PTSD symptoms in returning hostages as compared with returning soldiers. Although soldiers and hostages both had contact with the enemy every day, for soldiers, it was not knowing the when or the where of coming under fire—the contact, the constant threat of IEDs and snipers that is so invasive. For soldiers, it was the daily roller coaster of emotions, the level of vigilance required to protect their own life as well as the lives of their fellow soldiers. It was the intensity of battle; it was sometimes being the hunter and yet always being the hunted. For the hostage, after the abduction, it is the confinement and the torture that are the cause of the emotional roller coaster and the accompanying sense of helplessness.

The intention of this book is to provide travelers who may become victims of a kidnapping with a better understanding of how that situation may affect them when they return home. It is also to prepare the family of the released hostage with some insight as to potential adjustment issues. Hopefully, it provides a similar psychological inoculation for both the returning hostage and his family.

First of all, it is vitally important to the health of returned hostages and their families to know that not all survivors of traumatic events develop any of the symptoms of PTSD. Actually, a large majority do not. For combat-related PTSD it is around 8% and the prevalence in the general population ranges from 1-2%. (Basoglu p. 363) As mentioned earlier in chapter 13, susceptibility depends upon a number of factors: personality traits, age, education, religious beliefs and faith, family ties, and the individual's experience with problem-solving strategies.

I was fortunate while on one particular UN mission that my knowledge of PTSD allowed me to recognize early symptoms of PTSD developing in some of my fellow police officers. Although I held a senior executive position and could have sent them home immediately, I knew how much longer they were scheduled to remain "in country" and the kinds of daily exposure their present positions would subject them to. I was confident their symptoms would not progress to unsafe levels and they would readjust quickly when back at home.

Police officers on mission are able to change into civilian clothes after shift, whereas military personal often do not. Often soldiers remain in regulation uniform both on and off duty. Does this make a difference? I believe the parallels between police officers and soldiers on peacekeeping missions and resulting PTSD symptoms deserves further study.

Many psychologists recommend that freed hostages sit and talk to a friend they know will be understanding, discreet, and supportive without being judgmental. This is often a very helpful first step. This is why many war veterans will open up only to other veterans, believing only they can understand.

YOUTH HOSTAGES AND PTSD

Discreet information-sharing is vitally important to any young girl or boy who was abducted and confined and suffered any sort of physical or sexual abuse. To these young people, who knew virtually nothing of sexuality prior to their abduction and yet were exposed to physical practices or demeaning sexual activities, a variety of treatments, both personal and professional, may be required. A young person may find it more comforting to speak with a priest, pastor, or other religious leader than with a family doctor. A child might worry that a doctor might tell his parents a few things he's said, even if he's told that that what he says will be held in strict confidence, especially if he knows his parents tend to be a little pushy. On the other hand, the child may trust that his religious leader will keep everything secret. A child will believe this person when told that what happened to him was not his fault, there is nothing to be ashamed of, he has not sinned, and there is nothing to forgive.

For a child, it is critical that any suggestion of fault or blame be immediately rejected. A child does not have the necessary experience in dealing with a range of complicated social and emotional situations and, therefore, has not yet developed the essential problem-solving skills. It is this same lack of problem-solving skills that is responsible for so many suicides among all ages in our society. Even teenagers, who often think they are all grown up, don't always have the necessary problem-solving skills to figure out how to solve their "complicated" social problems.

Because childhood, adolescent, and adult PTSD symptoms are often specific to their age group, treatments are also age-specific; treatment for PTSD is rarely a one-size-fits-all approach.

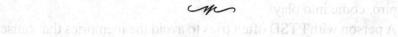

PTSD can be immediate, delayed or cumulative; PTSD can affect a person directly or indirectly. The development of characteristic symptoms of PTSD is the same for someone who has personally experienced an extreme stressor as for someone who learns of or witnesses a violent death or serious harm befalling a close friend or a family member. Some common symptoms are:

- a sense of foreboding, doom, or tragedy
- flashbacks of the event when a person is exposed to triggering events that are similar or identical to those of the initial traumatic event (generalizing)
- impaired social functioning or the avoidance of social functions
- emotional numbing or immobilizing fear
- being hypervigilant, overcautious, almost paranoid
- startling easily and overreacting to relatively mild stimuli
- having difficulty concentrating, seeming to daydream more often
- being irritable and overreacting with outbursts of anger
- experiencing poor sleep patterns because of heightened anxiety and the inability to forget the traumatic event

The reader may recall my earlier analogy of a newly released hostage acting as though he had developed new phobias; these PTSD symptoms are characteristic of a phobic person's overreaction to a seemingly innocuous stimulus.

Often, PTSD sufferers will recount how the traumatic experience plays over and over in their mind like replaying a movie over and over again; they can't seem to stop it.

These memories need to be understood in order to be properly processed. The event must be recognized as a memory, understood for what it is, and appropriately filed away. This is where cognitive-behavioral therapy (CBT) and the relatively new eye movement desensitization and reprocessing (EMDR), developed by Francine Shapiro, come into play.

A person with PTSD often tries to avoid the memories that cause him to overreact. He might do this in any number of ways—the worst of which is substance abuse—to drown his memories or dull his reactions to those memories. The affected person initially drinks to forget the memories, but soon the drinking leads to depression and a sense of helplessness; this leads to more drinking to avoid the feelings of depression and into a downward spiral of hopelessness. Hopelessness can often lead to suicide. This cycle of substance abuse, depression, and helplessness needs to be broken. When this type of destructive or avoidance problem-solving begins, it is often time for professional help. This help is available from a number of sources. The first step may be contacting your FLO or media relations person because you have a previous relationship with him and he will put you in contact with the right people. There is no stigma to seeking professional help after enduring, and surviving, a life-and-death situation; it is a sign of strength.

Many military veterans, victims of criminal or domestic violence and people who have experienced disasters have been able to put their memories away like a book on a shelf, but not everyone can do this easily. But doing so is an important first step for them to understand their experiences and begin to put them into context. Sometimes memories are like viruses; they can infect the brain in the same way a virus can infect the body. Just as with anyone who has been diagnosed with a serious illness, the first step is to find out everything you can about it; the next step is undergoing treatment and then start the healing process.

THE TRAUMA HONEYMOON FACTOR

On December 31, 1999, the millennium New Year's Eve, Dr. Richard Yu was the physician on call at St. Michael's Hospital in Toronto, Canada. He was taken hostage in the hospital by a man holding a pellet gun to his head. In a later presentation to the Canadian Critical Incident Association, Dr. Yu told the audience of negotiators and tactical team members how he considered the damage a pellet gun would cause at close range. He was familiar with both the ballistic capacities of the gun and the neurological damage it could inflict relative to the particular part of his brain the gun was pointed. He considered his life as a quadriplegic, never being able to practice medicine. He thought of his life insurance policy and whether his premiums were paid up and how his family would be taken care of. He thought of how his family would react to his death or paralysis. His hostage taker was subsequently killed by the Toronto Police Emergency Task Force (ETF).

As a medical doctor, Dr. Yu knew about PTSD and felt he could personally handle the symptoms that might eventually present themselves. However, a few months later and despite his best efforts, he sought professional help. Dr. Yu was a hostage for only seventeen minutes (personal communication).

This example is extremely important when considering how to handle a newly released hostage or a victim of a serious crime. As a serious crime investigator, I have personally been involved with victims of serious crimes, specifically sexual assault and murder. After the initial victim interview and all the necessary forensic exhibits have been collected, the victim and her family leaves with the understanding that you will be contacting her again, as there are always a few questions that will arise. Later, maybe in a week or two, I would call and ask to speak with the victim. To my surprise, I would be told by a family member something like "We want to thank the police for all you've done, we really do appreciate it, but [X] doesn't want to talk to the police. [X] wants to forget all about it and get on with her life."

While giving a PTSD presentation to approximately two hundred Canadian and American negotiators and tactical personnel, I asked how many had found themselves in the very same situation; three quarters of the audience put up their hand.

Like Dr. Yu, most victims of a serious crime believe they can handle the aftermath as they expect it to unfold. They expect to have some trouble sleeping or the odd nightmare, but they understand what happened and they can deal with it. After a week or so, they realize they are having difficulty handling what is happening to them. The memories are stronger than they expected, the events keep playing out in their head, and the nightmares aren't going away. All this is taking its toll on their day-to-day mental faculties as they are feeling exhausted, irritable, and more afraid. This situation can be exacerbated by family members or well-meaning friends who verbalize the many what-ifs and maybes of the victim's ordeal. In their efforts to handle these problems, victims decide that maybe the best way to get over this is to forget about it—not talk about it and act like it never happened. This time between when the victim leaves the interview room and the police officer calls and is told she doesn't want to talk about it is what I call "the post-trauma honeymoon factor." From a police perspective, you've just lost your best witness.

This is why the first few days after a hostage's release are so important. Everyone—the government, the negotiation team, the hostage, and his family—understands that the hostage is free; he has been returned home. All is well. What could go wrong?

The transition from being a hostage to being free once again is a delicate time. What happens in the first few days of freedom will have a profound effect on the rest of the person's life.

SUICIDE

Suicide is often the result of not being able to effectively deal with what is bothering you.

Again, this topic is worth the years of research and the many books on the subject by authors much more qualified than I. However, suicide remains a factor in the overall mental health of a released hostage.

The best line I have ever heard from a negotiator came from a Catholic priest in Toronto (unfortunately, I cannot recall his name) who, when counseling a person who was considering suicide asked, "Do you really want to die or do you just want to live differently?" Of course, the person answers that he wants to live differently. As soon as the person tells you that he wants to live differently, you ask what he wants to change. Now you have a direction; you have a goal.

You can achieve that goal step by step as you approach the situation from solving one problem at a time. Does he need a warm place to sleep? We can do that. Does he need help with substance abuse? We can do that. Does he need to speak with a member of the clergy and confess something that has been bothering him for a long time? We can do that. Does he need to speak with family member and apologize for something he said or did? We can do that. We can do the same for anyone with symptoms of PTSD. What this priest does and what hostage negotiators, or any negotiators around the world do, is have knowledge of what alternatives, opportunities, and solutions are available to apply to particular problems. Hostage negotiators simply assist people in crisis by availing them of the particular services that can help solve their problem.

It is sad and bewildering to learn that a hostage, who has suffered untold mental and physical abuses while confined for months or years, found his will to live and fought off thoughts of suicide during confinement, only to come back to the family and the freedom he so desperately longed for yet succumbed to thoughts of suicide at home.

Certainly, the numbers of suicidal events by freed hostages are nowhere near the numbers of suicidal war veterans, but in many respects, they suffer from the same demons. Returning hostages and their families need to be able to recognize symptoms of PTSD and learn how to work through them. This is why government support for released hostages must continue for months and years after their return home. As I mentioned earlier, some hostages can handle abduction and confinement better than others, and some hostages can handle reentry and reintegrate into society better than others. Some released hostages may require regular meetings with a psychologist or psychiatrist, and some may require only a periodic visit—a checkup.

I recall speaking with a police officer about a year after he had been caught on the inside of a twenty-four-hour prison takeover by inmates. He had undergone the prescribed company mental health regimen of treatment for PTSD, was deemed fit, and had returned to the job. After only a few minutes of speaking with me, he admitted he was still having problems and that he could really use another visit with the doctor. I had obviously asked the right questions, but why hadn't someone else? Standard physical medical practice after being "cured" of any major biological illness requires periodic checkups with blood tests, body scans, and so on. This medical practice is designed to confirm that the physical disease has indeed been eliminated. PTSD is no different; it requires periodic aftercare checkups and reassessment.

As a newly freed hostage or as a family member of one, don't look upon meetings with mental health professionals with suspicion or skepticism. I strongly recommend that you look forward to these meetings in the same way as you look forward to an annual checkup with your family doctor. As I wrote earlier, it is a sign of strength that you go to these meetings. The medical profession continually tells us that early detection is the best strategy to identify and treat any illness; it is also great when the doctor tells you to keep doing what you're doing because you're just fine. Take advantage of their expertise. Go to these appointments with a positive outlook and an open mind. Just like physical healing is not always immediate, neither is psychological healing. After returning from an experience such as yours, these visits are often refreshing and reassuring. They will provide personal and family confidence for the future.

THE EFFECTS OF PTSD ON FAMILY MEMBERS

Much that is written about PTSD focuses on the survivor of the event, and rightfully so. However, research has shown that a person suffering from unresolved PTSD can also influence the development of PTSD symptoms in his household and in his children.

> Torture can also have severe effects on the families of survivors. Living with someone who may be irritable, paranoid, distrustful, and unable to connect with other human beings also takes a significant toll. A study of eighty-five children whose parents had been tortured in Chile (Cohn et al. 1985) showed 68 percent had emotional disorders, physical symptoms, or both. Thirty-four of the 85 children had insomnia and nightmares, 34 suffered from anxiety, 5 had tics, 12 complained of chronic stomach aches and 13 of headaches, 15 wet their bed, 13 suffered

from anorexia, 4 had impaired memories, and 16 demonstrated "behaviour difficulties."

Studies of the children of torture victims from Chile, Argentina, and Mexico have found chronic fear, depressive mood, clinging and overdependant behaviour, sleep disorders, somatic complaints and an arrest or regression of social habits and school performance.

Studies of Holocaust survivors have found that their children and even their grandchildren have higher rates of clinical depression and suicide than the population at large. (Conroy 2000)

Released hostages need time to recover from the physical, mental, and emotional difficulties they faced. However, it is important to keep in mind that human beings are highly resilient and can persevere in spite of tragedy. Research shows that positive growth and resilience can occur following trauma (Wessely 2005; Hanbury 2013).

My rule of thumb on treatment of returning hostages and PTSD is, consider **a hostage's body can be immediately released, but certain aspects of their mental self may act as if still in confinement**. Hostage events can never be forgotten; they can only be understood.

CHAPTER 20
FAMILY SURVIVAL STRATEGIES

During protracted hostage ordeals, the mental health of family members cannot be overlooked. Just as the traveler has become a victim of kidnapping, so has the family. The hostage's days were often spent wondering if he would ever return home alive; for the families too, their days were often spent wondering if their loved one would ever return home alive. In my experience, families are just as likely to require mental health assistance during the hostage ordeal as after the ordeal.

Consider the day-to-day life of a family member who has no idea if her loved one is even alive, let alone being held hostage. Her days are filled with the anxiety of wondering whether the next phone call will be from some government representative telling her a body has been found. Then again, even if she does know her loved one is being held hostage—somewhere—there are the almost daily television reports about hostages being taken and hostages having been executed. With every televised news report about hostages, family members search the screen in the hope of catching a glimpse of their loved one. In many ways, this mental torture is as terrible as the mental torture the hostage might be suffering, not knowing what's coming next during the weeks, months or even years.

Here are a few survival strategies for family members:

1. The FLO or media relations officer must work with the family to script their replies to media requests and prepare a script that family members can use when friends and curious locals inquire. The media will want to interview family members as soon as the news of the event is made public. However, during these early times, all media contact must be coordinated

by the FLO or the media relations officer. To do otherwise may expose the unprepared family to press coverage that is harmful to a hostage's treatment or negotiations. Later on, the FLO or media relations officer will discuss with the family how a family media spokesperson should be selected and why. During any and all media reports or interviews, the family must be seen to be speaking with one voice.

2. Consider getting a separate cell phone and private phone number to use for calls with the FLO, selected government representatives or employer representatives such as the dedicated human resources representative.

   Considering the increased number and duration of phone calls that the hostage family will receive on their usual phone line from family, friends, and well-wishers, the hostage's spouse will need a dedicated line. It would be continuously bothersome while speaking on the usual phone line to have to hang up on one call to pick up an incoming call, only to find out the first call was more important. With a separate phone and number, the spouse can go about her daily business, knowing she is always available for important hostage-related calls.

3. Family members should discipline themselves to watch the television news on one particular channel and only once or twice daily. A family will only suffer repeated torment by watching repetitious newscasts all day long without the benefit of learning anything new. This constant reminder of the ordeal will soon overwhelm the viewer and contribute to increased anxiety and mental exhaustion. A family should have sufficient confidence in the FLO and their government contacts that they will be advised prior to any relevant news item that may contain updated information.

4. The family may require legal assistance to access necessary finances. If proper financial arrangements were not made prior to the hostage's travel, the family may require legal representation. Every province, state, and country requires some sort of legal order to direct a bank or other financial institution to release funds or permit a spouse access to her

absent spouse's personal bank account. The legal department at the hostage's place of employment may be a good place to inquire about how they can assist the family in this regard plus any other legal concerns.

5. I strongly recommend that families consider professional health assistance at the earliest sign of social turmoil or disorder within the family. Considering the extreme pressures on a family affected by a hostage situation, the likelihood of family disagreements is almost a certainty. The larger the extended family, the more likely there will be a variety of strong opinions on what should be done and by whom. We all recognize that there is a pecking order or hierarchy in any family. During times of stress within a family—be they financial, medical or social—there is often competition, opportunity, jealousy, or favoritism. We all know of family arguments over Thanksgiving or Christmas dinners or who gets which weeks at the family cottage. But to a family living under the constant stressors of a family member taken hostage and possibly faced with an impossible ransom request or impending death, the situation requires professional support and guidance. A family that recognizes the need for professional guidance early in their ordeal is more likely to survive as a strong and supportive family unit regardless of the outcome.

CORPORATE FAMILY ASSISTANCE STRATEGIES

As mentioned in earlier chapters, the hostage's employer can play a significant role in assisting the family during these times. These assistance strategies complement those responsibilities in predeployment planning.

1. The employer should consider absorbing the costs for the spouse's dedicated cell phone as a legitimate business expense.

2. The employer may wish to assist the family by providing for a weekly cleaning service and yard maintenance.

Considering the increased traffic through the hostage's residence as family members meet, and considering that much of the spouse's time and focus is spent on so many other concerns, a weekly cleaning would be a significant gesture of kindness and support.

3. The employer may consider assisting the family with the numerous driving responsibilities once handled by the hostage employee. Any employee with young children or teens will have the numerous pickup and drop-off responsibilities at dance class, baseball or hockey practice, school dances or study groups, plus the occasional sleepovers or doctor's appointments that must now be handled in some other way.

These employer assistance strategies allow the family to function in a way that is as close to normal as possible—to help fill in the gaps. I am certainly not suggesting that their help implies that the company is in some way morally responsible or liable. I suggest these strategies because nowadays, being a responsible corporate employer is what the more successful employers are doing. They recognize their employees are not their employees for only eight hours a day; they are their employees for twenty-four hours a day.

From the family's perspective, their world has been turned upside down and inside out. A father and husband, a mother or wife, a son or daughter, a sister or brother has been kidnapped. The family has no idea if the person is dead or alive and, if alive, for how long. They have the police and the media asking questions; they have family and extended family members visiting and spending too many hours on the phone discussing the many what-ifs and maybes. They have no experience in this sort of thing, and they are going through every emotion in the book. They are mentally and physically exhausted.

The family has become captive by the media attention and the social impact of everyone knowing their business. The family is captive because they can't seem to go anywhere without arousing the attention of so many people. They can't go on vacation because they feel they are abandoning the hostage and they may not be there for that important phone call; the family feels guilty if they laugh or celebrate any event.

⁓

Closing note: US President Obama has recognized the shortcomings of the United States government in a number of areas with respect to American hostages and its service to hostage families. (See appendix 5.)

CONCLUSION

The world is becoming a more dangerous place. It is not safe for people traveling domestically or internationally, whether for business or for pleasure. It is no longer safe to visit our local coffee shop, attend a sporting event, walk our own streets, or even for our children playing at school.

More recently, hometown or domestic terrorism is being carried out by many seeking "celebrity criminal" status, for which the media are happy to oblige. When we can't find a reasonable explanation for a person's actions, we label them as sick or crazy because we can't get back to our normal lives until we convince ourselves it's a mental flaw; it's really nobody's fault, and therefore, we don't have to act. But science has proven that many are not sick or crazy. So are these dangers a product of gratuitous Hollywood violence? Are they a cry for social recognition or the product of terrorist propaganda?

The international media have become the abused victims of terrorism. The media hate the terrorists for what they do, but they need the terrorists for what they provide—the "Breaking News" reports; the sensational stories of love, hate, death, and drama, which give their stories legs. There are the documentary spin-offs; the behind-the-story specials; the investigative reports; and so on. They stay, they watch, and yet they do not have the courage to leave. The terrorists thrive on this relationship and have learned to exploit it. One terrorist attack in any part of the world provides an immediate incentive to other terrorists to commit a terrorist act through what I see as media-induced momentum. (The media calls them copycats.) After a major terrorist attack, a smaller terrorist attack can piggyback onto the media attention caused by the first event and reap more media attention than it would have attracted alone. A third terrorist attack within a short timeline of the first and second event reaps even more attention . . . and so on. Persons traveling to regions at risk are wise to factor in this trend.

Improving our personal security, whether at home or away, is largely our own responsibility. Each of us must become better informed and more aware; each of us must be prepared and vigilant. A traveler who is better prepared and more security-conscious is less likely to become a victim of a hostage taking. It is up to each of us to learn and practice these travel security measures. Practice them when traveling at home while in relative safety so that by the time you travel further afield, you are more comfortable and you are safer.

If your cruise ship is docking in a port that makes you feel uncomfortable, nothing says you have to go ashore. If you want to go ashore but are anxious or uneasy, go in a group and stay close to the ship where there is always an increased police presence. If you are in a foreign hotel, don't be shy about asking the concierge about local security issues and ask for safety recommendations.

When visiting a new city or a new country, don't be tempted to explore off the beaten path. Too often we feel we have to visit all the "must see" attractions or the trip isn't a success. A busy schedule distracts us from attention to our safety. When you do visit these attractions, take only recommended guided tours and don't fall for the cheaper tours sold by hawkers. If we agree to a smarter and safer trip prior to our departure, we will be more comfortable throughout our trip. Predeployment education helps us make better travel decisions.

From local television news reports, we know that more and more people are being abducted every day. Mothers and fathers are abducting their own children, and lonely and mentally unstable people are abducting children to serve as companions or replacements for absent spouses. From international news reports, we are reminded daily of politicians, businesspeople, and soldiers being kidnapped and murdered from too many conflicts in too many places. Globally, over one hundred people are kidnapped every day. There are the even sadder reports of hundreds of children taken as political or religious prisoners or as child soldiers or child wives. Don't join these television news reports; don't join these statistics.

This book is a toolbox of strategies that hostages can apply to their individual circumstances. The hostage strategies that were explained in this book are based upon actual survivor reports, hostage debriefings, and proven science. Some strategies are specific to a hostage's physical needs, others to his mental needs, and the behavioral strategies are directed toward a hostage's day-to-day demeanor and frame of mind. It is up to the hostage to select the particular strategies he feels able to successfully apply to his unique situation. Humans are social by nature, although social norms differ from culture to culture; science tells us there are core similarities. It is these core similarities upon which these strategies were built.

Make no mistake—just because you've read a book about survival strategies doesn't guarantee that if taken hostage, you will somehow have a better time of it. You are still in for a world of trouble, and regardless of what you do, you may not survive. History tells us that for many, it was in fact just by chance that one prisoner was sent one way and another prisoner was sent another way; one died and one lived. The better option is to do everything possible not to become a hostage in the first place.

In a few short years, terrorist groups have become more adept at abducting, confining, and ransoming hostages. More powerful terrorist groups like ISIS and al-Qaeda have become highly skilled not only at kidnapping and confining hostages but also at dehumanizing hostages. In an effort to counter survival strategies, they are hardening their own people against developing any sense of sympathy toward hostages or any feelings of remorse for the treatment or execution of hostages. Their brutality knows no bounds. The best safety strategy when it comes to groups like ISIS is to stay far away, because the chances of your survival may rely on nothing more than a coin toss.

This book educates the international and domestic traveler, NGO employees, volunteers, and soldiers who put themselves in harm's way. It educates their families and prepares them for their own survival during a potential hostage ordeal. This book provides information for the employers and the governments of those hostages with respect to their corporate social responsibilities and their training obligations prior to travel, as well as for the media and medical professionals whose services will be required during hostages' confinement and upon their release. Many countries and corporations have the appropriate policies in place, but for one reason or another, they don't always apply them well or consistently. As employees, we must remind them of these obligations.

The strategies presented in this book provide travelers and their families with opportunities for education and understanding; they offer hostages and their families suggestions on how to cope and survive during a hostage ordeal. They also guide families in preparation for a hostage's return home so that they may better reintegrate a changed person into a changed family. A family must remember a hostage's body might be free and back at home but he may sometimes act as though he is still in confinement.

When we travel, we check the weather and select our activities and clothing accordingly, but we never research travel and safety advisories and adjust those activities accordingly. The excitement of reading the travel brochures must be tempered with also reading government travel information and security warnings. We can no longer afford to travel and leave our security to fate.

This book is a foundation on which to build your own travel safety awareness and travel education checklist, because the best hostage survival strategy remains not to be taken hostage in the first place.

If you are kidnapped, think of your situation as having fallen into a deep well. It makes no sense to wonder how you could have been so stupid not to have seen the well, why you didn't see it coming even when you were warned the well was nearby. It makes no sense to feel sorry for yourself because that won't get you out of the well; it makes no sense to blame someone else because that won't get you out of the well. You can sit at the bottom of the well and spend all your time looking up and wishing someone would throw you a rope, or you can start thinking about how you can get out of the well by yourself. If someone throws you a rope in the meantime, great, but what is the likelihood of that happening? So start thinking and start doing everything about getting yourself out. Relax, think, and plan. Focus on your goal: survival.

AUTHOR'S AFTERWORD

I wrote this book in my negotiator voice—calm and understanding. A negotiator must always speak in this manner or the person on the other end won't listen to what he has to say; he'll tune out and hang up. If that happened, I would not have accomplished anything; I would not have done my job. Writing in this voice, I hoped the reader would continue to read, continue to learn and learn how to survive a hostage situation. I would not have accomplished what I set out to do if I lectured, scolded or threatened the reader along the way. On the other hand, I hope my calm voice did not understate the danger we all now face when travelling, especially to the regions of the world where hostage taking is a daily occurrence and is increasing exponentially.

I wrote this book as a guide for the families of hostages, because I have witnessed the kind of horror that makes a loved one tremble in emotional pain while crying in fear. I have witnessed the daily anguish, the dread, and the frustration that such an ordeal imposes upon the families. It is my hope that the information in this book and the associated family strategies will assist everyone in understanding the difficulties that lie ahead and help affected families to better deal with those difficulties.

A word to those with a desire to travel to faraway lands and ease the suffering of people who are victims of wars, victims of human rights abuses, or victims of corruption. Firstly, my compliments on your desire to selflessly serve others—not everyone can. Be aware, however, your desire to travel is often kindled by the rising sense of adventure and independence typically felt by young adults. And a word of caution—the longer you stay, the more likely it is that you will be kidnapped. In lands where for many locals daily survival is everything, no opportunity can be overlooked. You may be that opportunity. Experienced media personnel stay only as long as they absolutely have to—get in and get out. Don't let the news story be your kidnapping or your death. If you are taken hostage, the suffering you may have lessened on others far away will be multiplied and laid upon the members of your own family, every day and every night—maybe forever. You will never know how many tears your family will shed.

Every day as you sit as a hostage, wondering what will happen to you and whether you will ever see your family again, your family also sits wondering what will happen to you and whether they will ever see you again. Every night, your family will go to bed wondering where you are and whether you're cold and hungry. Your family becomes as much a hostage as you are. Reconsider traveling to these dangerous regions, at least for the near future anyway. Look for ways you can reduce these people's suffering from a variety of activities closer to home. After all, the best hostage and family survival strategy is not to be taken hostage in the first place.

APPENDICES

This first news article, by Tu Thanh Ha, was published on March 16, 2015, in *The Globe and Mail*. It recounts how two Spanish journalists were treated by their ISIS captors and how other hostages were treated. It shows how terrorists in that part of the world, on which my example scenarios for this book are based, have learned to dehumanize their hostages and routinely subject them to a range of mental and physical tortures. These atrocities committed by terrorists against noncombatants, civilians, journalists, and aid workers are as recent as early 2014.

Ex-hostages Share Grisly Tales of Islamic State's Answer to Guantanamo

The Globe and Mail, Tu Thanh Ha, March 16, 2015

New accounts by two Spanish journalists have provided more details about the Islamic State's creation of its own version of Guantanamo, where foreign hostages endured repeated mock executions, psychological and physical torture and other abuses, leaving some emaciated like walking skeletons while another victim underwent a mental breakdown from his suffering.

The reports, which appeared in the Spanish newspapers Sunday and Monday, were written separately by Javier Espinosa and Marc Marginedas, two former hostages who were captured in September, 2013.

"The apparent intention of the hijackers was to recreate a Guantanamo for Western prisoners," Mr. Marginedas wrote in the Barcelona paper El Periodico.

Mr. Espinosa similarly said he was held in what he dubbed *"El Guantanamo islamista."*

Writing in El Mundo, Mr. Espinosa said the detainees were part of a systematic effort by Islamic State that came to include journalists and aid workers from 11 different countries who had been captured after they entered civil-war-torn Syria.

"They had designed the project for a long time," Mr. Espinosa said he was told by James Foley, an American freelance reporter who had been held since November, 2012, with British journalist John Cantlie.

"The Iraqi sheik himself explained from the first moment they thought of kidnapping Westerners to lock them in a high security prison, with cameras, numerous guards . . . They told us we were going to [be] held for a long time because we were the first prisoners captured."

After enduring a mock execution at the hands of the militant known as Jihadi John, Mr. Espinosa said "that encounter confirmed the psychopathic character of my interlocutors."

Despite the brutality, some the prisoners held on to their wit and humanity, the accounts said.

Mr. Foley and Cantlie tried twice to escape. On one occasion, Mr. Foley could have run away but let himself be recaptured when he saw that Mr. Cantlie couldn't make it, Mr. Espinosa said, recalling that Mr. Foley said "I could not just leave John."

Because he endured the torture with stoicism, Mr. Foley was singled out by his guards, who beat him and waterboarded him for weeks, Mr. Espinosa said.

Mr. Marginedas said their guards came at night to force them to memorize phrases from the Quran.

"Learning Islam with these people is like learning Christianity with the Ku Klux Klan," one hostage later quipped, Mr. Marginedas recalled.

Mr. Marginedas said he and 18 other western prisoners were put together in a mansion near the Turkish border. They were the responsibility of a group of Muslims of British origin they dubbed the Beatles.

The prisoners had to wear orange jumpsuits and had to memorize in Arabic a number written on their back.

"From that moment we are not called by name, but by our identification number," Mr. Marginedas said.

Mr. Espinosa said his prisoner's number was 43.

"You, Spaniard, what's your name?" a guard would ask.

"I am Number 43," he replied.

The guard corrected him. He had to say "Sir."

"Yes sir!"

"Louder, louder!"

"Yes sir!"

After being brought to the mansion, Mr. Espinosa said he was reunited with other foreigners. Among them he recognized Didier François, a French reporter. "His story was horrifying. They spoke of systematic torture, deprivation and hunger."

Mr. François told him he had been tied to a radiator without food or water for four days until he was delirious and started screaming.

Two aid workers, the Italian Federico Motka and the Briton David Haines, looked like "walking skeletons," Mr. Espinosa added.

The two men worked for Acted, a French aid agency delivering water, food and tents to refugee camps near the Turkish–Syrian border.

Mr. Motka was beaten merely for having a tattoo of a Buddhist symbol, Mr. Espinosa said.

He said Mr. Haines, who once had been an aircraft engineer for the Royal Air Force, had been subjected to such beatings that he suffered from constant diarrhea and vomiting.

Mr. Marginedas wrote that, for their amusement, their guards forced the hostages to stand facing their cell wall and sing a version of *Hotel California*, the 1977 hit song by the Eagles. The lyrics had been modified to say: "Welcome to Osama's lovely hotel; / Such a lovely place, / Such a lovely place. / Welcome to Osama's lovely hotel; / but you could never leave, / and if you try / you will die . . ."

Mr. Espinosa recalled more sinister moments when he was targeted by Jihadi John, who has been identified by *The Washington Post* as a Kuwait-born former Londoner named Mohammed Emwazi.

Barefoot, shaven-headed and with his beard grown out, Mr. Espinosa had to sit on the ground while Jihadi John pressed a sword to his neck.

"It is cold, right?" the militant asked as he talked in details about how much pain Mr. Espinosa would feel when the blade would cut him, how he would bleed and squirm "like pigs."

Jihadi John then pressed a pistol against Mr. Espinosa's head and pulled the trigger three times.

The gun went click, click, click. The safety catch was on.

Jihadi John then told another guard to point a Kalashnikov rifle at another hostage, the Spanish photographer Ricardo Garcia Vilanova.

"You prefer me to shoot your friend? Want to be responsible for his death?" he shouted at Mr. Espinosa.

On another occasion, a guard forced Mr. Espinosa to look at a photo of the remains of Sergei Gorbunov, a Russian engineer who was kidnapped in October, 2013, and held until he was shot in the head in March, 2014.

Mr. Gorbunov, who had several broken teeth and fingers, had been tortured so much that he lapsed between moments of lucidity and periods where he hid under a blanket and laughed non-stop, Mr. Espinosa said.

The three Spanish journalists, Mr. François and Mr. Motka were released last spring.

Mr. Foley and Mr. Haines, whose countries have policies against paying ransoms, were beheaded.

Mr. Cantlie remains in captivity, his fate uncertain after he appeared in a series of Islamic State videos.

APPENDIX 2

Kayla Mueller, an American aid volunteer, was kidnapped in 2013. At the request of the US government, her family kept her kidnapping a secret until after she was killed in an airstrike on February 6, 2015. Her parents spoke to the media and were critical of the US government's efforts to secure her freedom. This appendix and the first part of appendix 3 are media stories regarding these events.

US Hostage's Parents Slam US Ransom Policy

ISIS fighters claimed Kayla Mueller, who was seized in the Syrian city of Aleppo in August 2013, was killed in a February 6 coalition air strike that buried her in rubble. It would be many days later that the American government could confirm her death. The Mueller family kept Kayla's hostage taking a public secret for 18 months.

Amy B Wang reported on the Muellers' appearance on NBC television's *Meet the Press* in the newspaper *The Arizona Republic*, Monday, February 23, 2015:

Carl and Marsha Mueller, Kayla's parents, and Eric Mueller, Kayla's brother, spoke with NBC's *Today* show for an exclusive interview.

A preview of the Muellers' interview online showed Carl Mueller saying the United States government "put policy in front of American citizens' lives." The U.S. has a policy of not paying ransoms to extremist groups.

"We understand the policy about not paying ransom," he said. "But on the other hand, any parents out there would understand that you would want anything and everything done to bring your child home."

Today show co-anchor Savannah Guthrie followed by asking the family, "Do you feel like the government did enough to help you?"

"I think I wanted to," Marsha Mueller answered quietly. "But I think, again, (it's) the policy. And I don't think anyone had any idea this group would be as powerful as they were."

APPENDIX 3

The following are letters released by the families of hostages to the press in February 2015.

First is Kayla Jean Mueller's letter, written in the spring of 2014 and recently released by her family. Following this letter is an excerpt from an updated article about her. Following this are letters home from Peter Kassig and James Foley, both of whom were murdered by the terrorists.

Everyone,

If you are receiving this letter it means I am still detained but my cell mates (starting from 11/2/2014) have been released. I have asked them to contact you + send you this letter. It's hard to know what to say. Please know that I am in a safe location, completely unharmed + healthy (put on weight in fact); I have been treated w/ the utmost respect + kindness. I wanted to write you all a well thought out letter (but I didn't know if my cell mates would be leaving in the coming days or the coming months restricting my time but primarily) I could only but write the letter a paragraph at a time, just the thought of you all sends me into a fit of tears. If you could say I have "suffered" at all throughout this whole experience it is only in knowing how much suffering I have put you all through; I will never ask you to forgive me as I do not deserve forgiveness. I remember mom always telling me that all in all in the end the only one you really have is God. I have come to a place in experience where, in every sense of the word, I have surrendered myself to our creator b/c literally there was no else . . . + by God + by your prayers I have felt tenderly cradled in freefall. I have been shown in darkness, light + have learned that even in prison, one can be free. I am grateful. I have come to see that there is good in every situation, sometimes we just have to look for it. I pray each [*sic*] day that if nothing else, you have felt a certain closeness + surrender to God as well + have formed a bond of love + support amongst one another . . . I miss you all as if it has been a decade of forced separation. I have had many a long hour to think, to think of all the things I will do w/ Lex, our first family camping trip, the first meeting @ the airport. I have had many hours to think how only in your absence have I finally @ 25 years old come to realize your place in my life. The gift that is each one of you + the person I could + could not be if you were not a part of my life, my family, my support. I DO NOT want the negotiations for my release to be your duty, if there is any other option take it, even if it takes more time. This should never have become your burden. I have asked these women to support you; please seek their advice. If you have not done so already . . . can contact . . . who may have a certain level of experience with these people. None of us could have known it would be this long but know I am also fighting from my side in the ways I am able + I have a lot of fight left inside of me. I am not breaking down + I will not give in no matter how long it takes. I wrote a song some months ago that says, "The part of me that pains the most also gets me out of bed, w/ out your hope there would be nothing left . . ." aka— The thought of your pain is the source of my own, simultaneously the hope of our reunion is the source of my strength. Please be patient, give your pain to God. I know you would want me to remain strong. That is exactly what I am doing. Do not fear for me, continue to pray as will I + by God's will we will be together soon.

All my everything,
Kayla

$\mathcal{M}$

Recently, information came to light about Kayla Mueller, revealing that she had been "married" to Abu Bakr Baghdadi, the leader of ISIS, who frequently raped her, as described in the following article.

US Intelligence Says Hostage Kayla Mueller Repeatedly Raped by ISIS Leader

Global News, Ken Dilanian. August 14, 2015

WASHINGTON—American hostage Kayla Mueller was repeatedly forced to have sex with Abu Bakr Baghdadi, the leader of the Islamic State group, U.S. intelligence officials told her family in June.

The news is but the latest in a litany of horrors perpetrated by the Islamic State group, which has beheaded, burned and crucified male captives while passing around women as sex slaves.

Mueller was held for a time by Islamic State financier Abu Sayyaf and his wife, known as Umm Sayyaf. Al-Baghdadi took Mueller as a "wife," repeatedly raping her when he visited, according to a Yazidi teenager who was held with Mueller and escaped in October 2014.

The 14-year-old made her way to Iraqi Kurdistan, where she talked to U.S. commandos in November 2014. Intelligence agencies corroborated her account and American officials passed it on to her parents in June.

"They told us that he married her, and we all understand what that means," Carl Mueller, Kayla's father, told The Associated Press on Friday, which would have been his daughter's 27th birthday. Her death was reported in February.

Her mother, Marsha Mueller, added, "Kayla did not marry this man. He took her to his room and he abused her and she came back crying."

Umm Sayyaf confirmed that al-Baghdadi had "owned" Kayla during Umm Sayyaf's lengthy American interrogation in Iraq, the Muellers said they were told by American officials.

A U.S. official confirmed their account, first reported by London's Independent newspaper. The official was not authorized to be quoted by name and spoke on condition of anonymity.

Abu Sayyaf was killed in a Delta Force raid of his Syrian compound in June, which resulted in a treasure trove of intelligence about the Islamic State group. Umm Sayyaf has been turned over to the Iraqi Kurds for trial.

The Muellers have been told she can be expected to serve a long prison sentence, said a family spokeswoman, Emily Lenzner.

Mueller was held with three other women, all Yazidis, the Muellers were told. All were sexually abused. When al-Baghdadi visited, he would take Mueller to his room, the witness told American officials. She would tell her fellow captives— sometimes tearfully—what had happened.

"Kayla tried to protect these young girls," her mother said. "She was like a mother figure to them."

When the teenaged Yazidi girl escaped with her sister, she asked Mueller to accompany her, the parents were told, but Kayla refused, worrying that her obvious Western appearance would lead to their capture.

By the time the Yadizi escapee reported the situation to Delta Force commandos in Iraq, Kayla had been moved, her parents were told.

U.S. intelligence officials found information on Sayyaf's computer indicating that Mueller, who spoke some Arabic, had been searching for information about fertility to help Umm Sayyaf, who was trying to get pregnant, according to two U.S. officials who refused to be quoted because the information is classified.

Mueller, from Prescott, Arizona, was taken hostage with her boyfriend, Omar Alkhani, in August 2013 after leaving a Doctors Without Borders hospital in Aleppo, Syria, where he had been hired to fix the Internet service for the hospital.

Mueller had begged him to let her tag along because she wanted to do relief work in the war-ravaged country.

Alkhani was released after two months, having been beaten.

The Islamic State group claimed Mueller was killed in a Jordanian air strike near Raqqah, the group's self-declared capital in Syria. U.S. officials confirmed the death but not the circumstances.

Peter Kassig's letter was written while he was in captivity, and it was released by his family in the November following his death. He was 26.

It is still really hard to believe all of this is really happening . . . as I am sure you know by now, things have been getting pretty intense. We have been held together, us foreigners . . . and now about half the people have gone home . . . I hope that this all has a happy ending but it may very well be coming down to the wire here, and if in fact that is the case then I figured it was time to say a few things that need saying before I have to go.

The first thing I want to say is thank you. Both to you and mom for everything you have both done for me as parents; for everything you have taught me, shown me, and experienced with me. I cannot imagine the strength and commitment it has taken to raise a son like me but your love and patience are things I am so deeply grateful for.

Secondly, I want you to know about things here and what I've been through straight from me so you don't have to wonder, guess, or imagine (often this is worse than the reality). All in all I am alright. Physically I am pretty underweight but I'm not starved, & I have no physical injuries, I'm a tough kid and still young so that helps.

Mentally I am pretty sure this is the hardest thing a man can go through, the stress and fear are incredible but I am coping as best I can. I am not alone. I have friends, we laugh, we play chess, we play trivia to stay sharp, and we share stories and dreams of home and loved ones. I can be hard to deal with, you know me. My mind is quick and my patience thinner than most. But all in all I am holding my own. I cried a lot in the first few months but a little less now. I worry a lot about you and mom and my friends.

They tell us you have abandoned us and/or don't care but of course we know you are doing everything you can and more. Don't worry Dad, if I do go down, I won't go thinking anything but what I know to be true. That you and mom love me more than the moon & the stars.

I am obviously pretty scared to die but the hardest part is not knowing, wondering, hoping, and wondering if I should even hope at all. I am very sad that all this has happened and for what all of you back home are going through. If I do die, I figure that at least you and I can seek refuge and comfort in knowing that I went out as a result of trying to alleviate suffering and helping those in need.

In terms of my faith, I pray everyday and I am not angry about my situation in that sense. I am in a dogmatically complicated situation here, but I am at peace with my belief.

I wish this paper would go on forever and never run out and I could just keep talking to you. Just know I'm with you. Every stream, every lake, every field and river. In the woods and in the hills, in all the places you showed me. I love you.

James Foley, 40, asked a fellow hostage who was being released to memorize this letter and dictate it to his family. Foley was killed in August 2014.

Dear Family and Friends,

I remember going to the mall with dad, a very long bike ride with mom. I remember so many great family times that take me away from this prison. Dreams of family and friends take me away and happiness fills my heart.

I know you are thinking of me and praying for me. And I am so thankful. I feel you all, especially when I pray. I pray for you to stay strong and to believe. I really feel I can touch you even in this darkness when I pray.

Eighteen of us have been held together in one cell, which has helped me. We have had each other to have endless long conversations about movies, trivia, sports. We have played games made up of scraps found in our cell . . . we have found ways to play checkers, chess, and Risk . . . and have had tournaments of competition, spending some days preparing strategies for the next day's game or lecture.

The games and teaching each other have helped the time pass. They have been a huge help. We repeat stories and laugh to break the tension.

I have had weak and strong days. We are so grateful when anyone is freed; but of course, yearn for our own freedom. We try to encourage each other and share strength. We are being fed better now and daily. We have tea, occasional coffee. I have regained most of my weight lost last year.

I think a lot about my brothers and sister. I remember playing Werewolf in the dark with Michael and so many other adventures. I think of chasing Mattie and T around the kitchen counter. It makes me happy to think of them. If there is any money left in my bank account, I want it to go to Michael and Matthew. I am so proud of you, Michael and thankful to you for happy childhood memories and to you and Kristie for happy adult ones.

And big John, how I enjoyed visiting you and Cress in Germany. Thank you for welcoming me. I think a lot about RoRo and try to imagine what Jack is like. I hope he has RoRo's personality!

And Mark . . . so proud of you, too, Bro. I think of you on the West Coast and hope you are doing some snowboarding and camping. I especially remember us going to the Comedy Club in Boston together and our big hug after. The special moments keep me hopeful.

Katie, so very proud of you. You are the strongest and best of us all!! I think of you working so hard, helping people as a nurse. I am so glad we texted just before I was captured. I pray I can come to your wedding . . . now I am sounding like Grammy!!

Grammy, please take your medicine, take walks and keep dancing. I plan to take you out to Margarita's when I get home. Stay strong, because I am going to need your help to reclaim my life.

Jim

APPENDIX 4

The following media article is from the *Washington Post*. It outlines the attempted rescue operation for the American hostages Kayla Mueller as well as James Foley, Steven Sotloff, Luke Somers, Peter Kassig, and others from Somalia, Yemen, and Syria. It contains information and statements from some parents regarding the efforts of the American government to rescue their children and President Obama's comments to the contrary. This appendix is relevant and instructive to chapter 14, "Escape"; chapter 16, "Rescue"; and chapter 17, "Release."

The Anatomy of a Failed Hostage Rescue Deep into Islamic State Territory

The Washington Post, Karen DeYoung, Feb. 14, 2015

On the evening of Thursday, June 26, the Pentagon sent a bold hostage rescue plan to the White House for approval. Dozens of Special Operations forces would fly into Syria under the barest sliver of moonlight, set down in the heart of Islamic State territory and snatch four Americans being held by the militants.

The landing took place almost exactly a week later. Yet the commandos who rushed through gunfire into the makeshift prison found only half-eaten meals and a wisp of hair. The hostages had been there. But they were gone.

By the end of the year, the Islamic State had brutally killed three of the Americans, posting their videotaped beheadings online. The last hostage and the only woman, Kayla Mueller, was declared dead last Tuesday after the militants sent photographs of her body to her family.

The finality of that news has given rise to painful questions about whether more could have been done to

353

save them. Grieving relatives of the victims, some of whom have accused the administration of waiting too long to launch a rescue mission, have also criticized the U.S. policy of non-negotiation with hostage takers.

The administration has acknowledged it could do better at communicating with the families, notwithstanding its ongoing rejection of paying ransom, and has launched a review led by the National Counterterrorism Center. "We will do everything we can, short of providing an incentive for future Americans to be caught," President Obama said in an interview last week with BuzzFeed.

But some of those who worked on the rescue mission say they believe the White House itself is at least partly to blame for the failure. They charge that there were delays in bringing the plan to Obama's desk, and that, as a result, the rescuers missed the hostages by a matter of days, or even hours.

In interviews with *The Washington Post* and in other published accounts, a number of operational-level U.S. intelligence and military officials, speaking on condition of anonymity to voice criticism of higher-ups, have said their disappointment at the failure of the mission was mixed with frustration over the decision process.

Obama himself acknowledged in the BuzzFeed interview that they "probably missed [the hostages] by a day or two." But, he said, it was inaccurate "to say that the United States government hasn't done everything we could."

Senior administration officials strongly denied there was any delay in the approval, especially once it reached the White House.

Instead, four senior officials directly involved in the decision, and several others with close knowledge of it, said that one of the most complex and dangerous such efforts ever undertaken had moved through the planning, approval and execution process at what one called "warp speed."

To prove their point, the officials revealed new details about a rescue mission that, once it failed, was never intended to be made public.

"For us, the clock starts when they tell us they have an operation that they want the president to review and approve," said Susan E. Rice, Obama's national security adviser. The clock on the mission to rescue James Foley, Steven Sotloff, Peter Kassig, and Kayla Mueller "began on a Friday and ended on a Saturday evening" when the president, meeting with his top advisers, gave the "go" order.

"It can't happen any faster than that . . . particularly given the complexity of the risk," Rice said.

A senior Defense Department official said he understood the frustration of intelligence operatives, planners and "the guys ready to go."

But this "was a risky operation, deep into Syria, where we hadn't been before," he said. "It involved a lot of people," with substantial danger to both the troops and the hostages themselves. "It wasn't a nice little surgical operation."

Moreover, while the rescuers found evidence at the site that the hostages had been there, the mission was launched with no definitive intelligence confirming their presence.

"There wasn't a hot, smoking trail," the Pentagon official said.

Deputy White House national security adviser Ben Rhodes acknowledged the feeling that "if the timing had been different, maybe the outcome would have been different. The fact of the matter is, if you're talking about a major military operation inside Syria, the notion that you shouldn't have any review of the plan before it goes to the president for signature is contrary to how things should be done."

"Frankly, the president made an incredibly risky decision," Rhodes said. "In some respects, it was more risky than the bin Laden operation."

Hostages in Somalia and Yemen

"Hostage rescues are the hardest thing we do," the senior Pentagon official said. "It's twice as hard as capturing a prisoner" in a hostile environment overseas, as Special Operations forces have done successfully on a number of occasions during the Obama administration.

If the target prisoner gets killed in the process, he said, "it's no big deal."

Osama bin Laden, whether or not it was part of the plan, ended up dead. Terror suspects captured by U.S. raids into Libya—Nazih Abdul-Hamed al-Ruqai in 2013 and Ahmed Abu Khattala in 2014—both ended up in U.S. prisons.

But a rescue mission is a different story. According to a range of officials involved in such actions, the factors weighed begin with the level of certainty about where the hostage is located. There was only one case among attempted and successful rescues in recent years, officials said, when there was absolute knowledge of where a hostage was and the conditions of captivity.

The January 2012 rescue of American aid worker Jessica Buchanan and her Danish colleague was considered a relative piece of cake. With substantial overhead and ground intelligence, the Pentagon assured Obama that they were completely confident of her position in the wilds of north-central Somalia. They knew the al-Shabaab [sic] fighters holding her were lightly armed and poorly trained and that there were no reinforcements nearby.

A team of Navy SEALs dropped into the camp. One jumped atop Buchanan to shield her, the others killed a number of her guards. The successful operation was over in minutes.

Last fall, long after the Buchanan operation and the failed summer raid in Syria, U.S. commandos made two attempts to rescue American photojournalist Luke Somers, kidnapped by al-Qaeda in Yemen in 2013.

In planning for the first attempt, in late November, officials believed that several hostages were being held in a cave, although they were not sure Somers was among them. There was no information that his life was in immediate danger, but the location was considered easy and the risk to U.S. forces was judged to be fairly low. The operational plan was presented to the White House on Thursday; Obama approved it on Sunday.

All of the presumed terrorists at the site were killed. One of the rescuers was wounded in the arm. Somers was not there.

Less than two weeks later, new intelligence located Somers in a compound of buildings in the southern Yemeni province of Shabwah, and there was a "clear indication he was about to be killed," the senior Pentagon official said. Intelligence on the location was good, although the assessed risk was high. Significant components of the previous attempt were still in place, and Obama's approval came within a day.

The Dec. 6 mission resulted in the deaths of Somers and another hostage the Americans said they did not know was being held with him, South African aid worker Pierre Korkie. Both were shot by

their captors, who were alerted to the landing force
before U.S. commandos could reach the site on foot.
Korkie's family and employer later said the failed
rescue mission came just as they were negotiating his
release.

Intelligence on Americans

In March and April of last year, Islamic State militants
in Syria released at least six European hostages.
Although the exact circumstances of their freedom
remain murky, most if not all are presumed to have
been exchanged for ransom.

At least some of them had been held with the
Americans. The Islamic State frequently moves its
captives, but after debriefing the released Europeans,
U.S. intelligence officials believed that at least Foley,
and possibly more, were at a location outside the
militants' de facto headquarters in the north-central
Syrian city of Raqqa. On that basis, the Joint Special
Operations Command, or JSOC, began drawing up a
rescue plan.

The hostage site was described as a compound
of buildings, including a small oil refinery, on the
city's outskirts. A substantial concentration of
militant troops was said to be nearby, along with the
main Islamic State force in Raqqa, whose pre-war
population totaled about 220,000 civilians.

At the time—months before U.S. airstrikes would
begin in September—there was virtually no air
surveillance over Syria and little desire to risk engaging
Syrian government air defenses. Information from the
released hostages, the administration believed, was
inconclusive and intelligence from inside the country,
particularly from areas wholly occupied by the Islamic
State, was scant at best. The Tampa-based Central

Command, presented with a preliminary proposal by JSOC, was hesitant.

Meanwhile, the hostages' families had been gathering their own intelligence. To them, the situation seemed far more clear-cut than it did to the administration, which they believed was dragging its feet.

Some remain bitter. "Nothing was done to save our young Americans," Diane Foley said in an ABC News interview last week. Her son and the others were "held for nearly two years and there were many opportunities along the way: several times when the captors reached out, several times when returning hostages brought sensitive information," she said.

"It is no secret that the administration neglected this case," Barak Barfi, the principal hostage adviser to the Sotloff family said in an interview. "It never dedicated the necessary resources to locate the Americans. ... The administration was always two steps behind us as we were the first to debrief European hostages as well as receive information from Syrians who had been held with the Americans."

For the administration, the breakthrough that pushed the rescue plan forward came in mid-June with the release of another European, Danish photojournalist Daniel Rye Ottosen. After a ransom of what Danish newspapers said was about $2.3 million was paid, Ottosen was taken by the Islamic State from the Raqqa prison on June 17.

He was released from a militant safe house near the Turkish border on June 19, and on June 22, FBI agents interviewed him in Denmark. Ottosen helped solidify the information learned from the other released hostages. He had been with all four of the Americans just days before and provided a description of the prison site so exact that planners had enough certainty of where it was, and what the rescuers would encounter when they touched down, that the plan began to move up the military chain of command.

The Central Command signed off, despite ongoing doubts about the quality of the intelligence, the large amount of troops and other assets involved, and the fact that Syria was unknown territory, administration officials said. From the Central Command it went to the Joint Staff, and then to Defense Secretary Chuck Hagel, who signed it and sent it to the White House.

The raid into Syria

The plan, by all accounts, was unprecedented in its degree of difficulty and hazard. More than 100 Special Operations forces were to be involved, along with an array of fixed-wing aircraft and helicopters.

"It required more resources, more effort, more time to stage and prepare" than any previous such operation and involved representatives of all U.S. military services, a Pentagon official said. "It was so freaking complicated."

Because of the presence of a large force of Islamic State fighters, this official said, the plan involved several "diversionary elements" designed to "distract the handlers from the site."

"We had to have the assistance of some countries in order to stage assets," a senior administration official involved in the process said. "That is not a decision that the Defense Department or JSOC can make." Other officials said the operation was launched from Jordan.

"We had information that made us think they could be there," the senior administration official said of the Raqqa prison site. "But we also didn't know what they were walking into. We didn't have a huge intelligence base. We didn't have overwatch. We didn't have a lot of what you might have in other operations." The risk to both the hostages and the commandos was assessed as high.

For the Special Operations forces readying to take action, the wait was nerve-racking. "These guys are snake eaters," the Pentagon official said. "They move quickly, they don't want to be slowed down for anything. They don't live in the world" of policy decisions.

Senior representatives from all national security departments and agencies convened at the White House early on Friday, June 27. Later that day, their Cabinet-level principals met to examine the plan so that it could be presented to the president with all questions answered and risks assessed.

On Saturday, it was forwarded to Obama, with a recommendation for approval, by his top national security team. "I frankly expected the president to say, being presented with such a high risk, complex operation, okay, thank you, let me sleep on it," said a senior official who was present at the meeting in the White House situation room. But Obama signed off before the meeting ended.

Presidential approval set a series of events in motion. Jordan needed to be briefed on the final plan and agree to it. Special Operations forces assigned to the mission had to be gathered at their home base at Fort Bragg and transported to the Middle East. Aircraft had to be positioned to carry the rescuers in and out, participate in the diversions and conduct overhead surveillance while the operation was underway. The weather and phases of the moon had to be studied, to ensure cover of darkness.

The commandos would fly in heavily armed Black Hawk helicopters from the Army's 160th Special

Operations Aviation Regiment, known as the "Night Stalkers."

When the force landed in the early morning of July 4 [later corrected to July 3] in Syria, their stay was brief. What one military official said was "a good number" of militants were killed. One U.S. service member received a minor injury when Islamic State fire hit a helicopter.

There were no hostages. Despite later conjecture that they might have been moved only a few hours earlier, and Obama's estimate of a day or two, several senior administration and military officials said it could have been days, or a week or more. "We don't know," said one. "We know that they were there, based on what we found. But we don't know" when they left.

News of the raid, and its failure, would not become public until Aug. 20, the day after the Islamic State posted a video of Foley's beheading.

A similar video of Sotloff's killing was posted on Sept. 2, followed by Kassig on Nov. 16. Last week, when Mueller's death was announced, the administration confirmed that she, too, had been one of the four held at the prison outside Raqqa. U.S. and Jordanian officials denied that she had been killed, as the militants claimed, by a coalition airstrike.

"I understand the frustrations of folks who are working their hearts out, removed from what goes on in the Pentagon, in the White House, in the State Department. I get that," one senior official said of the failed rescue mission.

"I don't think it was too long a time," the official said. "I think it is heart-breaking that they weren't there."

Adam Goldman contributed to this report.

APPENDIX 5

Shortly after learning of the death of Kayla Mueller in 2015, her parents made Kayla's earlier 2014 letters available to the public and held a press conference criticizing the American government's handling of her rescue. Subsequent statements by President Obama confirmed the government was not doing a good enough job dealing with the families. This report in *The Washington Post* outlines US future activities in that regard.

U.S. Considers New 'Fusion Cell' to Deal with Overseas Hostage Situations

The Washington Post, Adam Goldman, April 7, 2015

The Obama administration is considering the creation of a "fusion cell" of law enforcement, intelligence and other officials to better coordinate its response to hostage situations. Its mission would be to focus exclusively on developing strategies to recover American captives being held overseas.

The proposal is described in a letter sent to the families of American hostages and is one of several ideas the administration is considering as it gets closer to concluding its review of hostage policies. That review was launched in December amid frustration at the government's response from families of American hostages, some of whom were held and later killed by the Islamic State and other terrorist groups.

The new fusion cell would oversee a "whole-of-government response to hostage events," according to the letter, a copy of which was obtained by *The Washington Post*. It would involve subject-matter experts from agencies including the FBI, the Defense Department, the State Department and those in the intelligence community.

Although all of those agencies already get involved when Americans are taken hostage overseas, the possible creation of a unified group underscores perceived gaps in a response that families describe as often bewildering.

Under another proposal, according to the letter, a senior-level policy group, chaired by the National Security Council staff, would review hostage policies and recovery strategies proposed by the fusion cell. That group would report to Cabinet officials and the president to "ensure sustained, high-level government-wide attention to hostage cases and policies."

The letter does not address the U.S. ban on paying ransoms to terrorist groups—a policy that has drawn criticism from families and others, particularly in light of other countries' willingness to pay for the release of their citizens. The administration has said it will not alter the policy, citing concerns that ransoms would reward hostage takers and encourage them to target more Americans.

At the same time, U.S. officials have expressed an interest in finding ways to better communicate with families about efforts to recover their loved ones. The letter says the administration is considering establishing a "family engagement team" to ensure that families have continuous, direct access to officials who can provide "timely information and other necessary support during and after a hostage crisis."

Some families have said that support was lacking in their cases.

Sara Berg, the sister of Nick Berg, an American contractor who was kidnapped and killed in Iraq in 2004, said she did not know what had happened to her brother until a video surfaced online depicting his beheading.

Sara Berg, one of dozens of family members interviewed as part of the administration's review, said she thought the letter sent by the administration reflected its interest in "consensus-making and being open to input." That, she said, "is very positive."

U.S. officials, according to the letter, hope to meet in person with families in May to solicit their feedback on the review.

"We have heard concerns expressed by some family members about their interaction and communication with U.S. government officials and the amount of information that can be shared," said Kathleen C. Butler, a spokeswoman in the Office of the Director of National Intelligence. "We have spoken with 22 families, provided them with updates on the review, and sought their feedback on an initial set of proposals."

Author's Note 1

On June 25, 2015, the US Department of State announced President Obama's new policy directive, known as PPD-30, which allows American families to negotiate and pay ransoms for American hostages without fear of criminal prosecution.

This new policy essentially changes nothing because there was never any real intention to prosecute American families. The law was on the books, but it was never enforced. What was not mentioned in PPD-30 was how this "change" in policy affects how US law enforcement will work with those families in other than an administrative role. Early reports say federal authorities will now assist families with negotiations.

There is some evidence to suggest that hostages from countries that do pay ransoms are not held as long as American hostages or hostages from countries that do not pay ransoms. These longer-held hostages are kept for their propaganda value and as an effort to entice American or Western governments to commit to a hostage rescue. ISIS has not yet been successful in luring the Americans into a military ground war. Therefore, their only chance to capture an American soldier is during a hostage rescue attempt.

Author's Note 2

For readers who may wish to learn more about the United States' hostage policies that were significant topics in appendices 2, 3, 4, and 5, they can be found in the *U.S. Department of State, Foreign Affairs Manual*, vol. 7. (CT: CON-142; 07-26-2006, United States Department of State, 2006).

To highlight only a few:

- 7 FAM 1823 (07-26-2006)—the US government will make no concessions to individuals or groups holding official or private US citizens hostage.

- 7 FAM 1825.1 (07-26-2006)—identifies a consular officer as the point of contact with family members of the hostage.
- 7 FAM 1825.4 (08-11-2014)—outlines contact with the victim's family.
- 7 FAM 1821 e.1 (06-29-2012)—says that should a private citizen or company wish to pay a ransom, the US government will limit its participation to basic administration services.
- 7 FAM 1821 e.2 (06-29-2012)—goes on to say that such citizens or companies do so without the cooperation of the US government.
- 7 FAM 1821 e.4 (06-29-2012)—strongly urges families not to pay ransom.

Author's Note 3

To learn more about the international obligations for the governments of the countries in which a hostage has been taken, refer to United Nations Treaty Collection (1984), listed in the References.

REFERENCES

Basoglu, Metin. 1992. *Torture and Its Consequences, Current Treatment Approaches.* Cambridge University Press.

Berry, A. et al. 2015. *Hope: A Memoir of Survival in Cleveland.* New York: Penguin Publishing Group.

Breault, M. and M. King. 1993. *Inside the Cult: A Member's Chilling, Exclusive Account of Madness and Depravity in David Koresh's Compound.* New York: The Penguin Group.

Brom, D. & Kleber, R.J. 1989. *Prevention of post-traumatic stress disorder.* Journal of Traumatic Stress, 2, 235-51.

Buchanan, Jessica and Erik Landemalm with Antonio Flacco. 2014. *Impossible Odds.* Atria Paperback, Simon & Schuster, Inc.

Callahan, S. 2002. *Adrift: 76 Days Lost at Sea.* Mariner Books.

Cohn, J., et al. 1985. A study of Chilean refugee children in Denmark. *The Lancet*, 2(8452), 437–438.

Conroy, J. 2000. *Unspeakable Acts, Ordinary People: The Dynamics of Torture.* New York: Random House.

Cornum, R. with P. Copeland. 1993. *She Went to War: The Rhonda Cornum Story.* Presidio Press.

Council of the European Union, the. 2002. *Council Framework Decision on Combating Terrorism.* Official Journal L 164, 0003–0007.

Country Reports on Terrorism 2014. Title 22, United States Code, Section 2656f.

Criminal Code of Canada, RSC. 1985. Section 83.01.

Curry, D., and H. Mercer. 2002. *Prisoners of Hope: The Story of Our Captivity and Freedom in Afghanistan.* New York: Doubleday.

De Becker, G. 1997. *The Gift of Fear.* New York: Dell Publishing.

Dilanian, K. 2015. US intelligence says hostage Kayla Mueller repeatedly raped by ISIS leader. *Global News*. http://globalnews. ca/news/2167086/us-intelligence-says-hostage-kayla-mueller-repeatedly-raped-by-isis-leader.

Epictetus.[12] http://www.goodreads.com/author/show/13852.Epictetus.

Faber, I., H. Harlow, and L. West. 1957. Brainwashing, conditioning, and DDD (debility, dependency, and dread). *Sociometry*, 20, 271–85.

Federal Bureau of Investigation. 1932. *Federal Kidnapping Act*. 18 U.S.C. § 1201.

Flight Safety Foundation. 2015. Aviation Safety Network. http://aviation-safety.net/statistics/period.

Fowler, R. 2011. *A Season in Hell*. Toronto, Ontario: Harper Collins.

Fung, M. 2011. *Under an Afghan Sky: A Memoir of Captivity*. Toronto: Harper Collins.

Goldman, A. 2015. US considers new "fusion cell" to deal with overseas hostage situations. *The Washington Post*. https://www.washingtonpost.com/world/national-security/us-considers-new-fusion-cell-to-deal-with-overseas-hostage-situations/2015/04/06/9d575834-dc8e-11e4-be40-566e2653afe5_story.html.

Guardian, The. 2015. "Even in prison, one can be free." From Kayla Mueller's letter to her family. http://www.theguardian.com/

---

[12] Born in Pamukkale (formerly Hierapolis, Phrygia), Turkey, Epictetus was a Greek Stoic philosopher. He was probably born a slave at Hierapolis, Phrygia (present-day Pamukkale, Turkey), and lived in Rome until his exile to Nicopolis in Northwestern Greece, where he lived most of his life and died. His teachings were noted down and published by his pupil Arrian in his *Discourses*. Philosophy, he taught, is a way of life and not just a theoretical discipline. To Epictetus, all external events are determined by fate and are thus beyond our control, but we can accept whatever happens calmly and dispassionately. Individuals, however, are responsible for their own actions, which they can examine and control through rigorous self-discipline. Suffering arises from trying to control what is uncontrollable or from neglecting what is within our power. As part of the universal city that is the universe, human beings have a duty of care to all fellow humans. The person who followed these precepts would achieve happiness.

us-news/2015/feb/10/kayla-mueller-letter-i-have-learned-that-even-in-prison-one-can-be-free.

Hanbury, R., and D. Romano. 2013. American Psychological Association.

Hoffman, B. 2006. *Inside Terrorism*. New York: Columbia University Press.

Human Rights Voices. n.d. UN 101: There Is No UN Definition of Terrorism. www.humanrightsvoices.org/EYEontheUN/un_101/facts.

Knight, M. with M. Burford. 2014. *Finding Me: A Decade of Darkness, A Life Reclaimed*. Toronto: Harper Collins.

Kruglanski, A. et al. 2013. Terrorism—a (self) love story: redirecting the significance quest can end violence. *American Journal of Psychology*, 68(7), 559–575.

Layton, J. 2015. "What Causes Stockholm Syndrome?" *How Stuff Works*. http://health.howstuffworks.com/mental-health/mental-disorders/stockholm-syndrome.htm.

Lee, M., and B. Klapper. 2015. Report shows Iran terrorism threat on the rise as nuke deadline nears. *Washington, Associated Press* in *The Globe and Mail*.

Liman, D., P. Crowley, and R. Gladstein (producers) and D. Liman (director). 2002. *The Bourne Identity* (motion picture). United States: Barrandov Studios.

Lindhout, A. and S. Corbett. 2013. *A House in the Sky: A Memoir*. New York: Simon & Shuster, Inc.

Loney, J. 2011. *Captivity: 118 Days in Iraq and the Struggle for a World without War*. Toronto: Alfred A. Knopf.

Marvasti, J., ed. 2008. *Psycho-Political Aspects of Suicide Warriors, Terrorism and Martyrdom: A Critical View from "Both Sides" in Regard to Cause and Cure*. Springfield, Illinois: Charles C. Thomas.

Metin, B., ed. 1992. *Torture and Its Consequences: Current Treatment Approaches*. Cambridge University Press.

Pilkington, E. 2009. "Betancourt Vilified by Fellow Hostages." The *Guardian.* http://www.theguardian.com/world/2009/feb/26/ingrid-betancourt-colombia-hostage-farc-book.

Post, J. 2007. *The Mind of the Terrorist: The Psychology of Terrorism from the IRA to al-Qaeda.* New York: Palgrave MacMillan.

Pryce-Jones, D. 1989. *The Closed Circle: An Interpretation of the Arabs.* Ivan R. Dee.

Ralston, A. 2004. *127 Hours: Between a Rock and a Hard Place.* Atria Books.

Rasmussen, O. 1990. "Medical Aspects of Torture." *Danish Medical Bulletin 37,* Supplement no. 1, 1–88.

Sciolino, E. 1992. "Female P.O.W. Is Abused, Kindling Debate." The New York Times. http://www.nytimes.com/1992/06/29/us/female-pow-is-abused-kindling-debate.html.

Sherwood, E. 1986. The power relationship between captor and captive. *Psychiatric Annals,* 16(11), 653–5.

Smart, Elizabeth. 2013. *My Story.* St. Martin's Press. New York, NY.

Speckhard, A. et al. 2005. "Stockholm Effects and Psychological Responses to captivity in hostages Held by Suicidal Terrorists." In *Psychological Responses to the New Terrorism: A NATO Russia Dialogue.* IOS Press. pp. 29.

Statistica, Nail McCarthy. 2015. http://www.statista.com/chart/3855/the-most-dangerous-countries-for-aid-workers.[13]

Taylor, Scott. 2003. *Unembedded.* Vancouver, Canada: Douglas and McIntyre.

Tebbutt, Judith. 2013. *A Long Walk Home,* London: Faber & Faber Ltd. p.85.

United Nations, General Assembly Official Records. 1979. International Convention Against the Taking of Hostages, G.A.

---

[13] The Statista "Chart of the Day," made available under the Creative Commons License CC BY-ND 3.0, may be used and displayed without charge by all commercial and noncommercial websites. Use is, however, only permitted with proper attribution to Statista.

Res. 146 (XXXIV), U.N. GAOR, 34th Sess., Supp. No. 46, at 245, U.N. Doc. A/34/46, entered into force June 3, 1983.

United Nations, General Assembly Working Group. 2014. Sixth committee, first meeting, sixty-ninth General Assembly.

United Nations, Global Compact. 2000. *United Nations Global Compact.* https://www.unglobalcompact.org.

United Nations, Office of the High Commissioner. 2000. *Guiding Principles on Business and Human Rights: Implementing the United Nations "Protect, Respect and Remedy" Framework.*

United Nations, Treaty Collection. 1984. Convention against Torture and Other Cruel, Inhuman or Degrading Treatment or Punishment. https://treaties.un.org/pages/ViewDetails.aspx?src=TREATY&mtdsg_no=IV-9&chapter=4&lang=en.

United States Department of State. 2006. *Foreign Affairs Manual.* CT: CON-142; 07-26-2006.

United States Department of State. 2015. *Worldwide Caution.* US Department of State: Bureau of Consular Affairs. US Passports and International Travel. http://travel.state.gov/content/passports/english/alertswarnings/worldwide-caution.html.

United States Institute of Peace. 1993. *Report of the Chilean National Commission on Truth and Reconciliation.* Released by copyright owner Kaluf, R. H., into the public domain on March 12, 2007.

Waite, T. 1997. *Footfalls in Memory.* Doubleday.

Wessely, S. 2005 Victimhood and Resilience. *New England Journal of Medicine,* 353: 548–550.

INDEX

employers of, 17, 49–50, 53–54, 56–
59, 62–63, 65, 67–68, 70–71,
73, 75–77, 81–82, 146, 287, 302,
306, 326–28, 333, 358
family of, xv, 36, 43–50, 52–54,
56–59, 61–71, 76–77, 81–83,
93–94, 114–15, 118, 130, 161–
62, 164–68, 180–83, 190–91,
236, 238–41, 270–72, 286–87,
290–92, 296–302, 305–8, 312–
18, 320–23, 325–29, 334–36,
342–48, 350, 364–65
released, 43, 293, 299, 301, 305–12,
314–15, 318, 320–21
survival strategies, xix–xxi, xxv,
113, 119
transport, 8, 109
hostage takings, expressive, 16
human shields, xxv, 3, 6, 11, 116, 200,
226, 276

I

ideologies, 34
IEDs (improvised explosive devices),
96, 315
instrumental hostage takings, 16
international business travel, 74
interrogations, xxvi, 113, 115, 118,
121–22, 125–26, 131–32, 136,
143, 145, 147–48, 162, 177–78,
189, 217, 229, 231, 233, 347
interrogators, 35, 119–22, 130–31,
134, 145–49, 163, 177–80, 199,
217, 230

ISIL (Islamic State of Iraq and the
Levant), 14, 17, 95–96
ISIS (Islamic State of Iraq and al-
Sham), xxiv, 14–15, 37, 39, 41,
62, 117, 164, 205, 276, 333, 337,
342, 346, 366, 370
Islamic State, xxiv, 14, 37, 69, 95, 172,
276, 337–38, 341, 346–48, 353,
358–60, 362–63
Islamist fundamentalists, 34
isometrics, 224–25

J

jihad, 116–17, 172
Jihadi John, 338, 340
jihadists, xxiv, 13, 116, 158, 161

K

Kassig, Peter, 240, 344, 348, 353, 355
kidnap situations, 8
Koran, the, 14–15, 29, 116, 142, 144–
45, 151–52, 155, 159, 164, 168,
171, 180
Korean War, 1, 200, 210
Korkie, Pierre, 283, 357
Kruglanski, 34, 371

L

Laporte, Pierre, 28
law enforcement, 69, 93, 148, 281,
297, 363, 366
life insurance, 77, 271, 319
lightning kidnappings, 12